A History of The Baronetage
by
Francis W. Pixley F.S.A.

A facsimile copy produced and privately printed by
The Armorial Register Limited
2016

First Published in 2016
by
The Armorial Register Limited
All rights reserved

Text & Images Copyright The Armorial Register
Limited

ISBN: 978-0-9568157-5-0

British Library Cataloguing-in-Publication Data
A catalogue record of this book is available on request
from the British Library

A HISTORY OF
THE BARONETAGE

BY FRANCIS W. PIXLEY

LONDON

DUCKWORTH AND COMPANY

1900

.

Edinburgh : T. and A. CONSTABLE, Printers to Her Majesty

TO

SIR CHARLES H. STUART RICH

FOURTH BARONET OF SHIRLEY, F.S.A.

FOUNDER OF THE

HONOURABLE SOCIETY OF THE BARONETAGE

THIS WORK, AS A TOKEN OF OUR

CLOSE FRIENDSHIP OF TWENTY-FIVE YEARS

IS AFFECTIONATELY

DEDICATED

PREFACE

ALTHOUGH close upon three centuries have elapsed since the erection of the degree of Baronet by King James I. of England and VI. of Scotland, yet, so far as I have been able to ascertain, no history of this hereditary dignity has ever been attempted. To endeavour to supply this deficiency in literature is consequently a task of considerable difficulty, accompanied by many misgivings.

A writer undertaking a history of the Peerage could begin by surrounding himself with works innumerable, from each of which he could cull something wherewith to enrich his own, but to break fresh ground requires more research ; and when his work is completed, the author has the uneasy feeling that there is concealed in many unknown localities much information which he would like to have included in his history, as being essential to its completeness, had he only been aware of its existence.

I have, however, done my best to gather together from various sources the hitherto disconnected documents which form the history of the sixth hereditary degree of the higher nobility of the United Kingdom of Great Britain and Ireland ; and I can only claim that however incomplete my work may be, it will be the means of presenting many documents printed for the first time. I also hope that it will cause many erroneous ideas in connection with the Baronetage to disappear for ever.

Amongst these may be mentioned the idea that the Baronetcies first created by King James 1. were sold to persons of no social standing for the purpose of providing funds for the King's private expenditure; the extraordinary error, which has been perpetrated even by Kings of Arms and Heralds, that the Baronetage is an 'Order,' whereas it is a Degree of Dignity Hereditary; also, that 'Bart.,' the popular nickname for a member of the Football Club of a well-known Metropolitan medical hospital, is a proper abbreviation of the word Baronet.

I must express my deep thanks to many Baronets who have given me assistance in my work; also to Sir Arthur Vicars, C.V.O., F.S.A., Ulster King of Arms, and Sir John Balfour Paul, F.S.A. (Scot.), Lyon King of Arms, for their courteous replies to many inquiries; to Captain Francis Fletcher-Vane for the copy of the grant to Sir Ralph Fane (or Vane), together with its translation; to the Rev. R. E. Cole of Doddington Rectory, Lincoln, for the document which enabled me to give an example of the fees paid on the creation of a Baronet; to Mr. Frederick P. Pelham for the loan of many interesting documents in connection with the 'Committee of the Baronetage for

Privileges,' originated by his relative, the late Richard Broun; to many courteous officials of the Reading Room of the British Museum, of the Public Record Office, and of the Guildhall Library ; and, above all, to Lady Shuckburgh for her great kindness in allowing me to examine the documents at Shuckburgh Hall handed to the late Sir Francis Shuckburgh, Baronet, who was the Treasurer of the 'Committee of the Baronetage for Privileges.'

It was, however, with great regret that I discovered that the minute-book of the Committee was not amongst these papers, and all efforts to trace its whereabouts have been in vain. By means, however, of reports, circulars, etc., issued by this Committee, I have been enabled to give an account of its proceedings, and can only regret that, owing to the absence of the minute-book, I have been unable to make it more complete.

FRANCIS W. PIXLEY.

LONDON, 1st May 1900.

CONTENTS

CHAPTER I

THE ERECTION OF THE DEGREE

CHAPTER II

THE CREATION OF A BARONET

CONTENTS

CHAPTER VI

LATER HISTORY OF THE BARONETAGE

A HISTORY OF THE BARONETAGE

CHAPTER I

THE ERECTION OF THE DEGREE

THE Baronetage as now existing dates from the 22nd May 1611, when the first Patents were granted by King James I. on the erection of this degree. The dignity is evidently of older date, as Sir Thomas de la More, who belonged to the Court of Edward II., when describing the battle of Barrenberg, fought in 1321, wrote, 'Capitur in campo comes Lancastriæ, Barones et Baronetti commilitones ejus et milites circa 95, reliquis fuga servatis'; and in the thirteenth year of the reign of Edward III. that monarch by Letters Patent conferred the dignity of a Baronet on William de la Pole and his heirs in return for a sum of money, of which the King was greatly in need for military purposes. Other Baronetcies were similarly created, and they were for some time numerous, particularly in Ireland ; but with the exception of a few cases in Ireland, the dignity had not been regularly hereditary, and long before the reign of James I. it had become practically unknown. It is believed that the discovery of William de la Pole's patent by Sir Robert Cotton was the cause of the revival of the title of Baronet in 1611. Others give the credit to Sir

Thomas Shirley of Wiston, as in 1615 his son made a claim on account of his father's services in connection with the erection of the dignity.

The word Baronettus, Anglice Baronet, at the time of the institution of the dignity by James I., was consequently not a new word, but had been used in France as well as in England. It frequently occurs in our old writers and records, and as a word implying a name of dignity, as Selden, Spelman, and others have observed. In England it had been used in two senses for a knight banneret, and for baronet when that has expressed (as it often did in the olden times) a parliamentary baron.

As an example of the former meaning, Thomas Walsingham, who lived and wrote under Henry VI., when describing the battle of Strivelin, which took place in 1313, between Edward II., King of England, and Robert I., King of Scotland, says of the English : 'Capti sunt autem et in custodia detenti barones et baronetti viginti duo, milites sexaginta octo, etc. Summa vero totalis quam comitum baronum et baronettorum quam militum inter fectorum et captorum ibidem centum quinquaginta quatuor,' etc.

As an example of the word Baronet being used for banneret, as expressing a Baron or Lord of Parliament, the fourth clause of the second statute of the fifth year of the reign of Richard II. commands every archbishop, duke, earl, baronet, etc., on summons to appear in Parliament according to ancient use on pain of amercement.

Owing either to a similarity of sound, or for some other reason, many have supposed the word Baronet is a modern pronunciation of Banneret ; but this is entirely wrong, and may be at once disposed of. Previously, however, to describing the method of creation of a Knight Banneret, the following Memorandum contained in *State Papers, Domestic Series, James I.*, vol. lxvii. No. 119, shows that the same confusion existed at the time of the erection of the Baronetage :—

' *Reasons.*

' ffrom the worde of the Patent.

' Dignitatem statum et Gradum Baronetti   Where we may reasonably fixe & settle our degree, there wee must have our dignitye & state.

' The Degree is proved by the name Baronett. for Baronet is not a name introduced by the slipp of a Penn : but commonly used & knowne for the name of the degree, wch was also knowne by the name Bannerett.

' Anncient originall Manuscriptes of the times of Ed. 1. 2. 3. & R. 2.

' The booke of the Abbies of Tewxburye : Lecester : E— login & Adam Merimouth.

' Manuscriptes in the Heraldes office.

' Liber illust. ordinis diui Georgii : the booke where in is entred the names & armes of those wch were at the siege of Berwicke by Ed. 3   We have also a rowle of the armie wch went wth him into France.

' *Law*

' Statutes written french 2 printed in french & Inglishe 5° & 14°, R. 2.

' *Common Law*

' Pleadinges in 35 H. 6. pb. 8.

' *Storie*

' Camden. Hollinshead

so as from time to time successively all writters have used the name as a knowne name for a Degree.

'What Degree

'We prove what degree by Comparinge them one w^(th) an other. for we finde one booke of the order of St. Geo. hath Baronett, an other in the same artickle hath Banerett.

'One Rowle of K. Ed. 3 journey into France hath Baronett, an other of the same Bannerett.

'Sir John Shandos who is famousely knowne to be a Banerett is in the rowle called Baronett.

'The same statuts of R. 2. one booke hath Baronett another booke & the recorde hath Bannerett.

'and therefore Mr. Camden in his Book might well say as he dothe Baneretti qui aliis Baronetti.

'This is the first proofe of our degree & Consequently of our dignity & state.

'The next is place : for place is properly to a degree : place is twofowle place amongst men : & place amongst degrees.

'our place is amongst Bannerettes & therefore wee are to have our dignity & state amongst them.

'The rather because this is given as an honour to incite us to be forward in his Ma^(ties) service in peace & warr, w^(ch) will not take that operacion yf wee bee not in dignityes & state equall to those amongst whome wee goe.

'Agayne if wee have not dignity & state equall to our place then is not his Ma^(ties) grace of equall vallue to all w^(ch) have received it : for those gentl. w^(ch) were no K^(tes) & our posteritie in like case know not what they may Challendge whether so much as an ordinarie K^t.

'This is the reason from the place in the first kinde. the second is from the Covenante.

'The K. Covenanteth he will not ordayne &c. any degree betweene us & Baron superior or equall to Baronett.

'In the plaine wordes wee conceave that wee now are Covenanted to bee the next degree to Baron, & so we Come into the anntient place of Bannerett.

'It will be said this Covenante is intended of a new Created degree : but not ment of Bannerett the Ancient Degree.

'I answere : then the wordes are not Cleere but ambiguous for yf the meaninge were that Baneret as an anntient Degree showlde interceade betweene Baron & Baronet then should it have beene said he would not ordayne any degree betweene Bannerett & Baronett, for to name Baron & Baronet as the duo stermini & meane Bannerett & Baronet : we thinke is not proper but an obscure speeche & wee must presume of the playne & Cleere speeche.

'This for the place. other reasons are drawne from Consideracion of the degree of Bannerett & from inconveniences.

'The degree of Bannerett was not meerely a Millitary Dignity, nor men Capable of that for deserte in warrs only but wth all for there estate in lande & revenues able to maintayne the state of a Bannerett & therefore wee shall finde many guyftes geven heeretofore by the K^{ts} to mayntayne the state of a Bannerett & wee reade of Sir John Shandos that he said he had landes & revenues suffitient to mayntayne the state of a Bannerett as an argument why he desired that degree.

'& that argument wee may urge the K. hath directed to Chuse men of bloade & estate, and I thinke our number 200 our bloode & state may be thoughte fitt, nay, may require that degree & all thinges wch doe belonge to the dignitie & state thereof.

'If wee bee not that degree : then must followe the Inconvenience of Novelty wch in no state is easey to be admitted & some have made a doubt whither a writt or pleadinge shall be defective for want of the title of Baronet before the law taketh knowledge of such a degree.

'besides as in all things Novelty disturbeth the former setled Course so in honour a new Degree interposed breedeth much envie & geveth Collour of greevance to all inferiour degrees when they thereby are thrust lower for these reasons as wee are perswaded that degree is Conveyed unto us so wee are induced to desire the same wth all rites & priviledges belonging there unto.

(Endorsed *in pencil*) '1611. Heraldic Baronets. Jas. 1. Notes of the conditions under which Baronets were created.'

A Banneret or Knight Banneret is a very ancient title of honour, said to have been instituted towards the end of the reign of the Roman Emperor Gratian and was subsequently adopted by different European nations. By Matthew of Paris, Knights Banneret were called *Milites vexilliferi*, and by the author of the *Dictionnaire de Trevoux*, *Milites vexillati* ; later on they have been styled Chevaliers à Banier.

The first Knight Banneret was made in England, according to Guillim, in the reign of King Edward 1. In France the Order appears to have been hereditary, but in England was confined to the life of him on whom the honour was conferred.

The Order was a purely military one, and was only bestowed for some heroic action performed on the field of battle.   The ceremony of creation was very impressive, and was usually as follows :—

The King, or very rarely the General, after a victory, received the Knight, having his pennon or guydon of arms in his hand, and led between two renowned Knights, or valiant men-at-arms, at the head of the army under the royal standard displayed, attended with all the field officers and nobles of the Court. In front of the Knight and his two supporters walked the heralds, who proclaimed his valiant achievements, for which he deserved to be made a Knight Banneret.

The King (or General) then called 'Advances toy Banneret,' and the point of the pennon was rent or cut off so as to make it a square, or into the shape of a banner. The new Knight then returned to his tent, the nobles and officers accompanying him, and trumpets sounding before him, where an entertainment took place.

In vol. 89 of the *State Papers, Domestic Series,* of the reign of James I., preserved in the Record Office, there is contained the following account of the making of a Knight Banneret :—

'BANNERET BANER

'A Kn^t that is to receive this honor shal be lead between 2 other Kn^{tes} before the K. or Generall bearing his Penon of Armes in his owne hand : and in prescence of all the Nobility & other Captains the Heralds shall say unto the K. or his Generall these words following :—

'May it please your Grace to understand that this Gentleman hath shewed himself valiant in the field and for so doing deserveth to be advanced to the degree of a Kn^t bannerett as worthy from henceforth to beare a baner in the warre.

'Then the K. or Generall shall cause the Points of his Penon or Guydon to be rent of, And the new Kn^t shall goe into his Tent conducted between 2 other Kn^{tes} the trumpets sounding all the way before him, there to pay fees, viz., to the Heralds 3^{li} 6s. 8d. And if he were before a Kn^t bacheler then he is to pay also to the Trumpetors 1^{li} I suppose the Scots do call a Kn^t of this Creation a Banerent for having his banner rent.

'Here is to be noted that no Kn^t banneret can be made but in the warr & the K. present or when the Standard royall is displayed in the field.

'A Baneret thus made and every Estate above him may beare his banner displayed if he be a Captayne : and set his Armes therein as Barons doe.

'A Banerets banner ought to be 3 foote square.

'The ould forme of the banner of a baneret was but 2 foot square, but now their worship & power is increased and therefore they have 3 foote as a Baron : which feet are to be understood to be in measure according to the Standard, as the measure of a weapon of duell ought to be.

'It is used to make the breadth of a banner less than the length, but that is without rule.

'Every Baneret and every Estate above him may have his baner displayed in the field if he be a chief Captaine.

'His Standard to be borne in battaill shal be 4 yards & half long & slit at one end.'

As a consequence of the cutting of the pennon so as to make it into a square or of the shape of a banner, it became the custom for Knights Banneret to bear their arms in a square shield instead of in one of the ordinary shape. They had no particular badge or embroidery worn on their garments to show their Order; but in England and most other countries they usually painted their arms on a banner placed in the paws of the supporters to their arms. In France they usually bore two banners with their arms in saltier behind the shield.

Even in times when it would be expected the difference between Baronets and Bannerets would be well known, many writers have stated that the word Baronettus was in earlier days always used in error for Bannerettus, and one of the examples quoted has been the Patent, so called, passed to Sir Ralph Fane, a Knight Banneret under Edward the Sixth.

Now this document commences with a recital to the effect that, for certain services rendered by him, Sir Ralph Fane, Knight, had stood erected, raised, and created by the King to the order, state, rank, honour, and dignity of a Baronet.

In the absence of proof such as could be afforded by a Patent of Baronetcy, we have to consider, in forming a judgment based on this recital, whether its wording applies to a ceremony performed on the field of battle, or to a hereditary dignity conferred by Letters Patent. The docu-

ment then goes on to fulfil its avowed purpose of making
'a grant to Ralph Fane and his heirs,' stating that this grant
(of a Manor and Advowson) is in order that he might be
the better enabled and empowered to sustain the burden of
his rank and state aforesaid, and as a further recompense for
his services.

It is difficult to say which is signified by such language,
whether rank for life or rank hereditary? It may surely be
one or the other : and the heading of the document leaves
us no clue, for, quite without excuse, it describes Sir Ralph
as if he were no more than a simple Knight. There appears,
however, to be no reason why it should be assumed that the
word 'baronetti' in Sir Ralph Fane's Grant was intended
to have been written ' banneretti.'

As this document, although alluded to, has never before
been printed, it is here given :—

'PRO RADULPHO FANE MILITE DE CONCESSIONE SIBI ET
HEREDIBUS

'Rex omnibus ad quos etc. Salutem. Cum in consideracione
fidelis et acceptabilis servicii nobis per dilectum servientem nostrum
Radulphum Fane Militem in guerris nostris tam in bello apud
Musskelboroughe contra inimicos nostros Scotos in apprehensione
Comitis Huntley inimici nostri per ipsum Radulphum ibidem
adtunc capti quam aliter antehac facti et impensi idem Radulphus
ad ordinem statum gradum honorem et dignitatem baronetti per
nos erectus sussitatus et creatus extiterit Quiquidem Comes Huntley
postea ab eodem Radulpho et e manibus suis per nos et ad usum
nostrum acceptus et detentus fuerit absque recompensacione per
nos eidem Radulpho pro redempcione dicti comitis adhuc facta
Sciatis quod nos tam in consideracione dicti servicii dicti Radulphi
Fane nobis in forma predicta et aliter antehac facti et impensi.

Et ut idem Radulphus onus gradus et status sui predicti melius sustinere valeat et possit quam in consideracione ac in partem recompensacionis per nos dicto Radulpho debite pro redempcione dicti comitis Huntley ·prisonarii sui per nos ab eodem Radulpho et e manibus suis ad usum nostrum capti et detenti ac pro aliis causis et consideracionibus nos ad presens specialiter moventibus de gratia nostra speciali ac ex certa sciencia et mero motu nostris Necnon de avisamento consilii nostri dedimus et concessimus ac per presentes damus et concedimus prefato Radulpho Fane Militi totum illud manerium nostrum de Penshurste ac advocacionem donacionem liberam disposicionem et jus patronatus ecclesie et rectorie de Cowden cum suis juribus membris et pertinentiis universis in comitatu nostro Kancie quondam parcellam terrarum tenementorum possessionum et hereditamentorum Edwardi Ducis Bukingham de alta prodicione attincti et convecti.

'In cujus rei, etc. Teste Rege apud Hynnyngham Castell vicesimo secundo die Julii
        per brevi de privato sigillo.'

The following is a translation of this interesting Document :—

'FOR RALPH FANE, KNIGHT, OF A GRANT TO HIM
AND HIS HEIRS.

'The King to all to whom, etc. Greeting. Whereas, in consideration of the faithful and acceptable service to us rendered and performed by our beloved servant, Ralph Fane, Knight, in our wars both in the battle of Musskelborough against our enemies the Scots, in apprehending the Earl of Huntley, our enemy, who was then and there taken by the said Ralph, as well as in other ways, the said Ralph was by us erected, raised, and created to the order, state, rank, honour, and dignity of a Baronet; which said Earl of Huntley was afterwards received and detained from the said Ralph and out of his hands, by us and to our use, without any recompense made by us, up to this present, to the said Ralph for the ransom of the said Earl, KNOW that we, both in

consideration of the said service of the said Ralph Fane to us in form
as aforesaid and otherwise heretofore performed and rendered, and in
order that the said Ralph may be the better enabled and empowered
to sustain the burden of his rank and state aforesaid, as also in consideration, and as part, of the recompense due from us to the said
Ralph for the ransom of the said Earl of Huntley his prisoner, by us
received and detained from the said Ralph and out of his hands to
our use, and for other causes and considerations us at this present
specially moving, of our especial grace, and out of our certain
knowledge and mere motion, as also with the advice of our Council
we have given and granted, and by these presents do give and grant,
to the aforesaid Ralph Fane, Knight, All that our manor of
Penshurste, and the advowson, and gift, free disposition and right of
patronage of the church and rectory of Cowden, With all its rights,
members, and appurtenances, in our County of Kent, formerly parcel
of the land, tenements, possessions, and hereditaments of Edward,
Duke of Buckingham, attainted and convicted of high treason.

'In witness whereof, etc.   Witness the King at Hynnyngham
Castle, the 22nd day of July.
'By writ of Privy Seal.'

The Baronets form the sixth division of the higher class
of nobility known as Nobiles Majores of the United
Kingdom of Great Britain and Ireland, the six being as
follows :—

> Duke.
> Marquess.
> Earl.
> Viscount.
> Baron.
> Baronet,

as there can be no question that the lower rank of nobility,
or the Nobiles Minores, are Knights, Esquires, and Gentlemen

entitled to bear Coat Armour not included in any of the above six ranks. In other words, in a division of the upper ranks of society between nobility and gentry it is wrong to consider the Baronets as forming the highest class of the ranks of the gentry.

The early members of the Baronetage who satisfied the conditions of James I. as referred to hereafter were called by him, previous to their receiving the honour of the dignity, 'principall Gentlemen of his Kingdom'; while very many, who were inferior in lineage to few others in the realm, were in the language of such authorities as Camden, Coke, Selden, and Blackstone, nobles by blood, or Nobiles Minores, and were raised on being created Baronets to the ranks of Nobiles Majores by virtue of the hereditary dignity with which the King invested them.

Their title is an hereditary one, and the question of treating as noblemen those only who have a seat in the House of Lords is clearly erroneous, as many Peers of Scotland and Ireland are universally admitted to be noblemen, although as such they have no right to seats in the Upper House of Parliament. They may, by the election of their own Peers, be deputed to sit in this house as representing their respective bodies, but the acquisition of this privilege no more confers upon them the rank of nobility than does the absence of it take away from them their undoubted possession of this distinction.

Another proof of Baronets being members of the Nobiles Majores is the manner in which their order of precedency was settled before the Union, this differing from that of

Knights, who could take place and precedency solely according to their priority of Knighthood. Nobiles Majores go below, as puisnes, those of the same degree in the nation in which they may be resident, as Barons of Ireland residing in England give place to all of the same degree of England; so in Scotland before the Union, the Scottish Barons, Dukes, etc., took place before the English, and *vice versâ*, in conformity to the law of nations.

Thus in the cavalcade of George I. on his arrival, Baronets of Great Britain took place of Baronets of Ireland or of Nova Scotia, an incontestable proof, as Sir Richard Broun contended, of their being considered as of the Nobiles Majores. While referring to this procession, it may be of interest to mention that the coaches of the Irish Baronets preceded those of the Attorney-General and Solicitor-General of England.

Again, can it be contended for one moment that in the seventeenth century the descendants of Hugh Lupus, Earl of Chester, were not included among the Nobiles Minores, and then that the elevation of this descendant into an hereditary degree did not confer upon him a higher rank? Would he not have scorned to accept this new dignity had it not been considered to place him in some higher rank than the one he already held?

In a pamphlet published anonymously in 1842, entitled 'British and Continental Titles of Honour,' occurs the following footnote :—

'The Great Barons of the Conqueror have long ago departed, excepting such of them as have received higher titles.   The senior Baron of the Peerage, Lord de Ros, goes no further back than 1264.   There are but comparatively few Peers whose titles bear date anterior to the Reformation.   Amongst the Baronetage and the Gentry, we find families who were Noble long prior to the Conquest, such as the Temples, Deerings, Titchbornes, Pennymans, Boothbys, Prideauxs, Poles, Frelfords, Chetwodes,—the twenty-eighth lineal descendant from Sir John Chetwode, Lord of the Manor of Chetwode, being the present Baronet. On the roll of Battle Abbey are the Burdetts, the Wakes, the Hazelriggs, Bedingfields, Shuckburghs, Tyrells, Pulestons, Wrottesleys, etc.   The names of the ancestors of the present Baronets of Colstoun and Riddell, Walterres le Brun and Gervasius de Ridell, occur (along with those of the Countess Matilda, afterwards Queen ; William, nephew of the Prince, Cospatrick, Earl of Dunbar, Alan de Percie, Walter de Lindesay, and others) as witnesses to one of the oldest Scottish documents extant, viz., the inquisition made by David, Prince of Cumberland (afterwards King David Ist), respecting the possessions of the see of Glasgow in 1116. Is it necessary to particularise the antiquity of the Gordons, Bruces, Stuarts, Setons, Ramsays, Sinclairs, Craufords, Wallaces, Cunninghames, Pringles, etc. ?—the Fitzgeralds, de Burghs, Cootes, Talbots, Shees, Butlers, Moores, etc. ?— or of the four Dukes, the seventeen Marquesses, the fifty-seven Earls, the fourteen Viscounts, and fifty-nine Barons, whose progenitors were Baronets long prior to their being raised to Peerage titles ? '

Later on, in the same work, the writer states that it is

recorded by Buchanan that Richard le Brun, John de Logie, and Gilbert Malherbe were three of the principal noblemen who headed a memorable transaction in Scottish history in the year 1320. Three hundred and sixty-six years later the representative of the first of these, who was of course as noble as his ancestor, received a Baronet's Patent. 'One feels at a loss,' adds the writer, 'to understand how this ennobled him, he being already noble when he received it.'

When a Baronet receives the title of Baron, he is in truth and in fact, and in the estimation of heralds, no more ennobled than is a Baron when he receives the title of Viscount. All he acquires thereby is an augmentation of dignity.

If one may judge of the eminency of a dignity by its rating for poll-taxes, that of a Baronet over two hundred and fifty years ago was very considerable. In the Ordinance of those persons who sat at Westminster in 1641 every Lord paid £40, every Baronet £30, while an Esquire paid but £10. In the Act of 17 Charles i. for disbanding the army, etc., a Baron paid £40, their eldest sons £30, a Baronet £30, and a Knight Bachelor £20.

In support of the obvious truth that Baronets are not mere Knights, and that the title of Knights-Baronets, so often applied to them, is incorrect, the following extract from Coke's *Reports* is given :—'That if an heir of a tenant in Knight's service, who was under age at his father's death, and so in ward, was made a Baronet by the King, it did not discharge such heir from being in ward, or if he was made a Knight, any more than if he had been made a Baron or an Earl.'

It is quite clear that it was the intention of James I. to create an hereditary dignity, the members of which, though lacking the legislative functions of those of the Peerage, and taking precedence after them, should nevertheless enjoy all the other established and recognised privileges of hereditary nobility.   He gave to Baronets and their eldest sons in 1612 the right to claim knighthood, but this was an afterthought and at best an added dignity.

The following document preserved in the Record Office among the *State Papers, Domestic Series, James I.*, vol. lxiii. No. 64, shows what was in the mind of that King and his advisers at the time of the institution of the Dignity :—

'A Project for erecting a new Dignitie beetween Barons & Knights in wch theese Circumstances . . . considerable what shall bee their name and their place.

'And upon what Condicions they shall have itt.

'Name.

'The partie that hath itt, shall beare the name of Baronet.   Hee shall have the same given him by Letters Patents to him and to the heires males of his body, Hee to bee called Sir and his wife Lady.

'Place.

'Hee shall goe above all Knights, banneretts not made under the Kinges Sta . . . in the ffeild displaied in his own presence and above the Knights of the Ba . . . and all other Knights under them.

'The same place shall bee retained by their wyves And their Sonnes and their Daughters, shall likewise take their places above the Children of all others t . . . are to goe beneath their ffathers.

'Condicions imposed upon the Partie that have the Dignitie.

'Hee shall bee Content to pay 30 foote after 8d. per diem for 3 yeares, towardes the servyce of Ireland and particularlie in regard of the plantacion of Ulster, and that reason shall bee expressed in the Patent Honoris gratia.

'The King to bee pleased to Covenant never to excede the numbre of 200.

'Thus-much to bee expressed in the body of the Patent.

'*Cautions concerning the former Project.*

'1. That none bee admitted except hee have of Certain yearlie revenue of Inheritance in possession 1000ᵗⁱ per annum de Claro, or of landes of old rent — good in accompt as 1000ᵗⁱ per annum of improvements or at least twoo parts in . . . of landes to the vallewe as aforsayd and the third in revercion expectant upon one life only holding by Dower or in Jointure.

'2. That none bee received whose Grandfather by the ffather did not beare Arms.

'3. That whosoever shall bee received upon death of an other without issue, shall Come in the lowest ranke.

'4. That hee must pay the mony downe for one yeares interteinment every yeare . . . hande.

'And for the order to bee observed in ranking those that shall receive this dignitie allthough it is to bee wished that those Knights wᶜʰ have now place before other Knights, in respect of the time of their Creation may bee ranked before others (cæteris paribus) yett because this is a dignitie wᶜʰ shall bee hereditarie wherein divers Circumstances are more Considerable then such a marke as is but temporary (that is to say of being now a Knight, in time before an other). It is his Maᵗⁱᵉˢ pleasure that the LL shall not bee so precise in placing those that shall receive this dignitie but that an Esqʳ of greate antiquitie and extraordinarie living may bee ranked in this Choyce before some Knights. And so of Knights a man of greater living more remarquable for his house, yeares and Calling in the Common wealth, now preferred before one in this dignitie that was made Knight before him.

'And lastlie that it may appeare that the partie wᶜʰ hath this dignitie hath not obtained it by any sordid, or base meanes, hee shall upon the delivery of his Patent, take his Corporall oath in the presence of the LL Comissioners in manner and forme following : viz. I, A. B. doe sweare, that neyther I nor any other to my knowledge, have, or hath given or promised, procured or consented to give, or to bee given any gift or reward directly, or indirectly to any person or persons whatsoever, for procuring his Ma^tes favour on my behalfe, to create mee a Baronet, or ranke mee before any other (those summes of money wch by my Patent I am tied to pay for the interteinm^t of 30 foote after 8d. per diem, for 3 yeares in Ireland only excepted). And that I will not give, nor any w^h my consent shall give or consent to bee given, any gift or reward, directly or indirectly, other than that wch I am so to pay in manner as aforesayd. So helpe me God.'

The following 'Memorandum' is contained in the same volume at the Public Record Office as the above 'Project,' but it belongs to a later date, 1612 :—

'Baronet.

'To maintaine 30 foot for 3 yeares for the defence of Ireland but especially for the plantacion of Ulster.

'His place to be immediately after the Younger Sonnes of Viscounts and Barons of England, & before all Kn^ts of the Bath & Kn^ts Bachelors, and all Kn^ts Bannerettes. Except only those Bannerettes that are made under the Kings owne Standard the King being present, or Bannerettes made by the Prince of Wales he then being present & his Banner displayed in open warre & not otherwise And that for terme of their lives onely, & not any others that shall happen after to be created. And except all Kn^ts of the Garter, Kn^ts of the privy Councell, &c.'

At that date the province of Ulster in Ireland was, as it had been on many former occasions, in a state of rebellion, and James I. was desirous of putting an end to this continual revolt, of settling and civilising its inhabitants, and of cultivating its soil. It occurred to him or his advisers to raise the necessary funds for this undertaking by the contributions of those on whom he should confer the new hereditary degree.

At the same time, the King was careful to bear in mind that as he was creating a new dignity of this nature, it was necessary, in order to invest it with the attributes of the degrees it was immediately to follow in social precedence, that none should be admitted to it who were not of gentle blood. He therefore prescribed that membership was only for those who were descended of a grandfather by his father's side who bore arms, and had a clear estate in lands of at least one thousand pounds a year. 'Or lands of the old rent, as good in account as one thousand pounds per annum of improved rents, or at least two parts in three to be divided of lands of the said values in possession, and the other third part in reversion, expectant upon one life only, holding by dower or in jointure.' An income of one thousand pounds from land in the year 1611 could only have been derived from very considerable territorial possessions, and it is therefore easy to realise that an inquiry into the social position of those who were the first to receive their Patents of Baronetcy proves conclusively that it was among the best of the gentle blood of England not already enjoying a title, and in many instances superior to that of families on whom had previously been conferred the honour of the Peerage itself.

A most absurd contention has frequently been put forward by writers to the effect that Baronetcies were indiscriminately sold to any one willing to provide funds for the royal founder's pecuniary necessities. This contention is easily

refuted by a short account of the families of those who
are now the senior members of the degree.

The ancestor of Bacon of Redgrave, who was created
Premier Baronet on the 22nd May 1611, was descended
from an ancestor who came to England at the time of the
Norman Conquest in common with William, Earl Warren,
to whom he was related.   He settled at Letheringsett,
near Holt, in Norfolk, and he and his descendants acquired
large possessions in Norfolk, Suffolk, and Gorhambury in
Hertfordshire.   It is related that when Queen Elizabeth
visited Sir Nicholas, the father of the first Baronet at Redgrave, she said it was too little for his lordship ; to which
he replied, ' No, madam, but your Highness has made me
too big for it,' and, acting on the suggestion, he is said
to have added the wings to the house at Redgrave.

It is quite enough to say of De Hoghton of Hoghton
Tower that the present Baronet resides on the property
which was in the possession of his family in the time of
Henry ii., and that from the time of Edward i. his ancestors
have frequently acted as Sheriffs of the county.

An ancestor of Shelley of Michelgrove was a Knight of
the Shire for Huntingdon in the time of William ii.
Sir Thomas Shelley, Knight, went as an Ambassador to
Spain in 1205, and Sir William Shelley was sent as an
Ambassador to the Emperor of Germany in the time of
Henry vii. ; and after their removal from Huntingdon,
nearly six and a half centuries ago, they went to Michelgrove
in Suffolk.

An ancestor of Musgrave of Edenhall also came over

with William the Conqueror, and the family was early
established in Westmorland, and gave their name to two
villages in that county. In the time of King John their
connection with this county was famous, they having served
as Members of Parliament for several divisions of the county
at various intervals; their residence was Hartley Castle. At
the restoration of Charles II. the Baronet of the day was
made Governor of Carlisle, and had a warrant for creating
him Baron Musgrave, but never took out the patent.

Cope of Hanwell is descended from John Cope, who was
granted by Richard II. the Manor of Denshanger, North-
amptonshire, and other properties, his descendants occupying
many positions about the Court until the time of Elizabeth,
when Anthony Cope, the eldest brother of Sir Walter
Cope, Knight, was Shire Sheriff of Oxfordshire, and received
from the Queen the honour of Knighthood. He was again
appointed Shire Sheriff of Oxfordshire by King James I.,
who, after knighting his eldest son William, conferred upon
the father the dignity of the Baronetage.

The ancestor of Gresley of Drakelowe was uncle of Rollo,
Duke of Normandy, whose descendants, Robert and Nigel,
accompanied William the Conqueror to England. Nigel
held Drakelowe, according to Doomsday Book, and
William Greisley, the son of Nigel, was the founder of the
Monastery of Greisley. The family from that time to the
present day have had Drakelowe in continual possession.

Although no attempt appears to have been made to
induce English gentlemen of position to become Baronets,
yet later on pressure was undoubtedly put upon gentlemen

of position in Scotland to accept the new honour, as will be
seen from the following letters of the King :—

'TO THE LARD OF TRAQUAIR

'Trustie and weilbeloved, &c., We, &c.—Thogh ther have
bene warning gevin to all the gentrie of that our kingdome by
publict proclamation, that they might in dew tyme come to be
created kynght barronettis, and not compleane heirefter of utheris
befoir whom they might expect to have place wer preferred unto
them, yet we have thoght fitt to tak particular notice of yow, and
the rather becaus it would seame that yow, not knowing or mistak-
ing our intention in a matter so much concerneing our royall
prerogative for the furthering of so noble a work did seik to
hinder the same : Therefor our pleasure is, that yow with diligence
embrace the said dignitie, and performe the conditions as others doe,
or that yow expect to be heard no more in that purpois, nor that
yow compleane no more heirefter of others to be preferred unto
yow. So not doubting but that, both by your selff and with others,
yow will use your best meanes for furthering of this work, wherby
yow may doe to ws acceptable service.—We bid, &c. Whythall,
24 March 1626.'

'TO THE LARD OF WAUCHTAN

'Trustie, &c. (as in the precedent till this place).—Yit we have
thoght fitt to tak particular notice of yourselff and house, desyreing
yow to performe the said dignitie of knyght barronet, and to performe the lyk conditions as otheris haveing the lyk honour doe,
which course we wish the rather to be takin by yow and others
in regaird that so noble a wark as the plantation of New Scotland
doeth much depend therupoun, and as your willingness to this our
request shall not be a hinderance bot rather a help to ane further
place that shalbe thoght fitt to be conferred upon yow ; so shall
yow heirby doe ws acceptable pleasur.—We bid, &c. Whythall,
24 March 1626.'

'TO THE LARD OF WEMYES

'Trustie and weilbeloved, We, &c.—Haveing determined that
the creation of knyght barronetts should proceid according as our

late dear father, with advyse of his Counsall, had agried upon ;
Thogh all the gentrie of that our kingdome had warning thairof
by publict proclamation, yit we ar pleased in regaird of the reputa-
tioun of your house to tak more particular notice of yow, and did
pass a signature of the said honour in your name, wherein we thoght
our favour would have bene acceptable unto yow : Therfoir these
presents ar to requyre yow to pass the said signatur, and to performe
the lyk conditions as others doe, or utherwayes doe not compleane
heirefter of the precedencie of others, whom we will the rather preferr
that by the embraceing of the said dignitie they be carefull to further
so worthie a work as doeth depend therupon, and as it is a nixt
steppe to a further title, so we will esteame of it accordinglie: Thus
willing yow to certefie bak your resolution heirin, with all diligence,
to Sir William Alexander, our secretarie, who will acquaint ws
therwith.   we bid you, &c.—Whythall, 24 March 1626.

The social position of the three gentlemen to whom
these letters were addressed shows that, anxious as the King
was to carry out his scheme of colonisation in Nova Scotia,
he was exceedingly particular in his selection of those who
were to help him.

Enough has, in fact, been said to prove beyond a doubt
that there is no foundation for the assertion so commonly
made by those who wish to depreciate the dignity, that it
was conferred in the first instance on any who cared to
purchase a title. It has been clearly shown that the first
holders of this title were of ancient lineage and possessed
of great territorial possessions, and who in return for receiving an hereditary dignity agreed to perform a military service
to the State. The title does not appear to have been on
any single occasion prostituted to reward Royal favourites,
nor to have been sold, like certain Peerages, in order to
provide for the private pecuniary necessities of Kings.

CHAPTER II

THE Baronetage is divided into five classes or creations, styled as follows :—

1. Baronets of England.
2. Baronets of Ireland.
3. Baronets of Scotland and Nova Scotia.
4. Baronets of Great Britain.
5. Baronets of the United Kingdom.

The Baronets of England were created between the 22nd May 1611 and 1707, of whom Sir Nicholas Bacon was the first, and whose descendant the present Baronet, Sir Hickman Bacon, still remains the premier Baronet of England and of the Baronetage.

The Baronets of Ireland were created between 30th September 1618 and 1801, of whom Sir Dominick Sarsfield was the first. The Reverend Sir Algernon Coote of Ballyfinn is now the premier Baronet of Ireland.

The Baronets of Scotland were created between 28th May 1625 and 1707, of whom Sir Robert Glendonwyn Gordon of Gordonstown and Letterfourie is the premier, his ancestor having been the first created.

After the Union of England and Scotland in 1707 no

further Baronets of England or Baronets of Scotland were created, the style being changed to Baronet 'of Great Britain,' the first so created being Sir Francis Dashwood of West Wycombe. The date of creation was 20th June 1707, and the descendant of Sir Francis, Sir Robert John Dashwood, still remains the premier Baronet of Great Britain. As Ireland remained a separate kingdom, the creation of Baronets of Ireland continued until Great Britain and Ireland were united in 1801 under the style of the United Kingdom. All holders of Baronetcies created after that date have borne the title of Baronets of the United Kingdom, Vavasour of Spaldington having been created, and still remaining, the premier Baronet holding this title.

It may be interesting here to point out that while from the date of the Union of Ireland with Great Britain the creation of Baronets of Ireland entirely ceased, yet peerages of Ireland are still created, the reason being that, while conferring the full rank and social dignity of the Peerage by such a creation, it does not confer on the holder the right to a seat in the House of Lords, but leaves him free, should he so desire, to seek the right of election to represent a constituency in the House of Commons.

The royal founder at the time of the erection of the dignity proposed to limit it to two hundred in number, and that when any of these Baronetcies became extinct others should not be created in their room, so that the number should diminish, to the greater honour of those that remained. This plan, however, was not adhered to, as shortly after a Commission was appointed to fill up the vacancies

and create others.   The Crown thereby revoked its engagement, and since then no limitation has been placed on the
number of Baronets, additional creations being entirely in
the discretion of the reigning sovereign.

The institution of a Baronet is by Letters Patent under
the Great Seal, to a gentleman, and the heirs male of his
body lawfully begotten, for ever, and sometimes the dignity
is further entailed, according to the pleasure of the sovereign,
as referred to hereafter.

Previous to the preparation of the early Letters Patent,
the following Memorandum and Warrant were issued :—

'MEMORANDUM

'After our very harty Comendacions Whereas —— —— of
—— in the County of —— hath out of his good affeccion
to his ma^{tes} service, offered to charge himself wth the yearely
intertaynement of 30^{tie} foote for three yeares after the rate
of 8d. per diem for the Plantacion of Ulster His Matie having
gratiously accepted of this his good service, is pleased in Recompence
thereof to conferr upon him the Dignity and place of a Baronnett
wth all Titles Preveledges and preheminences wch by his Ma^{tes}
favor is graunted unto others in the like case.   These shal be therefore to require yow to drawe a bill for that purpose fitt for us to
subscribe according unto the direccion given you and the authority
wch we have received by vertue of his Ma^{tes} Comission in that
behalfe, ffor wch this shal be yor warrant And soe we bid you hartely
farewell.

'ffrom Whitehall this   of   1611.

'Yor very loving freindes

'T. Ellesmere, Canc   Lenox

'R. Salisbury, T. Suffolke, Gibb, Shrewsbury,

'W. Knollys   E. Worcester, Fenton.

'Jul. Cæsar.'

'WARRANT

'Trustie and welbeloved wee greet yow well wheras wee are gratiouslie pleased to conferre uppon our trustie and welbeloved —— —— in our Countie of —— the Dignitie of Baronett of this our Kingdome and to entayle the same uppon the heire males of his bodie our will and pleasure is that you prepaire aswell a booke in due forme conteyncing our grant of the dignitie of Baronett unto the said —— —— and the heires males of his bodie as alsoe a warrant in usuall forme for discharging him of soe much money as is usuallie reserved in respect of that dignitie and that yow prepaire them both fitt for our signature for wch this shalbe yor warrant Given att ——.

'To the Clarke of our Signett now attending.'

The Patents of the first-created Baronets were in Latin and in the following form :—

'Rex Omnibus ad quos, etc. Salutem. Cum inter alias Imperii nostri gerendi curas, quibus animus noster assiduè exercetur, illa non minima sit, nec minimi momenti, de Plantatione Regni nostri Hiberniæ, ac potissimum Ultoniæ, amplæ et percelebris ejusdem Regni Provinciæ, quam, nostris jam auspiciis atque armis, fæliciter sub obsequii jugum redactam, ita constabilire elaboramus, ut tanta Provincia, non solum sincero Religionis cultu, humanitate civili, morumque probitate, verum etiam opum affluentia, atque omnium rerum copia, quæ statum Reipublicæ ornare vel beare possit, magis magisque efflorescat, Opus sanè, quod nulli progenitorum nostrorum præstare et perficere licuit, quamvis idipsum multa sanguinis et opum profusione sæpius tentaverint ; In quo opere, sollicitudo nostra Regia, non solum ad hoc excubare debet, ut Plantatio ipsa strenuè promoveatur, oppida condantur, ædes et castra extruantur, agri colantur, et id-genus alia ; Sed etiam prospiciendum imprimis, ut universus hujusmodi rerum civilium appartus, manu armatà, præsidiis videlicet et cohortibus, protegatur et communicatur, ne qua aut vis hostilis, aut defectio intestina, rem disturbet aut impediat : Cumque nobis intimatum sit, ex parte quorundá ex fidelibus nostris subditis,

quod ipsi paratissimi sint ; ad hoc Regnum nostrum inceptum, tam
corporibus, quam fortunis suis promovendum : Nos commoti operis
tam sancti ac salutaris intuitu, atque gratos habentes hujusmodi
generosos affectus, atque propensas in obsequium nostrum et bonum
publicum voluntates, Statuimus apud nos ipsos nulli rei deesse, quæ
subditorum nostrorum studia præfata remunerare aut aliorum animos
atque alacritatem, ad operas suas præstandas, aut impensas in hac
parte faciendas, excitare possit : Itaque nobiscum perpendentes atque
reputantes, virtutem et industriam, nulla alia re magis quam honore
ali atque acui ; omnemque honoris et dignitatis splendorem, et
amplitudinem à Rege tanquam à fonte, originem et incrementum
ducere, ad cujus culmen et fastigium propriè spectat, novos honorum
et dignitatum titulos erigere atque instituere, utpotè à quo antiqui
illi fluxerint ; consentaneum duximus (postulante usu Reipublicæ
atque temporum ratione) nova merita, novis dignitatum insignibus
rependere : Ac propterea, ex certà scientià et mero motu nostris,
Ordinavimus, ereximus, constituimus, et creavimus, quendam statum,
gradum, dignitatem, nomen et titulum Baronetti (Anglice of a
Baronet) infra hoc Regnum nostrum Angliæ perpetuis temporibus
duraturum. SCIATIS modo quod nos de gratia nostra speciali, ac
ex certa scientia et mero motu nostris, ereximus, præfecimus et
creavimus, ac per præsentes pro nobis, Heredibus, et successoribus
nostris, erigimus, præficimus, et creamus dilectum nostrum ——
—— de —— —— in comitatu —— virum, familia, patrimonio,
censu, et morum probitate spectatum (qui nobis auxilium et subsidium satis amplum, generoso et liberali animo dedit et præstitit, ad
manutenendum, et supportandum triginta viros in cohortibus nostris
pedestribus in dicto Regno nostro Hiberniæ, per tres annos intregros
pro defensione dicti Regni nostri, et præcipué pro securitate plantationis dictæ Provinciæ Ultoniæ) ad, et in dignitatem, statum, et
gradum Baronetti (Anglice of a Baronet) Ipsumque —— ——
Baronettum pro nobis, Heredibus, et successoribus nostris, præficimus, constituimus et creamus per præsentes, habendum sibi, et
heredibus masculis de corpore suo legitimè procreatis in perpetuum.
VOLUMUS etiam et per præsentes de gratia nostra speciali, ac ex certa
scientia et mero motu nostris, pro nobis, Heredibus, et successoribus

nostris concedimus præfato —— —— et Heredibus masculis de corpore suo legitime procreatis, Quod ipse idem —— —— et Heredes sui masculi prædicti habeant, gaudeant, teneant, et capiant locum atque Præcedentiam, virtute dignitatis Baronetti prædicti, et Vigore præsentium, tam in omnibus Commissionibus, brevibus, litteris patentibus, scriptis, appellationibus, nominationibus et directionibus, quam in omnibus Sessionibus, Conventibus, Cætibus et locis quibuscunque, præ omnibus militibus, tam de Balneo, (Anglice of the Bathe) quàm militibus Baccalaureis, (Anglice Bachelors) ac etiam præ omnibus militibus Banncrettis, (Anglice Bannerets) jam creatis, vel imposterum creandis, (Illis militibus Bannerettis tantummodo exceptis quos sub vexillis regiis, in exercitu regali, in aperto bello, et ipso Rege personaliter præsente, explicatis, et non aliter creari contigerit). Quodque uxoris dicti —— —— et Hæredum masculorum suorum prædictorum, virtute dictæ dignitatis maritorum suorum prædictorum, habeant, teneant, gaudeant, et capiant locum et præcedentiam, præ uxoribus omnium aliorum quorumcunq; præ quibus mariti hujusmodi uxorum, vigore præsentium habere debent locum et præcedentiam ; atque quod primogenitus filius, ac ceteri omnes filii et eorum uxores, et filiæ ejusdem —— —— et hæredum suorum prædictorum respectivè, habeant, et capiant locum et præcedentiam, ante primogenitos filios ac alios filios et eorum uxores, et filias omnium quorumcunque respectivè, præ quibus patres hujusmodi filiorum primogenitorum, et aliorum filiorum, et eorum uxores, et filiarum, vigore præsentium habere debent locum et præcedentiam. VOLUMUS etiam, et per præsentes pro nobis, hæredibus, et successoribus nostris, de gratia nostro speciali, ac ex certa scientia, et mero motu nostris concedimus, quod dictus —— —— nominetur, appelletur, nuncupetur, placitet et implacitetur per nomen —— —— Baronetti ; Et quod stilus et additio Baronetti apponatur in fine nominis ejusdem —— —— et hæredum masculorum suorum prædictorum, in omnibus Literis Patentibus, Commissionibus et Brevibus nostris atque omnibus aliis Chartis, factis, atque literis, virtute præsentium, ut vera, et legitima, et necessaria additio dignitatis. Volumus etiam, et per Præsentes pro nobis, hæredibus, et successoribus nostris ordinamus, quod

nomini dicti —— —— et Hæredum masculorum suorum prædictorum, in sermone Anglicano, et omnibus scriptis Anglicanis,
præponatur hæc additio, videlicet Anglice (SIR :) Et similiter quod
uxores ejusdem —— —— et hæredum masculorum suorum prædictorum, habeant, utantur, et gaudeant hac appellatione, videlicit
Anglice (Lady, Madame, and Dame) respectivè, secundum usum
loquendi. Habendum, tenendum, utendum, et gaudendum, eadem,
statum, gradum, dignitatem, stilum, titulum, nomen, locum, et
præcedentiam, cum omnibus et singulis Privilegiis, et cæteris
præmissis, præfato —— —— et heredibus masculis de corpore
suo exeuntibus imperpetuum. Volentes et per præsentes concedentes, pro Nobis Hæredibus et successoribus Nostris, quod
prædictus —— —— et hæredes sui masculi prædicti, nomen,
statum, gradum, stilum, dignitatem, titulum, locum et præcedentiam prædictam, cum omnibus et singulis Privilegiis, et
cæteris premissis successive gerant et habeant, et eorum quilibet
gerat et habeat, quodque idem —— —— et Hæredes sui Masculi
prædicti successive Baronetti in omnibus teneantur, et ut Baronetti
tractentur et reputentur, Et eorum quilibet teneatur, tractetur, et
reputetur. Et ulterius de uberiori gratia nostrâ speciali, ac ex certa
scientia et mero motu nostris Concessimus, ac per præsentes pro
Nobis, Hæredibus et successoribus Nostris concedimus præfato
—— —— Et Hæredibus suis masculis prædictis, quod numerus
Baronettorum hujus Regni Angliæ nunquam posthac excedet in
toto, in aliquo uno tempore, numerum ducentorum Baronettorum :
et quod dicti Baronetti, et eorum Hæredes masculi prædicti respectivè, de tempore in tempus in perpetuum, habebunt tenebunt et
gaudebunt locos et præcedentias suas inter se, videlicet, quilibet
eorum secundum prioritatem et senioritatem Creationis suæ Baronetti prædicti ; quotquot autem creati sunt, vel creabuntur Baronetti
per literas nostras Patentes, gerentes Datas uno et eodem die, et
Hæredes sui prædicti, gaudebunt locis et præcedentiis suis inter se
secundum prioritatem, quæ cuilibet eorum dabitur, per alias literas
nostras patentes in ea parte primo conficiendas, sine impedimento,
et non aliter, nec alio modo. Et insuper de abundantiori gratiâ
nostrâ speciali, ac ex certâ scientiâ et mero motu nostris concessi-

mus, ac per præsentes, pro nobis, hæredibus et successoribus nostris, concedimus præfato —— —— et hæredibus suis Masculis prædictis, quod nec Nos, nec Hæredes vel Successores Nostri, de cætero in posterum erigemus, ordinabimus, constituemus, aut creabimus infrà hoc Regnum nostrum Angliæ aliquem alium gradum, ordinem, nomen, titulum, dignitatem, sive statum, sub vel infra gradum, dignitatem, sive statum Baronum hujus Regni nostri Angliæ, qui erit vel esse possit superior, vel æqualis gradui et dignitati Baronettorum predictorem, sed quod tam dictus —— —— et Hæredes sui Masculi prædicti, quàm uxores, filii, uxores filiorum, et filiæ ejusdem —— —— et hæredum masculorum suorum prædictorum, de cætero in perpetuum liberè et quietè habeant, teneant, et gaudeant, dignitates, locos et præcedentias suas prædictas præ omnibus, qui erunt de talibus gradibus, statibus, dignitatibus, vel ordinibus in posterum, ut præfertur creandi respectivè secundum veram intentionem præsentium absq; impedimento nostro, hæredum, vel successorum nostrorum, vel aliorum quorum cunque. Et ulterius per præsentes declaramus, et significamus beneplacitum et voluntatem nostram in hac parte fore et esse, Et sic nobiscum statuimus et decrevimus, quod si postquam nos prædictum numerum ducentorum Baronettorum hujus Regni Angliæ compleverimus et perfecerimus, Contigerit aliquem, vel aliquos eorundem Baronettorum, ab hac vità discedere, absque Hærede masculo de corpore vel corporibus hujusmodi Baronetti vel Baronettorum procreato, quod tunc nos non creabimus, vel præficiemus aliquam aliam personam, vel personas in Baronettum, vel Baronettos Regni Nostri Angliæ, sed quod numerus dictorum Ducentorum Baronettorum ea ratione de tempore in tempus diminuetur, et in minorem numerum cedet et redigetur; Denique volumus, ac per præsentes, pro nobis, hæredibus et successoribus nostris de gratia nostra speciali, ac ex certa scientia et mero motu nostris concedimus præfato —— —— et Hæredibus suis masculis prædictis, quod hæ litteræ nostræ Patentes erunt in omnibus et per omnia firmæ validæ, bonæ, sufficientes et effectuales in lege, tam contra nos, hæredes, et successores nostros, quàm contra omnes alios quoscunque secundum veram intentionem earundem, tam in omnibus curiis

nostris, quam alibi ubicunque. Non obstante aliqua lege, consuetudine, præscriptione, usu, ordinatione, sive constitutione quacunque antehac editâ, habitâ, usitatâ, ordinatâ, sive provisâ, vel in
posterum ædendâ, habendâ, usitandâ, ordinandâ vel providendâ: Et
non obstante aliquâ aliâ re, causâ vel materiâ quacunque.

'Volumus etiam, etc. Absque fine in Hanaperio, etc. Eo quod
expressa mentio, etc. In cujus rei, etc. Teste Rege apud West-
monasterium vicesimo secundo die Maii, per ipsum Regem.'

The last Baronet created by a Patent in Latin was Sir
Gilbert Heathcote of London, the date of whose Patent
was the 17th January 1732. The next Baronet created was
Mr. Edward Turner of Ambrosden, whose Patent, dated
the 24th August 1783, is in English, and in the following
form, which form corresponds very approximately to the
Patents in Latin which succeeded the earliest Patents of
King James 1. :—

'George the Second by the Grace of God. To all to whom
these presents shall come Greeting. Whereas Our late Royal Progenitor King James the first made it one of the principal cares of
his Government to plant and improve his Kingdom of Ireland and
more especially Ulster a large province of that Kingdom which
by the conduct and Arms of his said late Majesty being happily
reduced to Obedience His said late Majesty laboured to establish in
such manner that so great a province might not only flourish with
the true Religion Civility and good manners but also with wealth
and plenty of all things which might advance the State of a Comon
Wealth In which undertaking his said late Majesties Royal
Care did not only endeavour that the Plantation itself might be
carried on Towns raised houses and Castles built and fields tilled
but also that so a new and extensive Establishment of Civil
Affairs should be protected and defended by an armed Force least
any Hostile force or intestine defection might disturb or hinder
the same And Whereas it was intimated to his said late Majesty

on behalf of some of his faithful Subjects that they should be
most ready to carry on that Royal undertaking both with their
lives and fortunes   And whereas his said late Majesty being
moved with the prospect of so good and pious a work and kindly
esteeming such generous affections and inclinations to his Service
and the publick good resolved within himself to be wanting in
nothing that might reward the said intentions of his Subjects or
which might stir up the minds and good wills of others to do their
endeavours and assist in that behalf therefore weighing and considering with himself that virtue and industry are best nourished
and encouraged by Honour and that all Honours and Dignityes
derive their original and increase from the King as from a Fountain
to whose Majesty and Regall State it properly belongs to erect and
institute new Titles of Honour and Dignity as from whom the
Ancient Titles flowed   He judged it proper to repay new meritts
with new Ensigns of Dignity   Wherefore of his certain knowledge
and mere motion after the manner of his Royal Progenitor of
famous memory who had and exercised this prerogative of creating
new Degrees of Honour amongst their subjects   He of his Royal
Power and Authority Ordained Erected Constituted and created a
certain State Degree Dignity name and Title of Baronett within his
then Kingdom of England to endure for ever and that the said State
Title Dignity and Degree of Baronett should be and be reputed to
be a middle State Title and Degree of Hereditary Dignity between
the Degree of a Baron and the Degree of a Knight   Now know
ye that We of our Especial Grace certain knowledge and mere
motion have erected appointed and created Our Trusty and Welbeloved Subject —— —— of —— —— in the County of ——
—— Esquire (a Man eminent for Family Inheritance Estate and
Integrity of manners who generously and freely gave and furnished
to us an Ayd and Supply large enough to maintain and support thirty men in our Foot Companys in our said Kingdom of
Ireland to continue for three whole years for defence of our said
Kingdom and especially for the security of the Plantation of our
said Province of Ulster, to and into the dignity state and degree
of a Baronett and him the said —— —— for Us Our heirs and

successors   We do erect appoint constitute and create a Baronett
by these presents   To hold to him and the heirs male of his body
lawfully begotten and to be begotten for ever   We will also and
do by these presents of Our especial grace certain knowledge
and mere motion for Us Our heirs and successors do grant unto
the said ―― ―― and to his heirs male aforesaid that he the said
―― ―― and his said heirs male may have enjoy hold and take
place and precedence by virtue of the dignity of a Baronett aforesaid and by force of these presents as well in all Commissions
Writs Letters Patent Writings Appellations Nominations and
directions as in all sessions meetings assemblies and places whatsoever next and immediately after the younger sons of Viscounts
and Barons of this our Kingdom of Great Britain and before
all Knights as well of the Bath as Knights Batchelors and also
before all Knights Bannerett now created or hereafter to be
created, except those Knights Banneret which shall happen to be
created under the Royal Banners displayed of Us Our heirs or
successors in Our Royal Army in open war and the King himself
being personally present and also all those Knights Bannerett which
shall happen to be created under the Royal Banners displayed of Us
Our heirs or successors in Our Royal Army by the first born son of
Us Our heirs or successors for the time being Prince of Wales
then personally present in Open Warr and not otherwise for the
term of their lives only and no longer respectively   And also except
all Knights of the Noble Order of the Garter   And all of the
Privy Council of Us Our heirs and successors The Chancellor and
Under Treasurer of Our Exchequer, The Chancellor of the Duchy
of Lancaster The Chief Justice of the King's Bench The Master
of the Rolls in Chancery The Chief Justice of the Comon Pleas
The Chief Baron of the Exchequer and all and singular Judges
and Justices of either Bench and the Barons of the Exchequer of
the degree of the Coif for the time being who all and singular by
reason of their Honourable Order and labour sustained in affairs
concerning the State and the administration of Justice shall have
take and hold place and precedence in all places and upon all
occasions before all Baronetts now created or hereafter to be created

any custom usage ordinance or any other matter to the contrary
in any wise notwithstanding And that the Wives of the said
———— ———— and of his heirs male aforesaid successively and respectively by virtue of the said dignity of their said Husbands shall
have hold enjoy and take place and precedence as well during
the lives of such their Husbands as after the deaths of the same
Husbands for and during the natural lives of such Wives next and
immediately after the Wives of the younger Sons of Viscounts and
Barons and the Daughters of Viscounts and Barons and before the
Wives of all persons before whom the Husbands of such Wives by
force of these presents ought to have place and precedence And
in regard that the said degree of Baronett is a degree of Hereditary
Dignity The first born Son or Heir Male apparent and all the rest
of the Sons and their Wives and the Daughters of the said ————
———— and of his said heirs Male respectively shall have and hold
place and precedence before the first born Sons and other Sons and
their Wives and the Daughters of all Knights of whatsoever degree
or order respectively And also before the first born Sons and other
Sons and their Wives and the Daughters of all persons respectively
before whom the Father's such first born Sons and other Sons and
Daughters by force of these presents ought to have place and precedence so that such first born Sons or Heirs Male apparent and
their Wives as well during the lives as after the deaths of their said
Husbands for and during their natural lives and such Sons, those
Sons following immediately and next after the Wives of the first
born Sons of such Baronetts shall have and take place and precedence
before the first born Sons and the Wives of the first born Sons
of every Knight of what degree or order soever And that the
Younger Sons of the said ———— ———— and of his said Heirs Male and
their Wives successively and respectively as well during the lives
as after the deaths of their said Husbands for and during their natural
lives shall in like manner have and take place and precedence next
and immediately after the first born Sons, and the Wives of the first
born Sons and before the younger Sons, and the Wives of the younger
sons whatsoever of Knights aforesaid We will also and do by
these presents for Us Our heirs and successors grant that the said

—— —— shall be named appealed called plead and be impleaded
by the name of —— —— Baronett and that the Style and
addition of Baronett shall be put at the end of the name of the
said —— —— and of his said Heirs Male in all our Letters
Patent Commissions and Writts and all other Charters Deeds and
Letters by virtue of these presents as the true lawful and necessary
addition of dignity   We will also and by these presents for Us
Our Heirs and successors do ordain that before the name of the
said —— —— and of his said Heirs Male aforesaid successively in
English Speech and in all English writings shall be used and set this
addition (to wit) Sir   And that in like manner the Wives of the
said —— —— and of his said Heirs Male shall use have and enjoy
this appellation (to wit) Lady Madam and Dame respectively
according to the manner of speaking   And moreover of Our more
abundant Grace and of our certain knowledge and mere motion
We have granted and by these presents for Us Our Heirs and
successors do grant unto the said —— —— and to his Heirs Male
aforesaid that they and their descendants shall and may bear in a
canton in their Coat of Arms or in an escutcheon at their pleasure
the Arms of Ulster to wit the Hand Gules or a Bloody Hand
in a Field Argent   And that the said —— —— and his Heirs
Male aforesaid successively and respectively shall and may have
place in the Armies of Us Our Heirs and successors in the Troop
nigh to the Banner of Us Our Heirs and successors in defence of
the same (which is the Middle Station between a Baron and a
Knight) and further We do hereby grant that the said —— ——
and his Heirs Male aforesaid shall have two Assistants of the Body
to support the Pall One as principal Mourner and four assistants to
the same principal Mourner in their Funerals   We will Moreover
and do by these presents of our more ample Grace certain knowledge and mere motion for us our Heirs and successors Covenant
and Grant to and with the said —— —— and his said heirs male
that We will immediately after the passing of these presents
create and make the said —— —— a Knight and that We our
Heirs and Successors will create and make the first born Son or
heir male apparent begotten of the body of the said —— —— and

of the bodyes of his heirs male aforesaid and every one of them a Knight as soon as he shall attain the age of One and Twenty Years although in the life time of his Father or Grandfather upon notice given thereof to the Chamberlain or Vice Chamberlain of the household of Us our heirs or successors for the time being or in their absence to any other officer or Member of Us our heirs or successors attending the person of us our heirs or successors. To have hold use and enjoy the same State degree dignity stile title place and precedence with all and singular the privileges and other the promises before granted to the said —— —— and his said heirs Male of his body lawfully begotten for ever Willing and by these presents for Us our heirs and successors Granting that he the said —— —— and his said Heirs Male and every of whom successively shall and may bear and have the same name state degree stile dignity title place and precedence with all and singular the privileges and other the promises And that the said —— —— and his said heirs Male and every of them shall successively be held Baronets in all things and shall be treated and reputed as Baronetts And further of Our more especial Grace certain knowledge and mere motion We have granted and do by these Presents for Us Our heirs and successors grant to the said —— —— and his said heirs Male that they and their heirs male respectively and other Baronetts made and hereafter to be made from time to time shall for ever have hold and enjoy their place and precedence among themselves according to the Priority and Seniority of his creation of a Baronet aforesaid and not otherwise nor in other manner And moreover of Our more abundant grace and of our certain Knowledge and mere motion We have granted and do by these presents for Us Our heirs and successors grant unto the said —— —— and his said heirs Male that neither We nor Our heirs or Successors will hereafter Erect Ordain Constitute or Create within this Our Kingdom of Great Britain any other Degree order name title Style dignity or state nor give or grant place precedence or pre-eminence to any person under or below the degree dignity or state of a Baron of Parliament of this Our Kingdom of Great Britain

who shall be or may be or accounted used or reputed to be
superior or equal to the degree dignity or place of a Baronet
aforesaid nor shall any person under the degree of a Baron (except
before excepted) by reason or colour of any Constitution order
dignity degree office service place business custom use or other
thing whatsoever now or hereafter have hold or enjoy place
precedence or pre-eminence before a Baronett aforesaid   But
that as well the said —— ——. and his said heirs Male as the
Wives Sons Daughters and the Wives of the Sons of the said
—— —— and of his said heirs Male respectively from henceforth for ever shall freely and quietly have hold and enjoy their
said dignity place precedence and privilege before all persons
(except before excepted) who shall hereafter be created of such
degree state dignity order name Stile or Title or to whom the title
place precedence or pre-eminence as aforesaid shall be given or
granted or who shall claim to have hold or enjoy any place or
precedence by reason or colour of any Constitution order dignity
degree office service place business custom use or other thing whatsoever and before their Wives and Children respectively according
to the true intent of these presents without the hindrance of Us
Our Heirs or Successors or any other persons whatsoever Saving
nevertheless and always reserving to Us Our Heirs and Successors
full and absolute power and authority to continue and restore to
any person or persons from time to time such place and precedence
as at any time hereafter shall be due to them which by any accident
or occasion whatsoever shall hereafter be changed any thing in
these presents or any other cause or respect whatsoever to the contrary thereof notwithstanding   We Will moreover and do by these
presents for Us Our heirs and successors grant and appoint that
if any doubt or question as to any place precedence privilege or
other thing touching or concerning the said —— —— and his
said heirs Male and their Wives the first born Sons and their
Wives the Younger Sons Daughters and Wives of the younger
Sons or any of them shall hereafter arise which neither by these
Our Letters Patent nor by other Letters Patent heretofore made
in this behalf are determined such doubts or questions shall be deter-

mined and adjudged by and according to such other rules customs and laws (as to place precedence or other thing concerning them) as other degrees of Hereditary Dignity are ordered governed and adjudged Lastly We will and do by these presents for Us Our Heirs and successors grant to the said —— —— and his said Heirs Male that these Our Letters Patent or the enrolment thereof shall be in and by all things good firm valid sufficient and effectual in the Law as well against Us Our heirs and successors as against all others whomsoever according to the true intent of the same as well in all Our Courts as elsewhere We will also &c. Without Fine in Our Hanaper, &c. In Witness, &c. Witness ourself at Westminster the —— day of ——

By Writt of Privy Seal.'

The long recital or preamble was later on abbreviated to the following, taken from a Patent, dated 16th January 1828 :—

'George the Fourth by the Grace of God &c. To all to whom these presents shall come Greeting. Whereas Our late Royal Progenitor King James the First ordained erected constituted and created a certain state degree and dignity name and title of a Baronet within his then Kingdom of England to endure for ever and that the said state title dignity and degree of a Baronet should be and be reputed to be a middle state title dignity and degree of Hereditary dignity between the degree of a Baron and the degree of a Knight. Now know ye that We, &c.'

On the 19th December 1827 George iv. revoked the promise and grant contained in the Letters Patent of James i. for knighting Baronets and their Heirs Male when they should attain the age of twenty-one, as referred to hereafter, and consequently in all Patents issued after that date the clause which had hitherto appeared conferring these honours has not been inserted.

Among the Baronets created on the 29th June 1611 (the second batch) was Sir Roger Dalyson of Laughton, Lincolnshire, but his original Letters Patent were omitted to be sealed. Accordingly, on the petition of his son Thomas Dalyson, a special warrant was granted on the 27th October 1624 to John, Bishop of Lincoln, Lord Keeper of the Great Seal for making, passing, and sealing Letters Patent, to bear date the 29th June 1611, creating Sir Roger a Baronet.

The following Memorandum preserved in the Public Record Office (*State Papers, Domestic Series, James I.*, vol. clxiv. No. 38) refers to this :—

'6 *May* 1624.

'SIR,—His Matie desires informacion from yow, touching that grant yow lately prepared for his Signature for the Baronetshipp of Sir Thomas Dallison ffor although his ffather Sir Roger Dallison was inrolled amongst the more ancient Baronettes, and paid the eleaven hundred poundes, having then a good estate in Land, but negligently forbare the passing of his Grant att that time : yett because the sonnes estate is much weakened & lesse then was required by the first institution, and that the number may be also otherwise full, His Matie desires to know what prejudice, or inconvenience may fall out by the passing of this grant and how it will stand with the orders sett downe in the institution of the Baronettes his Matie being well inclined to satisfie the Gentleman in this his sute if conveniently it may be done, & that in Justice he ought to have it. ffor the King would not for seemelines sake doe injustice.

'Excuse I pray yow the often trouble I give yow, and commaund in all yor uses.

'Yor assured friend to serve you

(No signature).

GREENWICH, 6 *May* 1624.

(Endorsed)   6 *May* 1624.

To MR. ATTURNEY.

The Form of Patent in use at the present time is of the simplest description, being as follows :—

'VICTORIA BY THE GRACE OF GOD of the United Kingdom of Great Britain and Ireland Queen Defender of the Faith TO ALL TO WHOM THESE PRESENTS SHALL COME GREETING know ye that We of Our especial Grace certain knowledge and mere motion have erected appointed and created Our trusty and well beloved —— —— of —— in Our county of —— Esquire to the dignity state and degree of a BARONET and him the said —— —— do by these Presents erect appoint and create and We have appointed given and granted and by these Presents for Us Our heirs and successors do appoint give and grant unto him the said —— —— the name dignity state degree style and title of Baronet aforesaid to have and to hold the said name dignity state degree style and title of Baronet aforesaid unto him the said —— —— and the heirs male of his body lawfully begotten and to be begotten WILLING and by these Presents granting for Us Our heirs and successors that the said —— —— and his heirs male aforesaid and every of them successively may bear and have the name dignity state degree style and title of Baronet aforesaid and that they and every of them successively may be called and styled by the name of Baronet and that he the said —— —— and his heirs male aforesaid and every of them successively may in all things be held and deemed Baronets and be treated and reputed as Baronets And also that he the said —— —— and his heirs male aforesaid may enjoy and use and every of them successively may enjoy and use by the name of Baronet aforesaid ALL and singular the rights privileges precedences and advantages to the degree of a Baronet in all things duly and of right belonging which other Baronets of England, Scotland, Great Britain, Ireland and the United Kingdom of Great Britain and Ireland have heretofore honourably and quietly used and enjoyed or as they do at present use and enjoy IN WITNESS whereof We have caused these Our Letters to be made Patent. WITNESS OURSELF at Westminster the —— day of —— in the —— year of our Reign.

BY WARRANT UNDER THE QUEEN'S SIGN MANUAL.'

Underneath is engrossed the name of the Secretary to the Lord Chancellor, and to the Patent is attached the Great Seal of England.

On the back of the Patent is endorsed the following, or words to the same effect :—

'The within Patent has been duly recorded in the College of Arms London pursuant to the tenor of a Royal Warrant bearing date the Third day of December 1783 for correcting and preventing abuses in the Order of Baronets and examined therewith this —— day of —— ——.'

This is signed by the Registrar of the College of Arms. The Royal Warrant referred to is given *in extenso* in Chapter VI.

The following is the Form of the Patent of creation of Baronets of Ireland when the Degree was first instituted :—

'Jacobus dei gratia Anglie Scotie Francie et Hibernie Rex fidei defensor, etc. Omnibus ad quos presentes littere nostre pervenerint salutem Cum inter alias Imperii nostri gerendi curas quibus animus noster assidue exercetur illa non minima sit nec minimi momenti de plantatione regni nostri Hibernie ac potissimum Ultonie magne et precelebris ejusdem regni provincie quam nostris jam auspiciis atque armis feliciter sub obsequii Jugum redactam ita constabilire elaboramus ut tanta provincia non solum sincero religionis cultu humanitate civili morumque probitate verum etiam opum affluentia atque omnium rerum copia que statum reipublice ornare vel beare possit magis magisque efflorescat opus sane quod nulli progenitorum nostrorum prestare et proficere licuit Quamvis id ipsum multa sanguinis et opum profusione sepius tentaverint In quo opere sollicitudo nostra regia non solum ad hoc excubare debet ut plantatio ipsa strenue promoveatur oppida condantur edes et castra exstruantur agri colantur et id genus alia sed etiam prospiciendum inprimis ut universus hujusmodi rerum civilium apparatus manu armata videlicet presidiis et cohortibus protegatur et communiatur Nequa aut vis hostilis aut defectio intestina rem disturbet aut impediat Cumque super intimationem nobis antehac factam Quod quidam ex fidelibus subditis nostris regni nostri Anglie paratissimi fuerunt ad hoc Regium nostrum inceptum tam corporibus quam fortunis suis promovendum Nos comoti operis tam sancti ac salutaris intuitu atque gratos habentes hujusmodi generosos affectos atque propensos in obsequium nostrum et bonum publicum voluntates perpendentes-que atque reputantes virtutem et industriam nulla alia re magis quam honore ali atque acui omnemque honorem et dignitatem splendorem et amplitudinem a Rege tanquam a fonte originem et incrementum ducere ad cujus culmen et fastigium proprie spectat novos honorum et dignitatum titulos erigere atque instituere ut pote a quo antiqui illi fluxerint consentaneum duxerimus postulantibus usu reipublice atque temporum ratione nova merita novis dignitatis insignibus rependere Ac propterea ex certa scientia et mero motu nostris more progenitorum nostrorum et predecessorum nostrorum celebris memorie qui potestatem hanc novus gradus inter subditos suos creandi habuerunt et exercuerunt de regali nostra potestate et authoritate ordinaverimus erexerimus constituerimus et creaverimus infra regnum nostrum Anglie quendam statum gradum dignitatem nomen et titulum Baronetti (anglice of a Baronett) infra dictum regnum nostrum Anglie perpetuis temporibus duraturum ac diversos fideles subditos nostros qui nobis auxilium et subsidium ad et versus defensionem dicti regni nostri et precipue pro securitate plantationis dicte provincie Ultonie prestiterint ad et in dictum dignitatis statum et gradum baronetti prefecerimus constituerimus et creaverimus per separales litteras nostras patentes Nos grata memoria recolentes fidelia servicia tam nobis quam precharissime nuper sorori nostre domine Elizabethe nuper Regine per quam plurimos subditos nostros dicti regni nostri Hibernie et progenitores suos non sine sanguinis et opum profusione prestita et impensa Necnon ipsorum animorum alacritatem et perseverantiam ad felicem statum dicti regni nostri Hibernie non solum continuandum sed in dies ampliandum considerantes justum et nobis honorificum futurum duximus paria merita et servicia paribus honoribus remunerare nostraque cura et pro-

videntia regali efficere ut dictum regnum nostrum Hibernie eisdem
legibus moribus religione et honoribus uti regnum nostrum Anglie
in dies magis magisque efflorescat   Nos igitur operis tam honorifici
complementum desiderantes ex certa scientia et mero motu nostris
ac ex regali nostra potestate et authoritate de assensu et consensu
predilecti et fidelis consiliarii nostri Oliveri St John militis deputati
nostri generalis dicti regni nostri Hibernie et secundum intentionem
et effectum letterarum nostrarum manu nostra propria signatarum
gerentium datum apud Apthorpe tricesimo die Julii Anno regni
nostri Anglie Francie et Hibernie decimo septimo et Scotie quinquagesimo tertio predicto deputato et aliis directarum et in Rotulis
Cancellarie nostre dicti regni nostri Hibernie Irrotulatarum quarum
quidem litterarum tenor sequitur in hec verba videlicet Right trustie
and welbeloved wee greete you well we have a purpose to make
a certaine nomber of Baronetts in that our kingdome of Ireland
accordinge the course in England soe much approved and intend-
inge it as a reward for vertue it shalbe our care to advance such men
onely to that dignitie as have well deserved of our Crowne either
in warre or peace to the end that a title of such honnor descending
to their posteritie may invite them to imitate the worth of their
Auncestors uppon whom for their merittes by our good grace and
favour it was worthily conferred Amongest the rest and before all
others in that kingdom as a singuller marke of our favour towardes
him wee have made choise of our trustie and right welbeloved ——
—— and send you a bill to be passed under the greate Seale of that
kingdome for the makinge of him a Knight Baronett signed for his
better grace and honnor with our owne royall hand which wee
require you to see performed according to this our pleasure   And
to lett him understand from us that findinge him soe faithfull and
industrious a servaunte to us and soe usefull to the commonwealth
in the place he holdeth we have freely bestowed this honnor uppon
him without any suite of his and shall uppon all occasions give him
such further testimony of that gratious opinion we have conceived
of him as may lett him understand howe much we value a man of
his honestie and able partes   And for what you shall doe herein
these our letters shalbe your warrant   Given under our signett at

Apthorpe the thirtieth day of July in the seaventeenth yeare of our
Raigne of England ffraunce and Ireland and of Scotland the three
and fiftieth   Ac etiam secundum tenorem et effectum bille predicte
in litteris nostris predictis specificate et in Rotulis Cancellarie predicte Irrotulate ordinavimus ereximus constituimus et creavimus
Ac per presentes pro nobis heredibus et successoribus nostris ordinamus erigimus constituimus et creamus quendam statum gradum
dignitatem nomen et titulum Baronetti infra regnum nostrum
Hibernie perpetuo futuris temporibus duraturum Quodque status
titulus dignitas et gradus predictus Baronetti sit erit et esse reputabitur status titulus dignitas et gradus dignitatis hereditarie loco
medius inter gradum Baronis et gradum militis Sciatis insuper quod
nos attendentes et gratiose considerantes quam plurima servicia nobis
per dilectum et fidelem nostrum prefatum ——— —— de ——
—— in comitatu nostro —— in dicto regno nostro Hibernie
antehac prestita ejusque fidem et alacritatem in plantatione dicti
regni nostri Hibernie antehac promovenda ac ad eandem imposterum
ampliandam et manutenendam de gratia nostra speciali ac ex certa
scientia et mero motu nostris de assensu et consensu predictis   Ac
secundum intentionem et effectum dictarum litterarum nostrarum
et bille predicte Ereximus prefecimus et creavimus eundem ——
—— ad et in dignitatem statum et gradum Baronetti (anglice of
a Barronett) dicti regni nostri Hibernie ipsumque —— —— Baronettum dicti regni nostri Hibernie pro nobis heredibus et successoribus nostris prefecimus constituimus et creamus per presentes habendum sibi et heredibus masculis de corpore suo legittime procreatis
imperpetuum volumus etiam et per presentes de gratia nostra speciali
ac ex certa scientia et mero motu nostris pro nobis heredibus et
successoribus nostris concedimus prefato —— —— et heredibus
masculis de corpore suo legittime procreatis Quod ipse idem ——
—— et heredes sui masculi predicti habeant gaudeant teneant et
capiant locum atque precedentiam virtute dignitatis Baronetti predicti et vigore presentium tam in omnibus commissionibus brevibus
litteris patentibus scriptis appellationibus nominationibus et directionibus quam in omnibus sessionibus conventionibus Cetibus et
locis quibuscunque proxime et imediate post filios Juniores vice-

comitum et Baronum dicti regni nostri Hibernie et pre omnibus
militibus tam de Balneo (Anglice of the Bathe) quam militibus
Baccalaureis (anglice Bachelers) ac etiam pre omnibus militibus
Bannerettis (anglice Banneretts) jam creatis vel imposterum creandis
Illis militibus bannerettis exceptis quos sub vexillis nostris regiis
heredum et successorum nostrorum in exercitu regali in aperto
bello et ipso Rege personaliter presenti explicatis Ac etiam illis
militibus bannerettis quos sub vexillis nostris regiis in exercitu nostro
regali explicatis per primogenitum filium nostrum Carolum nunc
Wallie principem Ibidem personaliter presentem in aperto bello
et non aliter pro termino vitarum eorum tantummodo et non diutius
creari contigerit respective Atque etiam exceptis omnibus militibus
preclari ordinis Garterii ac omnibus de privato consilio nostro
heredum et successorum nostrorum tam in regno nostro Anglie
quam in regno nostro Hibernie subthesaurio Scaccarii Capitali Justiciario de banco regis magistro Rotulorum cancellarie capitali
Justiciario de communi banco capitali Barone Scaccarii et omnibus
et singulis Judicibus et Justiciariis utriusque banci et Baronibus
Scaccarii in regno nostro Hibernie pro tempore existenti ac omnibus
aliis qui ante separales officiarios predictos aut eorum aliquem locum
et precedentiam habere debent qui omnes et singuli ratione talis
ordinis et in negotiis statum reipublice et Justitiam concernentibus
impensi locum et precedentiam in omnibus locis et omni de causa
pre omnibus baronettis dicti regni Hibernie imposterum creandis
habebunt capient et tenebunt aliqua consuetudine usu ordinatione
aut aliqua alia re in contrarium non obstante Quodque uxores dicti
—— —— et heredum suorum masculorum predictorum virtute
dicte dignitatis maritorum suorum predictorum habeant teneant
gaudeant et capiant locum et precedentiam tam durantibus vitis
hujusmodi maritorum suorum quam post eorundem maritorum
mortem pro et durante vita naturali hujusmodi uxorum proxime
et immediate post uxores filiorum Juniorum vicecomitum et
Baronum et filias vicecomitum et Baronum ac pre uxoribus omnium
quoruncunque pre quibus mariti hujusmodi uxorum vigore presentium
habere debent locum et precedentiam Et pro eo quod gradus iste
Baronetti gradus est hereditarius primogenitus filius sive heres

masculus apparens ac ceteri omnes filii et eorum uxores et filie ejusdem —— —— et heredum suorum masculorum predictorum respective habeant et capiant locum et precedentiam ante primogenitos filios ac alios filios et eorum uxores et filias omnium militum cujuscunque gradus seu ordinis respective ac etiam ante primogenitos filios ac alios filios et eorum uxores et filias omnium quoruncunque respective pre quibus patres hujusmodi filiorum primogenitorum, ac aliorum filiorum et filiarum vigore presentium habere debent locum et precedentiam Ita quod hujusmodi filii primogeniti seu heredes masculi apparentes et uxores sue tam in vita quam post mortem maritorum suorum predictorum pro durante vita eorum naturali et hujusmodi filie filiis istis imediate et proxime post uxores filiorum primogenitorum istiusmodi Baronettorum sequentibus habeant et capiant locum et precedentiam ante primogenitum filium et uxorem primogeniti filii cujusvis militis gradus seu ordinis cujuscunque Et quod filii juniores predicti —— —— et heredum masculorum suorum predictorum uxores sue tam in vita quam post mortem maritorum suorum predictorum pro et durantibus vitis suis naturalibus similiter habeant et capiant locum et precedentiam proxime et imediate post filios primogenitos et uxores filiorum primogenitorum et ante juniores filios et uxores juniorum filiorum quorumcunque militum predictorum volumus etiam et per presentes pro nobis heredibus et successoribus nostris de gratia nostra speciali ac ex certa scientia et mero motu nostris concedimus quod predictus —— —— nominetur appelletur nuncupetur placitet et implacitetur per nomen —— —— Baronetti Et quod stilus et additio Baronetti apponatur in fine nominis ejusdem —— —— et heredum masculorum suorum predictorum in omnibus litteris patentibus commissionibus et brevibus nostris atque in omnibus aliis chartis factis atque litteris virtute presentium ut vera legittima et necessaria additio dignitatis volumus etiam et per presentes pro nobis heredibus et successoribus nostris ordinamus Quod nomini dicti —— —— et heredum masculorum suorum predictorum in sermone Anglicano et in omnibus scriptis Anglicanis preponatur hec additio videlicet anglice Sir Et similiter quod uxor ejusdem —— —— et heredum masculorum suorum predictorum habeant utantur et gaudeant hac appellatione videlicet anglice (lady madame and dame) respective secundum usum loquendi Et insuper de abundantiori gratia nostra speciali ac ex certa scientia et mero motu nostris concessimus ac per presentes pro nobis heredibus et successoribus nostris concedimus prefato ——— ——— et heredibus suis masculis predictis Quod ipsi et eorum descendentes gestare possint et valeant aut in Cantone in insignibus suis Anglice in a canton in their coate of armes aut in scuto (Anglice an escutchion) ad libitum suum insignia Ultonie (Anglice the armes of Ulster) videlicet manum gules vel sanguineam manum in campo argenteo (anglice a hand gules or a bloody hand in a field argent) Et quod predictus ——— ——— et heredes sui masculi predicti habeant et habebunt locum in exercitu nostro heredum et successorum nostrorum in Turma prope regale vexillum nostrum heredum et successorum nostrorum in defensionem ejusdem que proportio media est inter Baronem et militem Et ulterius concedimus quod predictus ——— ——— et heredes sui masculi predicti habebunt duos assistentes corporis ad supportandum pallium (anglice two assistants of the body to assist the pall) unum principalem atratum anglice a principall mourner et quatuor assistentes eidem principali atrato in exequiis suis volumus insuper ac per presentes de ampliori gratia nostra certa scientia et mero motu nostris convenimus et concedimus prefato ——— ——— et heredibus suis masculis predictis Quod nos heredes et successores nostri aut deputatus noster heredum et successorum nostrorum dicti regni Hibernie filios primogenitos seu heredes masculos apparentes de corpore dicti ——— ——— ac de corporibus heredum masculorum dicti ——— ——— procreatorum et unumquemque eorum quamprimum etatem viginti et unius annorum attigerit licet in vita patris vel avi sui super notitiam inde eidem deputato aut camerario vel vicecamerario hospitii nostri heredum vel successorum nostrorum pro tempore existenti aut in absentia eorum alicui alii officiario seu ministro nostro heredum vel successorum nostrorum personam nostram heredum vel successorum nostrorum attendenti datam in militem creabimus et faciemus creabit et faciet habendum tenendum utendum et gaudendum eadem statum gradum dignitatem stilum titulum nomen locum et precedentiam cum omnibus et singulis privilegiis et ceteris premissis preconcessis prefato —— —— et heredibus masculis de corpore suo exeuntibus imperpetuum volentes et per presentes concedentes pro nobis heredibus et successoribus nostris Quod predictus —— —— et heredes sui masculi predicti nomen statum gradum stilum dignitatem titulum locum et precedentiam predictam cum omnibus et singulis privilegiis et ceteris premissis successive gerant et habeant et eorum quilibet gerat et habeat Quodque idem —— —— et heredes sui masculi predicti successive Baronetti in omnibus teneantur et ut Baronetti tractentur et reputentur et eorum quilibet teneatur tractetur et reputetur Et ulterius de uberiori gratia nostra certa scientia et mero motu nostris concessimus ac per presentes pro nobis heredibus et successoribus nostris concedimus prefato —— —— et heredibus suis masculis predictis Quod numerus Baronettorum dicti regni Hibernie nunquam posthac excedet in toto in aliquo uno tempore numerum centum Baronettorum et quod dicti Baronetti et heredes sui masculi predicti respective de tempore in tempus imperpetuum habebunt tenebunt et gaudebunt locum et precedentiam suas interse videlicet quilibet eorum secundum prioritatem et senioritatem creationis Baronetti predicti Quotquot autem creabuntur Baronetti per litteras nostras patentes gerentes datum uno et eodem die illi et heredes sui predicti gaudebunt locis et precedentiis suis inter se secundum prioritatem que cuilibet eorum dabitur per litteras nostras patentes in ea parte primo conficiendas sine impedimento et non aliter nec alio modo Et insuper de abundantiori gratia nostra speciali ac ex certa scientia et mero motu nostris concessimus ac per presentes pro nobis heredibus et successoribus nostris concedimus prefato —— —— et heredibus suis masculis predictis Quod nec nos nec heredes vel successores nostri de cetero imposterum erigemus ordinabimus constituemus aut creabimus infra dictum regnum nostrum Hibernie aliquem alium gradum ordinem nomen titulum stilum dignitatem sive statum nec dabimus aut concedemus locum precedentiam sive preheminentiam alicui persone sub vel infra gradum dignitatem sive statum Baronum parliamenti dicti regni nostri Hibernie qui erit vel esse possit aut habebitur usitabitur aut reputabitur esse superior anterior vel equalis gradui dignitati vel loco Baronettorum predictorum Nec persona

aliqua infra gradum Baronis (exceptis preexceptis) ratione seu colore
alicujus constitutionis ordinis dignitatis gradus officii servicii loci
negotii consuetudinis usus seu alterius rei cujuscunque nunc aut
imposterum habebit tenebit vel gaudebit locum precedentiam sive
preheminentiam ante Baronettos predictos sed quod tam dictus
——— ——— et heredes sui masculi predicti quam uxor filii filie et
uxores filiorum ejusdem ——— ——— ac heredum masculorum suorum
predictorum respective de cetero imperpetuum libere et quiete
habeant teneant et gaudeant dignitatem locum precedentiam et
privilegia sua predicta pre omnibus (exceptis preexceptis) qui nunc
sunt aut imposterum erint creati de talibus gradibus statibus dignitatibus ordinibus nominibus stilis vel titulis vel quibustalis locus
precedentia vel preheminentia ut prefertur dabitur vel concedetur
vel qui habere tenere et gaudere clamabunt aliquem locum sive
precedentiam ratione sive colore alicujus talis consuetudinis ordinis
dignitatis gradus officii servicii loci negotii consuetudinis usus seu
alterius rei cujuscunque ac pre uxoribus et liberis suis respective
secundum veram Intentionem presentium absque impedimento
nostro heredum vel successorum nostrorum vel aliorum quorumcunque Salva tamen et nobis heredibus et successoribus nostris
semper reservatis plena et absoluta potestate et authoritate con-
tinuandi et restaurandi alicui persone sive personis de tempore in
tempus talem locum et precedentiam qualia aliquo tempe posthac
sibi debita erunt que per aliquem casum sive occationem quamcunque imposterum mutabuntur Aliquam in presentibus aut aliqua
alia re causa sive respectu quocunque in contrarium nonobstante Et
ulterius per presentes declaramus et significamus beneplacitum et
voluntatem nostram in hac parte fore et esse et sic nobiscum
statuimus et decrevimus Quod si postquam nos predictum numerum
centum Baronettorum dictorum regni Hibernie compleverimus et
perfecerimus contigerit aliquem vel aliquos eorundem Baronettorum
ab hac vita decedere absque heredibus masculis de corpore vel
corporibus hujusmodi Baronetti vel baronettorum procreatis Quod
tunc Nos non creabimus vel perficiemus aliquem aliam personam
vel alias personas in Baronettum vel Baronettos dicti regni nostri
Hibernie sed quod numerus dictorum centum Baronettorum ea

ratione de tempore in tempus diminuetur et in minorem numerum
cedet et redigetur volumus insuper ac per presentes pro nobis
heredibus et successoribus nostris prefato ——— ——— et heredibus
suis masculis predictis convenimus et concedimus Quod si dubitationes sive questiones alique (quo-ad aliquem locum precedentiam
privilegium seu aliam rem) predictum ——— ——— et heredes masculos
de corpore suo et uxores eorum primogenitos filios et uxores suos
filias filios Juniores et Juniorum filiorum uxores sive eorum aliquem
tangentes sive concernentes imposterum orientur que per has litteras
nostras patentes jam determinate non existunt hujusmodi dubitationes sive questiones determinabuntur et adjudicabuntur per et
secundum hujusmodi usuales regulas consuetudines et leges (quo-ad
locum precedentiam privilegia seu alia ista concernentia) prout alius
gradus dignitatis hereditarie ordinantur reguntur et adjudicantur
denique volumus ac per presentes pro nobis heredibus et successoribus
nostris de gratia nostra speciali ac ex certa scientia et mero motu
nostris concedimus prefato ——— ——— et heredibus suis masculis
predictis Quod he littere nostre patentes erunt in omnibus et per
omnia firme valide bone sufficientes et effectuales in lege tam contra
nos heredes et successores nostros quam contra omnes alios quoscunque secundum veram intentionem earundem tam in omnibus
Curiis nostris quam alibi ubicunque Nonobstante aliqua lege consuetudine prescriptione usu ordinatione sive constitutione quacunque
antehac editis habitis usitatis ordinatis sive provisis vel imposterum
edendis habendis usitandis ordinandis vel providendis Et non obstante
aliqua alia re causa vel materia quacunque volumus etiam, etc.
Absque fine in hanaperio, etc.   Eo quod expressa mentio, etc.   In
cujus rei testimonium has litteras nostras fieri fecimus patentes
Teste prefato deputato nostro generali regni nostri Hibernie Apud
Dublin ultimo die septembris Anno regni nostri Anglie Francie et
Hibernie decimo septimo et Scotie Quinquagesimo tertio

Virtute litterarum domini Regis ab Anglia missarum et manu sua
propria signatarum.

The following is an example of the later Patent in
English of a Baronet of Ireland, and is the one used for

Sir Jonah Wheeler Denny Cuffe, the last creation of the Baronetage of Ireland :—

'GEORGE the Third by the Grace of God of Great Britain France and Ireland King, Defender of the Faith and so forth To ALL unto whom these presents shall come Greeting WHEREAS the Most Illustrious Prince King James the first of Blessed Memory for the Security of Our Plantation of Our Province of Ulster in our Kingdom of Ireland of his mere Motion and Royal Power and Authority ordained constituted and created a certain State Degree Dignity Name and Title of Baronet within our Kingdom of Ireland to continue for ever and that the said State Dignity Title and Degree of Baronet should be and reputed an hereditary State Dignity Title and Degree between the Degree of a Baron and the degree of a Knight KNOW YE therefore that We being well assured of the many and very faithful services of our Trusty and well beloved ——— ——— of —— in the County of   Esquire and being fully certified of his Faith and Industry and also of his Ability and Chearfulness in advancing our said Plantation in our said Kingdom of Ireland and in enlarging and maintaining the same for the future of our special Grace certain Knowledge and mere Motion by and with the advice and consent of our Right Trusty and entirely beloved Cousin and Counsellor CHARLES MARQUIS CORN-WALLIS our Lieutenant General and General Governor of our said Kingdom of Ireland and according to the Tenor and Effect of our Letters under our Privy Signet and Royal Sign Manual bearing date at our Court at Saint James's the fourteenth day of August one thousand seven hundred and ninety nine in the thirty ninth year of our Reign and now Enrolled in the Rolls of our High Court of Chancery in our said Kingdom of Ireland and remaining of Record in our said Court have advanced raised and created and by these presents We do for us our Heirs and Successors advance raise and create our said trusty and well beloved ——— ——— to the Dignity State and Degree of a Baronet in and of our said Kingdom of Ireland To HAVE HOLD and ENJOY the said Dignity unto him the said ——— ——— and the Heirs Male of his body lawfully begotten and our Will is and by these presents of our special Grace certain Knowledge and mere Motion for Us our Heirs and Successors We do grant unto the said —— —— and the Heirs Male of his body lawfully begotten that he the said —— —— and the Heirs Male of his body lawfully begotten may have hold enjoy and take place and precedence by Virtue of the Dignity of Baronet and of these Presents as well in all Commissions Writs Letters patent writings appellations Nominations Appointments and Directions as in all Sessions Conventions Assemblies and places whatsoever next and immediately after the younger sons of Viscounts and Barons of our said Kingdom of Ireland and before all Knights as well of the Bath as Knights Batchelors and also before all Knights Banneretts heretofore created and hereafter to be created these Knights Banneretts only excepted who shall happen to be created under the Royal Banner of Us our Heirs and Successors displayed in a Royal Army in open War the King himself being personally present by the Eldest Son of the King there personally present in open War and not otherwise and also except all Knights of the Most Noble Order of the Garter and all those of the Privy Council of Us our Heirs and Successors as well in our Kingdom of England as in our Kingdom of Ireland Vice Treasurers of our Exchequer Chief Justices of our Court of Kings Bench Masters of the Rolls Chancellors Chief Justices of our Common Bench Chief Barons of our Exchequer and all and singular the Justices and Judges of each Bench and Barons of our Exchequer in our said Kingdom of Ireland for the time being and all others who before the several Officers aforesaid or any of them ought to have place and precedence and who by means of such Order and Business concerning the State Common Wealth and Justice ought to have and take place and precedence in all places before all Baronets of our said Kingdom of Ireland created or hereafter to be created any Custom Use Ordinance or any other thing to the contrary notwithstanding and that the Wives of the said —— —— and of the Heirs Male of his body lawfully begotten and to be begotten by Virtue of the Dignity of their Husbands may have hold and enjoy and take place and precedence as well during the Lives of such Husbands

as after the death of the same Husbands for and during the natural
lives of such Wives next and immediately after the Wives of the
Younger sons of Viscounts and Barons and the Daughters of
Viscounts and Barons and before the Wives of all those before
whom the Husbands of such wives by Virtue of these presents ought
to have place and precedence   And in regard that the said Degree
of Baronet is hereditary to the Eldest Son or Heir Male apparent
that the eldest son and all other the sons and their Wives and the
daughters of the said —— —— and of his Heirs respectively may
have and take place and precedence before the Eldest Son and other
sons and their Wives and before the Daughters of all Knights of
what Degree or Order soever respectively and also before the Eldest
Son or other Sons and their Wives and the Daughters of all Persons
whatsoever respectively before whom the Father of such Eldest son
and other sons and their Wives and Daughters by Virtue of these
presents ought to have place and precedence so that such Eldest son
or Heir Male apparent and their Wives as well in the Lifetime as
after the death of their Husbands aforesaid for and during their
natural lives and such other sons and their Wives immediately and
next after the Wife of such Eldest son being a Baronet may have
and take place and precedence before the Eldest son and the wife of
the Eldest Son of any Knight of any Degree or Order whatsoever
and that the younger sons of the said —— —— and the Heirs Male
of their Bodies and their Wives as well in the Lifetime as after the
death of their Husbands aforesaid for and during their Natural Lives
may have and take place and precedence next and immediately after
the Eldest Sons and the Wives of the Eldest Sons and the younger
sons and the Wives of the younger sons of any Knights whatsoever
AND our further Will is and by these presents for us Our Heirs and
Successors We do grant that the said —— —— may be named
called stiled and may plead and be impleaded by the name of SIR
—— —— Baronet and that the Stile and addition of Baronet may
be added at the end of the Name of the said —— —— and of the
Heirs Male of his Body in all our Letters Patent Commissions and
Writs and in all Charters Deeds and Letters by Virtue of these
presents as a true legal and necessary addition of dignity   AND our

further Will likewise is and by these presents for Us our Heirs and
Successors WE Order that before the Name of the said ——— ———
and the Heirs Male of his body in English Discourse and in all
English Writing this addition that is to say 'Sir' shall be put and
likewise that the Wives of the said ——— ——— and of the Heirs
Male of his Body aforesaid may have use and enjoy these Titles
that is to say 'Lady, Madam and Dame' respectively according to
the manner of discoursing   MOREOVER of our abundant Special Grace
certain Knowledge and mere motion We have granted and by
these presents for Us our Heirs and Successors We do grant unto
the said ——— ——— and the Heirs Male of his Body aforesaid that
they and their Descendants may wear and bear in a Canton on their
Coat of Arms or in an Escutcheon at their Pleasure the Arms of
Ulster that is to say an Hand gules or a bloody Hand in a field
Argent and that the said ——— ——— and the Heirs Male of his
Body aforesaid may and shall have a place in the Army of Us our
Heirs and Successors in the Troop near the Royal Banner of Us
our Heirs and Successors in Defence of the same which is the
middle Degree or Station between Barons and Knights   AND
further We do grant that the said ——— ——— and the Heirs Male
of his Body aforesaid shall have two Assistants of the Body to
support the Pall a Principal Mourner and four Assistants to the
said Principal Mourner at their Funerals   AND our further Will
is and by these presents of our more abundant special Grace certain
Knowledge and mere Motion We have granted to the said ———
——— and the Heirs Male of his Body aforesaid that We our Heirs
and Successors or the Deputy of us our Heirs and Successors of our
said Kingdom of Ireland the Eldest sons or Heirs Male apparent
of the Body of the said ——— ——— and of the Bodies of the Heirs
Male of the said ——— ——— begotten or to be begotten and each
of them as soon as they shall attain to the age of twenty one
years although in the lifetime of their Father or Grandfather upon
Notice thereof to the said Deputy or Chamberlain or Vice Chamberlain of the Household of Us our Heirs or Successors for the
time being or in their Absence to any other Officer or Minister
of Us our Heirs or Successors attending upon Us our Heirs or

Successors shall make and create Knights To have hold and Enjoy
the said State Degree Dignity Stile Title Name place and precedence with all and singular the Privileges and other the Premises
before granted to the said —— —— and his Heirs Male of his
Body issuing for ever WILLING and by these Presents granting for
Us our Heirs and Successors that the said —— —— and the Heirs
Male of his Body aforesaid may bear and have and each of them
may bear and have the name State Degree Stile Dignity Honor
place and Precedence with all and singular the Privileges and other
the Premises successively and that the said —— —— and the Heirs
Male of his Body may successively be Baronets in all things and
may be treated and reputed and each of them may be deemed
treated and reputed as Baronets and that the said Baronets and their
Heirs male of their Bodies aforesaid respectively from time to time
for ever shall hold and enjoy their Places and Precedencies amongst
themselves that is to say each of them according to the Priority
and Seniority of his Creation but as many as shall be created by
our Letters patent bearing date on one and the same day and their
Heirs Male aforesaid shall enjoy without impediment their places
and precedences between themselves according to the Priority which
shall be given to each of them by our Letters patent in that behalf
first executed and not otherwise or in other manner And further
of our abundant special Grace certain knowledge and mere motion
We have granted and by these Presents for Us our Heirs and
Successors We do grant unto the said —— —— and the Heirs
Male of his Body aforesaid that neither We our Heirs or Successors
for the future shall make Ordain Constitute or create within our
said Kingdom of Ireland any Degree Order Name Title Stile
Dignity or State nor will We give or grant place precedence or
pre-eminence to any person under or below the Degree Dignity
or State of Barons of Parliament of our said Kingdom of Ireland
who shall or can be or shall be had used or reputed to be superior
or higher or equal to the Degree and Dignity or place of Baronets
aforesaid (except as before excepted) but that as well the said
—— —— and the Heirs male of his Body aforesaid as the Wives
Sons and Daughters and the Wives of the sons of the said —— ——

and of his Heirs Male aforesaid respectively for ever may freely and
quietly have hold and enjoy their Dignities Places Precedences and
Privileges aforesaid before all those (except as before excepted) who
hereafter shall be created by such Degree State Dignity Order
Name Stile or Title or to Whom such places precedences or pre-
eminences aforesaid shall be given or granted or who shall claim
to have hold or enjoy any place or precedence by means or colour
of any such Custom Order Dignity Degree Office Service Place
Business or any other Matter whatsoever and before their Wives
and children respectively according to the true Intention of these
Presents without any Impediment of Us our Heirs or Successors
or any others whomsoever saving and notwithstanding and always
reserving for Us our Heirs and Successors full and absolute Power
and Authority of continuing and restoring to any person or persons
from time to time such place and precedence as at any Time hereafter shall be due to him or them who for any Cause or Occasion
whatsoever hereafter shall be changed any thing in these presents
or any other thing cause matter or respect whatsoever to the contrary notwithstanding   AND our further Will is and by these
presents for Us our Heirs and Successors We do grant unto the
said ⸺ ⸺ and the Heirs Male of his body that if any Doubt
or Question shall hereafter arise as to any place precedence privilege
or other Matter aforesaid touching or concerning the said ⸺ ⸺
and the Heirs Male of his Body aforesaid and their Wives the Eldest
Sons and their Wives the younger sons and the wives of the younger
Sons or any of them which by these our Letters patent are not
now determined such Doubt or Question shall be determined and
adjudged by and according to such rules customs and Laws as concern such place precedence and privilege as other Degrees of
Hereditary Dignities are ordered ruled and adjudged   AND further
of our more abundant special Grace And by and with the advice
and Consent aforesaid We do declare and signify our Pleasure and
Royal Will in this behalf to be and so We have determined and
appointed that the said ⸺ ⸺ and the Heirs Male of his Body
lawfully begotten may be exonerated and discharged from all
Charges and Payments whatsoever and from all services of what

kind soever which are due or ought to be paid to Us our Heirs or
Successors by means or consideration of the Honor and Dignity
aforesaid any thing in these our Letters patent contained to the
contrary notwithstanding AND our Will is and by these presents
for us our Heirs and Successors of our special Grace certain knowledge and mere Motion We do grant unto the said ——— ——— and
the Heirs Male of his Body aforesaid that these our Letters Patent
or the Inrollment of them shall be in all things good firm valid
sufficient and effectual in the Law as Well against Us our Heirs
and Successors as against all others whomsoever according to the
true Intention of the same as well in all our Courts as elsewhere
wheresoever any Cause or Matter whatsoever to the contrary notwithstanding. LASTLY our Will is that the said ——— ——— Baronet
may and shall have those our letters Patent under the Great Seal
of Ireland without any Fine great or small for the same unto our
Hanaper to be rendered paid or made altho no express mention be
made in these presents of the free yearly value or Certainty of the
Premises or any of them or any other Gifts by Us or by any of our
Progenitors made to the said ——— ——— PROVIDED ALWAYS that
these our Letters Patent be inrolled in the Rolls of our High Court
of Chancery in our said Kingdom of Ireland within the space of
six Months next ensuing the date of these presents IN WITNESS
whereof We have caused these our Letters to be made Patent
WITNESS our aforesaid Lieutenant General and General Governor
of our said Kingdom of Ireland at Dublin the ——— day of ——— in
the ——— year of our Reign.'

The Patent of the Baronets of Scotland and Nova Scotia
is naturally of much greater length than any of the preceding, it having been the original intention that each Baronet
should obtain in addition to his dignity sixteen thousand
acres of land in Nova Scotia, all particularly bounded and
its limits ascertained in his Patent.

The following is the Patent in full of Sir Robert Gordon
of Gordonstown, the first Baronet created :—

'CAROLUS, Dei gratia, Magnæ Britanniæ, Franciæ, et Hiberniæ, rex, fideique defensor, OMNIBUS probis hominibus totius terræ suæ, clericis et laicis, salutem. SCIATIS, nos, cum consilio et consensu prædilecti nostri consanguinei et consiliarii Johannis Marriæ comitis, domini Erskine et Garioch, etc. magni regni nostri Scotiæ thesaurarii, computorum rotulatoris, collectoris, ac thesaurarii novarum nostrarum augmentationum, ac dilecti et familiaris nostri consiliarii, domini Archibaldi Napier de Merchingstoun, militis, nostri in eisdem officiis deputati, ac etiam dominorum nostri secreti consilii ejusdem regni nostri Scotiæ, nostrorum commissionariorum, pro propagatione religionis Christianæ infra bondas regni et dominii nostri Novæ Scotiæ, jacen. infra terminos Americæ, limitibus Novæ Angliæ confinis, per dilectum nostrum dominum Willielmum Alexander de Menstrie, militem, pro magnis suis sumptibus et impensis tam mari et navigationibus, quam terra, non ita pridem inventi, et supervisi, nunc hæreditarium proprietarium ejusdem regni, et dominii, et nostrum locum tenentem, et deputatum, infra easdem bondas, pro promptiori opere et auxilio in plantatione et policia ejusdem, et ad reducendum dictum regnum ad nostram obedientiam, proque bono et gratuito servitio nobis per dilectum nostrum DOMINUM ROBERTUM GORDON, militem, filium quondam Alexandri Sutherlandiæ comitis, et pro diversis aliis magnis et gravibus considerationibus, nos moven. Dedisse, concessisse, et disposuisse, tenoreque præsentis cartæ nostræ, cum consilio antedict. dare, concedere, et disponere, præfato prædilecto nostro DOMINO ROBERTO GORDON, militi, filio quondam Alexandri Sutherlandiæ comitis, *hæredibus suis masculis, et assignatis quibuscunque, hæreditarie,* TOTAM ET INTEGRAM illam partem et portionem dict. bondarum et terrarum regni et dominii Novæ Scotiæ, ut subsequitur, vulgari nostro sermone particulariter bondat. et limitat. To WITT, Beginnand on the sea-cost at the south-west part of land, upon the eastmost side of that bay callit Port de Montoun, and from thence going eastward thrie myllis alongst the cost, and from thence passing northward from the said sea-cost unto the mayn land, anent these thrie myllis, till the quantitie thairof extend to sexteen thousand acres of land, keeping alwayis thrie myllis in bried; cum castris,

turribus, fortaliciis, maneriarum locis, domibus, ædificiis extructis
vel extruendis, hortis, pomariis plantatis vel plantandis, toftis, croftis,
parcis, campis, pratis, molendinis, multuris, terris molendinariis, et
sequelis, silvis, piscationibus, tam rubrorum quam alborum piscium,
salmonum, aliorumque magnorum et parvorum piscium, tam in salsis
quam aquis dulcibus, advocatione, donatione, benificiorum ecclesiarum
et capellaniarum, et juribus patronatuum earund. annexis, connexis,
dependentiis, tenentibus, tenandriis, libere tenentium servitiis, una
cum omnibus et singulis fodinis, mineralibus venis, saxis latoniis,
tam metallorum et mineralium, regalium vel regiorum, auri et
argenti, infra dictas bondas et terras, quam aliarum fodinarum ferri,
chalybis, stanni, electri, cupri, plumbi, æris, aurichalchi, et aliorum
mineralium quorumcunque ; Una etiam cum omnibus et singulis
pretiosis lapillis, gemmis, margaritis, unionibus, chrystallis, aluminibus,
lie curell, et aliis ; Et cum plenaria potestate, privilegio, et jurisdictione liberæ regalitatis infra totas et integras prædictas bondas et
terras, omnium et singularum partium, pendiculorum, pertinentium,
privilegorium, et commoditatum earund. terrarum, aliorumque
supra mentionat.   CUM plenaria potestate et privilegio præfato
domino Roberto Gordon, suis hæredibus masculis, et assignatis,
venandi, tentandi, fodiendi, eruendi, ac scrutandi fundum dictarum
terrarum pro dictis fodinis, mineralibus, pretiosis lapillis, gemmis,
margaritis, unionibus, aliisque supra script. et utendi omni legitima
et ordinaria industria pro inventione et recuperatione eorundem, et
lucrandi, extrahendi, evelandi, purgandi, examinandi, re-examinandi,
et purificandi eadem, tam dict. aurum et argentum, quam alia
metalla, pretiosos lapillos, margaritas, uniones, et alia supra mentionat,
et eadem ad suos proprios usus convertendi et applicandi, similiter
et tam libere quam præfatus dominus Willielmus Alexander, sui
hæredes, et assignati, virtute originalis infeofamenti, ipsis desuper
fact. et concess. de data apud Windsor, decimo die mensis
Septembris, anno Domini millesimo sexcentesimo vigesimo primo
facere potuerunt.   RESERVATA tamen nobis, nostris hæredibus et
successoribus, decima parte regalium metallorum, communiter vocat.
lie ore auri, et argenti, lucrandorum, et obtinendorum, omnibus
temporibus a futuris, infra dictas bondas et terras, et reliquis metallis

mineralibus, pretiosis lapillis, gemmis, margaritis, unionibus, aliisque
quibuscunque, in usum et proprietatem præfati domini Roberti,
hæredum suorum masculorum, et assignatorum, in perpetuum integre
cessuris, per ipsos intromittendis, cum omnibus proficuis, divoriis, et
commoditatibus earund.   Cum potestate etiam præfato domino
Roberto Gordon, suis hæredibus masculis, et assignatis, ædificandi,
extruendi, et erigendi infra bondas ejusdem et fundi terrarum, super
quacunque parte earund. civitates, urbes, oppida, villas, burgos,
baroniæ liberos portus, sinus, navium habitationes, et stationes, infra
eosdem, castra, turres, fortalicia, munimenta, extructiones, valles,
aggeres, propugnacula, infra easdem bondas, terras, civitates, burgos,
stationes, portus, aliaque loca quæcunque, tam per mare et littora,
quam per terras, munita, supportata, et inhabitata, mœnibus, et
præfidiis militum et armatorum, pro fortificatione, roboratione,
tutela, et defensione earund.   Et similiter erigendi, et constituendi
nundinas, mercaturas, et mercemoniarium loca, infra dictas civitates,
burgos, urbes, villas, et baroniæ burgos, et infra aliquam aliam
partem omnium et singularum dictarum bondarum et terrarum,
vel in burgis, vel villis custodiend. observand. et manutenen.
quibus temporibus, particularibus diebus, anni temporibus, locis
et occasionibus, prout præfato domino Roberto, suis hæredibus
masculis, et assignatis, expediens videbitur ; et imponendi, exigendi,
tollendi, et recipiendi, omnes et quascunque tolonias, custumas,
anchoragia, primitias, lie vrymguilts, carmarum salaria, lie doksilver,
et alias divorias earundem civitatum, burgorum, oppidorum, villarum
portuum, stationum, nundinarum, et fororum, prout præfato domino
Roberto, suis hæredibus masculis, et assignatis, magis videbitur
expedien. cum omnibus et singulis privilegiis, libertatibus, et commoditatibus eisdem spectan.   Et similiter faciendi et constituendi
capitanos, imperatores, ductores, et gubernatores, majores officiarios,
præpositos, et balivos dict. civitatum, burgorum, urbium, villarum et
burgorum baroniæ regalitatis, portuum, stationum, castrorum et
munimentorum, una cum justiciariis pacis, constabulariis, aliis
officiariis, tam in causis criminalibus, quam civilibus, pro regimine,
vera et legitima administratione justiciæ infra easdem, et reliquas
bondas præscript, terrarum, bondarum, et littorum ; et si ipsis

videbitur eosdem magistratus et officiaros, pro promptiori et meliori
præfatarum bondarum regimine, alterand. et mutand. et ordinem
ineundi pro ipsorum regimine, prout ipsis expediens videbitur,
necnon faciendi, constituendi, et ordinandi hujusmodi particulares
leges, ordinationes, et constitutiones, infra totas et integras præfatas
terras et bondas, tam in burgis quam in villis, prout ipsis expediens
videbitur, omni tempore a futuro observandos, prævaricatores et
contravenientes eisdem castigandi, corrigendi, et conformiter
puniendi.   Ac etiam, ædificandi et extruendi naves, navigia, et
vasa, tam magna quam parva, tam bello quam mercimoniis apta;
vel infra dictum dominium Novæ Scotiæ, et partes dictarum
terrarum, præfato domino Roberto, suis hæredibus masculis, et
assignatis, specialiter supra designat.   Cum omni genere muni-
tionum, bombardarum magnarum seu parvarum, pulveris sulphurei,
globuli armorum, et omnium armorum, invasioni vel defensioni
convenien. et omnibus aliis ingenii et belli exercitationibus.   Et
similiter, transportandi eisdem, aut quibuscunque aliis navibus ad
dictum regnum Novæ Scotiæ, et speciales bondas supra designatas,
tormenta, semitormenta, lie cannonis, semicannonis, fusilia, et alias
munitiones, magnas seu parvas, pro defensione, salute, et tuitione
dicti regni.   Et similiter, cum expressa potestate, privilegio, et
licentia, præfato domino Roberto, suis hæredibus masculis, assignatis
et deputatis, vel aliis ipsorum nominibus, transportandi de dicto
regno Scotiæ, vel aliis nostris dominus, vel alio pro ipsorum arbitrio,
omnes et quascunque personas, milites, bellicosos colonos, artifices,
mercatores, vel alios strategos cujuscunque qualitatis, status, seu
graduum, cum suis bonis, supellectilibus, equis, catellis, bovibus,
ovibus, munitionibus, magnis seu parvis armis, provisionibus, et
commeatu ad dict. fundum et terras, pro meliori armatu et propagatione dictæ plantationis.   Et similiter, utendi et exercendi
omni legitimo genere mercemoniarum, pro meliori policia earundem
bondarum et terrarum, et excludendi, prohibendi, inhibendi, resistendi,
repellendi, et invadendi vi et armis, omnes et quascunque personas
intendentes plantationem, occupationem, vel possessionem dictarum
bondarum et terrarum, vel ad exercendum, utendum, mercandum,
aut negotiandum infra easdem, absque expresso avisamento, licentia,

et consensu dicti domini Roberti Gordon, suorum hæredum masculorum, assignatorum vel deputatorum, ad id effectum habito et
obtento, et confiscandi, intromittendi, detinendi, et authorendi
omnes et singulas naves, bona, catella, et supellectilia, vel per mare
vel terras usurpantium in contrarium, et eadem ad proprios usus,
utilitatem, et commodum dicti domini Roberti, suorumque prædict.
applicandi, cum expressis warranto et mandato omnibus nostris
vicecomitibus, senescallis, et balivis regalitatum, justiciariis pacis,
majoribus, senioribus, præpositis, balivis, et serjandis, constabulariis,
et justiciæ ministris quibuscunque, concurrendi, fortificandi, et
assistendi præfato domino Roberto, suisque præscript. in eisdem, et
in debita et legitima executione omnium et singulorum punctorum,
clausularum, et articulorum, dictæ cartæ et infeofamenti; Et
quod paratam habeant navigationem ad omnes occasiones, pro suis
hominibus, copiis, bonis, catellis, munitionibus, armis, loricis, commeatu, et præparationibus, ad et a dictis bondis et regni Novæ
Scotiæ, cum ipsis, si videbitur, suis rationabilibus sumptibus et
impensis, ut congruit. Cum potestate etiam præfato domino
Roberto, suis hæredibus masculis, assignatis et deputatis, in casu
rebellionis, tumultus, vel seditionis infra dictas bondas, fundum et
terras, vel in cursu itinerum, vel navigationum, ad vel ab iisdem, ut
si contigerit aliquam personam, vel personas, infra easdem bondas et
terras, et qui erunt sub imperio et mandato eorum in dictis itineribus,
et navigationibus, prævaricare et contraire ipsorum mandatis: In
hoc casu, vel aliquo eorum casuum, utendi, et exercendi potestatem
et privilegium omnium jurium militarium contra delinquentes, et
reos puniendi, et corrigendi eosdem hujus legibus, prout ipsis videbitur expediens. Excludendo per præfentis cartæ nostræ tenorem,
nostrum locum tenentem, et omnes alias personas quascunque, ab
usu et exercitatione quarumcunque legum militarium contra dictas
personas, vel earum aliquam infra dictas bondas, in dictis itineribus
et cursibus, in et abs eisdem; exceptis dicto domino Roberto, suis
hæredibus masculis, assignatis vel suis deputatis tantum. Ac etiam,
nos, pro nobis et successoribus nostris, cum consilio et consensu
antedicto, tenore præsentis cartæ eximimus, quiete clamamus, et
liberamus præfatum dominum Robertum, suos hæredes masculos,

et assignatos, ab omni pœna, arrestatione, tortura, et executione jurium vel legum militarium, quæ contra ipsos vel ipsorum aliquem, per nostrum locum tenentem, vel aliquam aliam personam, vel personas quascunque, instigi, intendi, vel exerceri, poterint. Et si contigerit etiam prædictas personas, vel aliquam ipsarum, sub imperio, manutenentia, vel dependentia dicti domini Roberti, suorumque præscript. abstrahere vel subducere se ipsos ab obedientia dicti domini Roberti, suorumque præscript. vel suis servitiis in dicta plantatione, et defensione ejusdem, vel per mare vel per terras, vel in ipsorum cursu et itinere ad et a dicto regno Novæ Scotiæ, vel subducere et abstrahere se ipsos, sua bona, vel catella, a ministerio et obedientia dicti domini Roberti, vel removere seipsos, vel bona, vel catella, a bondis et fundo earundem terrarum, vel ab hujusmodi partibus et portionibus earundem; tunc, in iis casibus, vel aliquibus eorum foris facien. perdent et ammittent ipso facto omnes et singulas possessiones, terras, bona, et catella infra dict. terras existentia. Et licitum erit præfato domino Roberto, suis hæredibus masculis, assignatis et deputatis, confiscare, recognoscere, et possidere easdem terras, bondas, possessiones, bona et catella, et applicare eadem suis propriis usibus, libere, absque periculo juris, vel aliqua ulteriore declaratura de eisdem. Et similiter, si aliquæ venditiones, alienationes, vel conditiones fiant inter præfatum dominum Robertum, suos hæredes masculos, assignatos, vel deputatos, cum quacunque alia persona seu personis, sive nativis dicti regni, sive extraneis, alienis, vel aliis personis quibuscunque, pro transportatione quorumcunque bonorum catellorum, mercemoniarium, mercium, ammunitionum, armorum, commeatuum, præparationum, vel aliorum quorumcunque, vel pro implemento cujuscunque facti vel factorum, præfato domino Roberto, vel suis præscript. vel infra dictum regnum Novæ Scotiæ, vel per mare cursum, vel transitum, in vel ab eodem regno, sub quibuscunque pœnis vel pecuniarum summis: Et si fregerint aut violaverint eadem pacta, contractus, fœdera, vel conditiones, vel defecerint in perficiendo et implemendo earundem, in damnum et detrimentum dicti domini Roberti, suorumque præscript. et impediant, et moram faciant dict. laudabili intentioni in sæpefata plantatione, et policia ejusdem, tunc, et in

iis casibus, vel in aliquo eorundem, licitum erit præfato domino
Roberto, et suis præscript. intromittere, uti, et possidere eadem
bona, catella, mercantia, pecuniarum summas, et alia, ad suos proprios usus, absque ulteriori processu aut declaratione juris. NEC
NON cum expressa potestate et privilegio præfatis domino Roberto,
suis hæredibus masculis, assignatis, et deputatis, suis hominibus,
tenentibus, et servis, infra dictas terras et bondas frequentandi,
utendi, et exercendi, mercandi, negotiandi cum nativis et silvestribus
dicti regni, et faciendi, capiendi, obcontrahendi pacem, et fidelitatem,
affinitatem, et fœdera cum ipsis, et familiaritatem et amicitiam cum
eisdem frequentandi, et cum ipsorum ductoribus, gubernatoribus,
et præcipientibus; et, in casu offensionis, violationis officii, pro-
missorum, vel amicitiæ suis partibus, capiendi et utendi armis ad-
versus eos omni hostili modo, tam per mare quam per terras, cum
potestate et privilegio etiam præfato domino Roberto Gordon, et
suis præscript. omni tempore a futuro, exportandi de dictis bondis
et regno Novæ Scotiæ, omnia mercimonia, mercantias, et commoditates quascunque, et importandi et inducendi eadem in dictum
regnum Scotiæ vel ad quascunque alias partes, pro ipsorum arbitrio;
nec non exportandi de dicto regno Scotiæ et aliis locis quibuscunque,
omnes mercantias, mercemonia, et commoditates quascunque, et
inducendi et inferendi easdem dicto regno Novæ Scotiæ, pro solutione summæ quinque librarum monetæ Scotiæ, custumæ pro quibuslibet centum libris tantum, absque solutione alterius cujuslibet
acustumæ, impositionis vel divoriæ cujuscunque, tollendi, capiendi,
vel inde exigendi per nos, hæredes, vel successores nostros, vel nostros
publicanos, seu custumarios deputatos, vel officiarios, vel per aliam
aliquam personam quamcunque, vel infra dictum regnum Scotiæ,
vel regnum Novæ Scotiæ.   Inhibendo, tenore præsentis cartæ
nostræ, nostros custumarios et officiarios, ne exigant ulteriorem
impositionem vel custumam ex eisdem, et de ipsorum officiis in hac
parte; cum potestate etiam sæpefato domino Roberto, suisque præscript, per seipsos suos deputatos, officiarios, et alios suis nominibus
levandi, exigendi, et recipiendi ab omnibus nostris, et successorum
nostrorum subditis, quos contigerit negotiari seu mercari infra dictas
bondas, fundum, et terras supra designatas, portus, et stationes earund.

quinque libras monetæ ante dict. custumæ pro quibuslibet centum
libris omnium bonorum, mercimoniarum, vel commoditatum, vel
importandorum eidem per ipsos, vel ipsorum aliquem, vel exeundi
reportandorum ; et summam decem librarum ab omnibus extraneis,
pro quolibet centum omnium bonorum, mercium, et mercimoniarum
exportandorum et importandorum per ipsos, vel ipsorum aliquem,
et id præter et ultra dictam summam quinque librarum, nobis, et
nostris successoribus, ut præmittitur, debitam. Et præterea nos
pro nobis, nostris hæredibus, et successoribus, cum avisamento et
consensu ante dict. tenore præsentis cartæ nostræ volumus, concedimus, ordinamus et declaramus, quod dicta summa quinque
librarum monetæ ante dict. custumæ designatæ, ut præmittitur,
solvend. nobis, hæredibus et successoribus nostris, custumariis nostris,
et deputatis, pro omnibus bonis, mercimoniis, mercantiis, et commoditatibus, vel exportandis de dicto regno Novæ Scotiæ, vel eidem
importandis, serventur et reddantur præfato domino Willielmo Alexander, suis hæredibus et assignatis, nostri dicti regni locum tenentibus,
et non aliis, pro spatio sexdecem annorum diem datæ præsentis
cartæ nostræ immediate subsequend.   Et in hunc finem, quod
licebit præfato domino Willielmo Alexander, et suis præscript. tollere,
exigere, petere, et recipere easdem acquittantias, et exonerationes
desuper dare et concedere, quas nos, tenore præsentis cartæ nostræ
pro nobis, hæredibus, et successoribus nostris, volumus et declaramus
sufficientes fore recipientibus dictarum acqittantiarum, et persol-
ventibus dictam summam quinque librarum custumæ. Et cum
potestate præfato domino Willielmo Alexander, et suis præscript.
durante dicto tempore, utendi et convertendi dictam summam quinque librarum pro quolibet centum, sic ut præmittitur, levandi, suis
propriis usibus et utilitati, prout ipsis videbitur expediens pro suo
meliori auxilio, ope, et manu tenenti suorum onerum et expensarum
in regimine dicti regni, et propagatione dict. plantationis. Et quamquam nullo modo licitum sit alieno nobili vel generoso, terras habenti
infra regnum Scotiæ, transire de eodem obsque licentia nostra, nos
pro nobis, hæredibus, et successoribus nostris, volumus, concedimus,
ac tenore præsentis cartæ nostræ declaramus, præsentem hanc
nostram cartam esse et fore sufficientem licentiam et warrantum,

omni tempore a futuro, præfato domino Roberto Gordon, et suis
præscript, et omnibus aliis personis læsæ majestatis non reis, vel
alioquin specialiter non inhibitis, cum ipsis vel eorum aliquo pro-
ficisci cupientibus dictis terris et bondis, libere eundi de dicto
regno Scotiæ et proficiscendi, et reparandi ad dictas terras et regnum
Novæ Scotiæ, absque aliquo periculo, inconvenientia ipsis, in suis
corporibus, terris, bonis, seu catellis penes quam nos, cum avisamento, ante dict. pro nobis, et nostris successoribus, dispensavimus,
ac per præsentis cartæ nostræ tenorem dispensamus in perpetuum.
ET PRÆTEREA, dedimus, concessimus, et declaravimus, tenoreque
præsentis cartæ nostræ pro nobis, hæredibus et successoribus nostris,
cum avisamento et consensu supra script.   Damus, concedimus,
volumus, declaramus, et ordinamus, quod omnes nostri subditi, et
aliæ personæ quæcunque, quæ subjicere sese nostrorumque hæredum, et successorum obedientiæ placebit, quæ quocunque tempore
imposterum profecturi sunt ad dictas bondas et terras, præfato
domino Roberto Gordon per præsentes dispositas, ad inhabitandum
easdem, vel aliquam earundem partem, cum licentia, consensu, et
permissu, dicti domini Roberti, suorum hæredum masculorum, et
deputatorum, quod omnes et singulæ dictæ personæ, cum suis
liberis et posteris respective habebunt, tenebunt, fruentur, gaudebunt, et possidebunt omnes et quascunque libertates, privilegia, et
immunitates liberorum, et naturalium subditorum dicti regni nostri
Scotiæ, aliorumque nostrorum dominiorum, ac si nati et procreati
fuissent infra eadem regna et dominia.   Et pro constitutione majoris
authoritatis, imperii, potestatis, et jurisdictionis omni tempore a
futuro, in persona dicti domini Roberti Gordon, hæredum suorum
masculorum, assignatorum et deputatorum, infra dictas terras, nos
pro nobis, hæredibus et successoribus nostris, cum avisamento et
consensu ante dict. dedimus et concessimus, tenoreque præsentis
cartæ nostræ, damus et concedimus hæreditarie præfato domino
Roberto Gordon, hæredibus suis masculis, et assignatis quibuscunque, justiciariam et vice-comitatum dictarum omnium particularium
bondarum et terrarum supra specificat.   Et fecimus et constituimus, tenoreque præsentis cartæ nostræ facimus, et constituimus
præfatum dominum Robertum Gordon, suos hæredes masculos, et

assignatos, nostros hæreditarios vicecomites, quæsitores, justiciarios, hæreditarie in perpetuum, infra omnes et singulas dictas particulares terras et bondas supra specificatas, et specialiter designatas, cum omnibus et singulis libertatibus, privilegiis, franchisis, immunitatibus, et commoditatibus dict. vicecomitatui et justiciariæ spectan. cum potestate dicto domino Roberto Gordon, suis hæredibus masculis, assignatis, vel deputatis, sedendi in judicio, cognoscendi, et decernendi, in omnibus et quibuscunque causis, tam civilibus quam criminalibus, infra dictas bondas et jurisdictionem earundem terrarum, similiter, et tam libere omnibus modis, tanquam aliquis alius justiciarius, quæsitor, vel vicecomes quicunque potest, vel poterit facere aliquo tempore præterito vel futuro. Et ne aliqua quæstio occurrat de tempore infra quod præfatus dominus Robertus, suique præscript. tanquam vicecomites vel justiciarii sedeant. cognoscant, et decernant in causis criminalibus post commissa crimina, nos pro nobis, hæredibus et successoribus nostris, cum avisamento et consilio ante dict. tenore præsentis cartæ nostræ volumus, concedimus, et declaramus, quod licitum et legitimum erit iisdem accusare quoscunque reos criminaliter offendentes infra dictas bondas et terras, pro quibuscunque criminibus per ipsos commiss. et sedendi, cognoscendi, judicandi, et decernendi de iisdem, quocunque tempore infra spatium sex mensium, diem commiss. criminis immediate subsequen. durante quo quidem spatio, licebit tantum præfato domino Roberto, et suis præscript, et non aliis, examinare, cognoscere, judicare, et procedere de eisdem, excludendo, durante dicto spatio, nostro locum tenente, et omnibus aliis personis quibuscunque, ab exercitatione cujuscunque judicii vel jurisdictioniis de eisdem, et ab attachiamento, arrestatione, adjuramento, vocatione vel conventione dictorum criminaliter offendentium, et crimina committentium, quocunque modo vel ratione. Proviso tamen quod si, post dictum spatium sex mensium excurrentium, dicta crimina et criminaliter offendentes non fuerint judicati nec examinati, vel discussi per dictum dominum Robertum, et suos præscript. in ea casu licebit deinceps nostrum locum-tenenti, suis hæredibus et assignatis, nostrum locum tenentibus, et suis deputatis, accusare, attachiare, arrestare, citare, et convenire dictas personas reas, et judicare et cognoscere de criminibus per ipsos commiss. prout ipsis expediens videbitur, cum potestate etiam dicto domino Roberto, et suis præscript. non obstante provisione supra script. post expirationem dict. sex mensium, omnibus temporibus, in absentia dicti domini Willielmi Alexander, suorum hæredum et assignatorum, nostrum locum tenentium, et eorum deputatorum, judicandi, cognoscendi, et decidendi in omnibus causis criminalibus, et puniendi omnes criminaliter offendentes infra dictas bondas, pro ipsorum arbitrio; et simili modo, in ipsorum absentia extra dictum regnum, vel infra spatium sex mensium, vel postea quocunque tempore, remittendi, et condonandi dict. crimina et criminaliter offendentes infra dictas terras et bondas, pro hujus-modi rationalibus causis et considerationibus, prout ipsis videbitur expediens. ET PRÆTEREA, cum potestate dicto domino Roberto, et suis præscript. sedendi, judicandi, et cognoscendi de omnibus criminibus et criminaliter offendentibus infra dictas bondas, et vel puniendi, remittendi, vel condonandi dicta crimina et criminaliter reos, prout ipsis videbitur expediens, omnibus temporibus dicto spatio sex mensium elapso, antequam præfatus dominus Willielmus, sui hæredes et assignati, nostrum locum tenentes, et sui deputati provo-caverint, citaverint, vel indictaverint dictos criminaliter offendentes, ad comparendum coram ipsis in judicio, quamquam in regno Novæ Scotiæ pro tempore fuerint, absque præjudicio tamen præfato domino Willielmo, suis hæredibus, et assignatis nostrum locum tenentibus, et suis deputatis, si primi fuerint citatores, post elapsos sex menses, sedendi, judicandi, cognoscendi, puniendi, vel remittendi dicta crimina et criminaliter offendentes, pro eorum arbitrio, ut præ-mittitur. Et similiter, tenore præsentis cartæ nostræ, ordinamus, quod si contingat præfatum dominum Robertum, vel suos præscript. condonare et remittere aliqua ex dictis criminibus, vel criminaliter, ut præmittitur, offendentes, quod tunc et in eo casu, eorum remissio et indulgentia sic conceden. publicabitur et proclamabitur infra dictas bondas, die et data concessionis ejusdem, per aliquem ex dict. particularibus officiariis per ipsos ad id effectum designandis; et post publicationem ejusdem, quod eadem remissio insumabitur in registro dicti domini Willielmi, suorum hæredum et assignatorum, nostrum locum tenentium ejusdem regni, infra spatium sexaginta dierum, publicationem ejusdem proxime subsequentem, ad minimum, quod eadem offeretur et praesentabitur, coram duobus fide dignis testibus, dicti registri custodi, si dicti registri clericus, vel custos ejusdem, in dicto regno Novæ Scotiæ pro tempore fuerit, cum plenaria potestate et privilegio similiter præfato domino Roberto Gordon, suis hæredibus masculis, assignatis et deputatis, in sempiternum sedendi, affigendi, et tenendi, vel tenere causandi, suis nominibus curias justiciariæ, vicecomitum curias, liberæ regalitatis curias, et baronis et baroniæ curias, infra et super totis et integris prædictis bondis, et terris ipsi, ut præmittitur, designatis, vel super aliqua parte earundem, omnibus temporibus et occasionibus prout ipsis visum fuerit, clericos officiaros, serjandos, adjudicatores, et alia curiæ membra quæcunque faciendi et creandi, æschetas et amerciamenta curiarum ordinandi, exigendi, levandi, recipiendi, et ad ipsorum proprios usus, prout ipsis expediens visum fuerit, applicandi, cum omnibus aliis et singulis privilegiis, libertatibus, commoditatibus et casualitatibus ad dicta officia et jurisdictiones justiciariæ liberæ regalitatis, et vicecomitatus, aliaque supra expressa spectan. vel juste cadere aut spectare poterint ; cum libera potestate, et privilegio etiam præfato domino Roberto, suis hæredibus masculis, et assignatis, vendendi, alienandi, et disponendi hæreditarie vel aliter, totas et integras prædictas bondas et terras supra designatas, pro ipsorum arbitrio ; cum omnibus et singulis libertatibus, licentiis, immunitatibus, et commoditatibus supra et infra expressis, tenore præsentis cartæ nostræ ipsis concess. vel cum tot et dictis libertatibus, commoditatibus, et aliis, quot ipsis et suis præscript. expediens videbitur, cuicunque alteri personæ vel personis, suis hæredibus, et assignatis sub nostra obedientia existentibus, tenen. de nobis, nostris hæredibus, et successoribus, vel de præfato domino Roberto, suis hæredibus masculis, et assignatis, pro arbitrio dicti domini Roberti, suorumque antedict. Quæ quidem terræ, bondæ, privilegia, aliaque supra expressa, vel aliqua pars earundem sic disposita per præfatum dominum Robertum, vel suos præscript, cuicunque alteri personæ, seu personis, tenen. de nobis, nostris hæredibus, et successoribus, nos, nostri hæredes et successores recipimus, et admittimus ipsos, et eorum unumquemque tanquam

nostros liberos vassallas et immediatos tenentes earundem ; et concedimus ipsis et eorum unicuique talia sufficientia infeofamenta
earundem, et cum eodem modo tenendi, qualia nunc concessimus
præfato domino Roberto, suis hæredibus masculis, et assignatis,
quandocunque eadem ipsi requisiverint, cum postestate etiam præfato
domino Roberto, et suis antedict. et singulis alteri personæ vel
personis, sub nostra obedientia existentibus, quibus ipsos alienare
et disponere aliqam partem seu portionem dictarum terrarum
contigerit, insignire et vocare easdem, vel aliquam partem seu
portionem earundem, per aliquod nomen seu titulum temporibus
futuris, prout ipsis expediens videbitur ; nec non licebit hæredibus
masculis, vel successoribus dicti domini Roberti quibuscunque,
et suis assignatis, intrare seipsos, tanquam hæredes suis predeces-
soribus, dictis terris et bondis aliisque quibuscunque præfato
domino Roberto concess. et disposit. vel ad aliquam partem
earundem, virtute hujus præsentis cartæ nostræ ; et id vel
per ordinem cancellariæ dicti regni nostri Scotiæ, per servitium
brevium, retornatuum, et præceptorum ex eadem directorum, et
modis in similibus casibus in hujusmodi materia usitatis et consuetis,
vel alioqui per ordinem capellæ et cancellariæ dicti regni Novæ
Scotiæ, pro arbitrio et optione hæredum masculorum, et successorum
dicti domini Roberti, et suorum assignatorum quorumcunque. Cum
POTESTATE etiam præfato domino Roberto, et suis præscript. et
eorum deputatis, omni tempore futuro, convocandi omnes et singulos
homines tenentes, servos et incolas suos quoscunque dictarum
omnium bondarum et terrarum supra designatarum, omnibus temporibus et occasionibus, prout ipsis visum fuerit pro bono, defensione,
et propagatione ipsorum, vel dictarum bondarum et terrarum, ad
resistendum exteris hostibus, ad reprimendum insolventias, et
crimina turbulentorum, seditiosorum, et populi rebellantis, ad
reducendum silvestres et aborigines ad conformitatem et debitam
obedientiam, et ob alias legitimas urgentes et necessarias causas
quascunque. ET PRÆTEREA, dedimus et concessimus, tenoreque
præsentis cartæ nostræ pro nobis nostris hæredibus et successoribus,
cum avisamento et consensu antedict. damus, concedimus, volumus,
ordinamus, et declaramus, quod præfatus dominus Robertus, suique

præscript. omni tempore a futuro habebunt suffragium et vocem
in condendis omnibus et singulis legibus, imposterum faciendis de
publico statu, bono, et regimine dicti regni Novæ Scotiæ, et in
omnibus comitiis, parliamentis, synodis, conciliis, et conventionibus
convocandis, conveniendis, vel in eum finem tenendis ; et quod
debite et legitime ad id effectum promovebunt, quod nullæ leges
de eisdem fient, statuent aut validæ erunt absque avisamento et
consensu dicti domini Roberti, suorumque præscript. et absque
consensu reliquorum baronettorum, parem et similem quantitatem
et proportionem terrarum infra dictum regnum habentium, ad ipsos
suosque hæredes hæreditariæ spectan. qualem, tenore præsentis
cartæ nostræ, præfato domino Roberto disposuimus, Viz. singuli
eorum sexdecem millium acrarum terræ ad minimum, absque avisamento et consensu majoris partis totidem eorum, qui convenient
simul ad ferendum voces et suffragia, super debita et legitima præ-
monitione ipsis desuper faciendo, concludendo, et proponendo prima
conventione et synodo, per ipsos, et nostrum locum tenentes, vel
eorum hæredes aut assignatos, tenenda, nostrum locum tenentes
pro condendis legibus et statutis dicti regni ; et quod nulla persona,
seu personæ quæcunque, quæ non fuerint hæredes quælibet ipsarum
sexdecem millium acrarum terrarum infra dictum regnum, habebunt vocem vel suffragium in condendis quibuslibet legibus dictum
regnum concernen. absque avisamento, consilio, et consensu dicti
nostri locum tenentis, hæredum suorum et assignatorum, nostrorum
successorum locum tenentium, et dicti domini Roberti, suorumque
præscript. et reliquorum baronnettorum.   INSUPER, si præfatus
dominus Robertus, suique hæredes masculi, et assignati præscript.
non fuerint personaliter præsentes in dictis parliamentis, comitiis,
consiliis, conventionibus, et synodis, quæ tenebuntur, vocabuntur,
et convenientur ad effectum supra script. infra dictum regnum
Novæ Scotiæ, tunc et in eo casu, deputati seu actornati, seu
habentes potestatem et authoritatem suam, ac habentes quantitatem
mille acrarum terrarum ipsis infra dictum regnum hæreditarie
spectan. habebunt similem vocem et suffragium, ac si ipsi personaliter interessent ; sed si aliaquæ conventiones vel synodi tenebuntur
ad id effectum, infra dictum regnum Scotiæ, si personaliter inter-

fuerint pro tempore infra dictum regnum, habebunt vocem et suffragium, tantum per seipsos, et non per delegatos, vel actornatos; sed casu absentiæ extra dictum regnum, hujusmodi temporibus, in eo casu, sui deputati et actornati, haben. suam potestatem et warrantum, habebunt similem vocem et suffragium, ac si persona-liter interessent. Et quod præfatus dominus Robertus, et reliqui nostri subditi et incolæ illius regni Novæ Scotiæ, omni tempore futuro, judicabuntur, regentur, et gubernabuntur, in omnibus causis civilibus et criminalibus, legibus dicti regni tantum, et non aliis, absque præjudicio tamen præfato domino Roberto, et suis præscript. per seipsos et suos deputatos, faciendi tales particulares leges, con-stitutiones, et statuta, infra proprias suas bondas particulariter supra designat. quæ sibi usui sint pro meliori policia, bono, et regimine earundem et inhabitantium ibid. et pro conservatione boni ordinis, et administratione juris et justiciæ ibidem. Et absque præjudicio dicto domino Roberto, et suis præscript, alterius cujusquam parti-cularis libertatis, privilegii, immunitatis, clausulæ seu conditionis qualiscunque supra vel infra express. in favorem ipsius concept. Proviso omni modo, quod quæcunque leges generales faciendæ et constituendæ modo præscript. publicum statum, bonum, et regimen dicti regni concernen. vel per præfatum dominum Robertum, et suos ante dict. in ipsorum particularibus bondis, ut præmittitur, fiant conformes, et æquales legibus dicti regni Scotiæ quoad con-venienter poterint, respectu habito ad circumstantias temporis, loci, et situationis ejusdem regni, et inhabitantium, et conditionum et qualitatis earund. Et præterea, tametsi per expressam condi-tionem dict. originalis infeofamenti nostrum locum tenenti concess. constitutum est, quod ipsi, et hæredes ac assignati sui, ut convocent omnes et singulos inhabitantes regni Novæ Scotiæ proclamationibus, vel aliter, modo et forma inibi specificat. nihilominus concessimus, voluimus, et ordinavimus, tenoreque præsentis cartæ nostræ, pro nobis, hæredibus et successoribus nostris, cum avisamento et con-sensu antedict, volumus, concedimus, declaramus, et ordinamus, quod nullo modo licitum erit nostrum locum tenenti, suis hæredibus, successoribus, vel assignatis, aut quibuscunque aliis nostri, seu nostrorum successorum, officiariis quibuscunque, vocare, convocare, cogere per proclamationem, vel aliter, dictum dominum Robertum, suos hæredes et assignatos, successores, deputatos, homines tenentes, servos, vel incolas dictarum particularium bondarum, præfato domino Roberto, sic ut præmittitur, dispositarum, nisi pro rationalibus, necessariis, et legitimis causis, quæ invenientur utiles et expedientes reipublicæ dicti regni, per legitimum nostrum locum tenentem, suosque prædict. cum avisamento et consensu dicti domini Roberti, suorumque antedict. et reliquarum personarum supra mentionat. designatarum, ut habeant vocem et suffragium in condendis legibus, ut præmissum est.   Quæ quædem personæ, et qulibet ipsarum, sui hæredes, successores, assignati, deputati, homines tenentes, servi, vel incolæ dict. separatarum bondarum, simili conditioni subjicientur; et similiter, non erit licitum nec legitimum dicto nostrum locum tenenti, vel suis præscript. vel quibuscunque aliis, nostris, hæredum vel successorum nostrorum officiariis, exigere, imponere, vel levare aliquam taxationem vel impositionem, a vel super dictum dominum Robertum, suos hæredes masculos, assignatos, deputatos, homines tenentes, servos, vel inhabitantes dictarum terrarum et bondarum particulariter supra dispositarum, vel super dictis suis terris, redditibus, bonis, seu catellis, absque speciali consensu dicti domini Roberti, vel suorum præscript. non obstante aliqua potestate nostro locum tenenti et suis antedict. per dictum originale infeofamentum concess. vel virtute cujuscunque alterius tituli vel juris fact. et concess. vel per nos, nostros hæredes, vel successores, præfato locum tenenti nostro, vel alicui alteri personæ cujuscunque faciendi vel concedendi, absque præjudicio tamen præfato domino Roberto, et suis præscript. infra bondas particulariter supra designat. et per præsentes sibi disposit. vocandi, cogendi, et conveniendi suos homines et incolas, omnibus temporibus et occasionibus, modo et propter causas supra expressas, ut præmittitur, ipsas tangen. Nec non dedimus, concessimus, et disposuimus, tenoreque præsentis cartæ nostræ, pro nobis et successoribus nostris, cum avisamento et consensu antedict. damus, concedimus, et hæreditarie in perpetuum disponimus, dicto domino Roberto, et suis præscript. omnia et quæcunque alia privilegia, libertates, licentias, commoditates, et immunitates, proficua, prærogativa, dignitates, et casualitates, generaliter

et particulariter in dicto originali infeofamento, præfato domino
Willielmo Alexander, et suis antedict. concess. specificat. et express.
et id tam plenario, libero, et amplo modo, et forma, ac si eadem
privilegia, prærogativa, immunitates, libertates, licentiæ, dignitates,
commoditates, et alia, cum omnibus clausulis et conditionibus, in
hac præsenti carta nostra ad longum specialiter insinuatæ et con-
tentæ essent, quatenus extendi et concerni poterint particulares
bondas et terras supra designatas, virtute hujus cartæ nostræ, præfato
domino Roberto, et suis antedict. tanquam hæredibus earund.
disposit.   Excepto omni modo et reservato præfato domino
Willielmo Alexander, suis hæredibus et assignatis, officio nostri
locum tenentis dicti totius regni et dominii Novæ Scotiæ, potestate
et privilegio cudendæ pecuniæ, officio principalis justiciarii generalis
ejusd. regni, in causis criminalibus, officio admiralitatis, faciendi
officiarios status, conferendi titulos honorum, cum plena potestate
et jurisdictione liberæ regalitatis, capellæ, et cancellariæ dicti regni,
et privilegio condendi leges publicum statum, bonum, et regimen
dicti regni concernentes, illi per suum originale infeofamentum
prædict concess.   Proviso tamen quod eadem reservatio et exceptio,
in favorem dicti domini Willielmi, suorumque præscript. nunc con-
cepta, nullatenus præjudicabit vel præjudicatio erit præfato domino
Roberto, et suis antedict. penes omnes, vel aliquod ex particularibus
privilegiis, licentiis, libertatibus, immunitatibus, commoditatibus,
aliisque supra et subtus mentionat. præfato domino Roberto, et suis
antedict, tenore præsentis cartæ nostræ concess. modo generaliter
et particulariter supra et subtus specificat.   Quæ Quidem terræ,
bondæ, advocatio et donatio beneficiorum ecclesiarum, et capellaniarum, fodinæ, mineralia, metalla, margaritæ, silvæ, piscationes,
molendina, multuræ, officia, privilegia, et jurisdictio liberæ regalitatis,
justiciæ et justiciariæ, vicecomites vicecomitatuum, et omnes alias
libertates, immunitates, privilegia, commoditates, licentiæ, custumæ,
casualitates, aliaque universa generaliter et particulariter supra
mention. debite et legitime resignatæ, sursum redditæ, et extra
donatæ fuerunt per dict. dominum Willielmum Alexander, et legitimum procuratorem suum, ipsius nominibus, in manibus nostris
tanquam immediati sui superioris, earundem per fustum, et baculum,

ut moris est, resignatione earundem facta, Apud Quhythall, vigesimo sexto die mensis Maii, anno Domini millesimo sexcentesimo vigesimo quinto ; una cum omni jure, titulo, interesse, et jurisclameo quæ seu quas in et ad easdem, aliquam earundem partem, habuit, habet, seu quovis modo in futurum habere vel clamare potuerat.   In et ad favorem dicti domini Roberti Gordon, suorum hæredum masculorum, et assignatorum quorumcunque, sub modo, provisionibus, limitationibus, exceptionibus, et reservationibus respective quibus supra.   Et id pro novo hoc nostro hæditario infeofamento, per nos præfato domino Roberto Gordon, suis hæredibus masculis, et assignatis quibuscunque, desuper dando et concedendo simul universum erigendis, uniendis, annexandis et incorporandis in unam plenam, integram, et liberam baroniam et regalitatem, in perpetuum, Baroniam de Gordon omni tempore a futuro nuncupandam, tenen. de nobis, hæredibus, et successoribus nostris, coronæ regni nostri Scotiæ successuris, in libera alba firma, pro solutione annuatim unius denarii usualis monetæ dicti regni nostri, super fundo dict. terrarum et bondarum, vel alicujus partis earundem, ad festum nativitatis Domini, nomine albæ firmæ, si petatur tantum, cum dispensatione etiam non introitus earundem omnium terrarum, bondarum et baroniæ, censuum, firmarum, proficuorum, et divoriarum earund. duran. eodem non introitu.   Et insuper de novo dedimus concessimus, et disposuimus, tenoreque præsentis cartæ nostræ, pro nobis et successoribus nostris, ex nostra certa scientia, et proprio motu, cum avisamento, et consensu prædicto, pro diversis bonis et gratuitis servitiis, per præfatum dominum Robertum nobis præstitis et impensis, proque aliis gravibus causis, et bonis considerationibus, nos moventibus, de novo damus, concedimus, et disponimus præfato domino Roberto, hædibus suis masculis, et assignatis, hæreditarie in perpetuum, Totas et integras prædict. terras, bondas, molendina, silvas, piscationes, advocationem, donationem beneficiorum et capellaniarum, ac ecclesiarum, necnon jura patronatus earund. fodinas, mineralia, metalla, pretiosos lapillos, cum potestate, privilegio, et jurisdictione justiciariæ et vicecomitatus, in omnibus causis civilibus et criminalibus, curias, eschetas, amercia-

menta, curiarum exitus, lie outlawis, et omnes et singulas alias
libertates, immunitates, licentias, custumas, casualitates, proficua,
divorias, aliaque quæcunque particulariter seu generaliter supra
specificat. quæ nos pro nobis hæredibus et successoribus nostris,
cum avisamento et consensu antedict. tenore præsentis cartæ nostræ
volumus, et reputamus tanquam in hac præsenti carta nostra specialiter et particulariter insinuata, repetita, inserta, et expressa, cum
particularibus exceptionibus, limitationibus, et reservationibus respective et specialiter supra script. Et de novo erigimus, unimus,
annexamus, et incorporamus, omnes et singulas prænominatas terras,
bondas, molendina, silvas, piscationes, advocationem, et donationem
beneficiorum, ecclesiarum, et capellaniarum, et jura patronatuum
earund. fodinas, metalla, mineralia, margaritas, gemmas, officia,
regalitatem justiciariam, vicecomitatum, libertates, licentias, privilegia, immunitates, custumas, emolumenta, casualitates, dignitates,
potestatem, jurisdictionem, et alia quæcunque generaliter et particulariter supra expressa, quæ nos pro nobis et successoribus nostris,
tanquam in hac præsenti carta nostra repetita, et particulariter
inserta, tenemus, cum specialibus exceptionibus, et reservationibus
particulariter supra mentionat. cum generalite in perpetuum dis-
pensando, in unam, integram plenarium, et liberam baroniam
et regalitatem de Gordon, tenen. et haben. præfato domino
Roberto Gordon, suis hæredibus masculis et assignatis, de nobis,
et nostris coronæ et regni nostri Scotiæ successoribus in libera
hæreditate, unius baroniæ et regalitatis in perpetuum, per omnes
rectas metas suas antiquas, novas, et divisas, prout jacent in longi-
tudine et latitudine, in domibus, ædificiis, boscis, planis, moris,
maresiis, viis, semitis, aquis, stagnis, rivulis, pratis, pascuis, et
pasturis, molendinis, multuris et eorum sequelis, aucupationibus
venationibus, piscationibus, petariis, turbariis, carbonibus, car-
bonariis, cuniculis, cuniculariis, columbis, columbariis, fabrilibus,
brasinis, braseriis, et genistis, sylvis, nemoribus et virgultis, lignis,
tignis, lapidiis, lapide et calce, cum curiis, et earum exitibus, here-
zeldis, bludwetis et mulierum mercheris, cum communi pastura,
libero introitu et exitu, et cum furca, fossa, soli sabthole, thaniæ,
vert wrak wair, veungsoun waiff, pitgalous, infangthief et out-

fangthief earund.   Et cum omnibus aliis et singulis libertatibus
commoditatibus, proficuis, asiamentis, privilegiis, prærogativis, dignitatibus, et casualitatibus, per nos vel nostros prædecessores cuicunque baroni majori vel minori infra dictum regnum Scotiæ antehac
concessis, aliisque omnibus in dicto originali infeofamento desuper
contentis, et quæ nos, per nos metipsos vel quemcunque alium ex
regiis nostris progenitoribus et antecessoribus, dedimus, concessimus,
et disposuimus, vel virtute quarumcunque cartarum, infeofamentorum, literarum patentium, donationum, et concessionum quibuscunque ex nostris subditis cujuscunque qualitatis, status vel gradus,
extiterint, vel quibuscunque societatibus, cætibus, vel aliis particularibus earundem membris, petentibus, ducentibus impetrantibus,
acquirentibus, conquirentibus, aut protegentibus, quascunque ex-
traneas terras vel colonias, dare, concedere, vel disponere poteruntis,
sub exceptionibus, reservationibus, et provisionibus specialit. supra
mentionatis; et tam plena, libera, et ampla forma, et modo, quam
eadem privilegia, libertates, commoditates, et immunitates, cum
omnibus et singulis clausulis, conditionibus, et provisionibus easdem
concernen. ad longum specialiter in hac præsenti carta nostra insinuata, inserta et comprehensa forent, una cum omni jure, titulo,
interesse, jurisclameo, tam petitorio quam possessorio, quæ nos,
nostri prædecessores vel successores, habuimus, habemus, seu quovis
modo habere, clamare, vel prætendere poterimus, ad easdem terras,
vel ad census, firmas, proficua, et divorias earundem terrarum
baroniæ, aliorumque specialiter et generaliter supra mentionat. de
quibuscunque annis et terminis præteritis, pro quacunque causa
seu occasione præterita.   Renunciando et quiete clamando eisdem,
cum omni actione et instantia nobis inde competen.   IN ET AD
favorem præfati domini Roberti Gordon, suorum hæredum masculorum et assignatorum in perpetuum, tam pro non solutione
divoriarum in dicto originali infeofamento content. quam quod non
fecerunt debitum homagium juxta tenorem ejusd. vel ob non
puram plectionem cujuscunque articuli ejusdem originalis infeofamenti, vel quod commiserunt aliquod factum, actum, omissum
vel commissum, præjudiciale ejusd. vel unde originale infeofamentum infringi, impugnari, vel in quæstionem legitime trahi

quocunque moto poterit; acquietando, et extra donando easdem simpliciter, cum omni actione quæ nobis, nostris hæredibus vel successoribus quomodocunque inde competit, vel competere poterit; et renunciando eisdem jure lite et causa, cum pacto de non petendo, ac cum supplemento omnium defectuum et imperfectionum tam non nominat. quam nominat. quæ tanquam pro re-express in hac præsenti carta nostra habere volumus. REDDENDO inde annuatim præfatus dominus Robertus Gordon, sui hæredes masculi, et assignati, nobis, nostris hæredibus, et dictæ coronæ et regni nostri Scotiæ successoribus, præfatam albæ firmæ divoriam unius denarii usualis monetæ dicti regni, super fundo dict. terrarum et baroniæ ad dictum festum nativitatis Domini nostri, nomine albæ firmæ, si petatur tantum, pro omnibus aliis divoriis, servitiis, quæstione, seu demanda quæ inde exigi, vel supra dictis terris et baronia imponi poterint; ET QUIA dictæ bondæ et regnum Novæ Scotiæ tanto intervallo distant, et separantur ab antiquo regno nostro Scotiæ, et quia idem regnum Novæ Scotiæ adhuc omnino destituitur notariis et tabellionibus publicis, pro authoritate danda sasinis et instrumentis conferendis de possessione ejusdem, necnon respectum habentes ad diversa et multifaria incommoda quæ inde accedere poterint, in defectu debitæ et tempestivæ sasinæ, vel sasinarum, super dicta carta, et similibus cartis et infeofamentis capiendarum de dict. terris et baronia præfato domino Roberto Gordon, suis hæredibus masculis et assignatis, dandis et concedendis, et quia dictum regnum Novæ Scotiæ et originale infeofamentum ejusd. de dicto antiquo regno Scotiæ tenetur in capite, nuperque inventum, supervisum, extentum, et acquisitum fit, per præfatum dominum Willielmum Alexander, nostrum locum tenentum, ejusd. suis propriis impensis nativum dicti regni nostri Scotiæ, et jam partum, plantatum et plantandum, cum colonis et nativis dicti regni nostri, et ob id appelatum, et nomen, stilum et titulum Novæ Scotiæ, juste promeren. unde fit ut idem regnum partem dicti regni nostri Scotiæ jam reputari et existimari oporteat; idcirco, cum avisamento antedict. tenore præsentis cartæ nostræ, decernimus, declaramus, et ordinamus, quod unica sasina, capienda apud *castrum Edinburgenum* tanquam locum dicti regni nostri Scotiæ maxime con-

spicuum et principalem, vel in arbitrio et optione dicti domini
Roberti, suorumque præscript. capienda super fundo et baronia de
GORDON, vel aliqua parte ejusdem, stabit, et sufficiens erit sasina
omni tempore a futuro, pro totis et integris eisdem terris et baronia,
vel aliqua earundem vel cujusdem parte seu portione; penes quam
dispensavimus, tenoreque præsentis cartæ nostræ dispensamus in
perpetuum; et pro omnibus et singulis privilegiis, et aliis specialiter
et generaliter supra mentionatis; ET QUUM dict. terræ et baroniæ
tenentur in libera alba firma, ut præmissum est, et cum in defectu
tempestivi et legitimi introitus hæredis, seu hæredum masculorum,
præfati domini Roberti Gordon, suorumque assignatorum, hujusmodi baroniæ et aliis succeden. qui difficulter, debite, et debito
tempore per ipsos fieri poterit, propter magnam distantiam earund.
a dicto regno nostro Scotiæ; unde fieri possit, quod eadem baronia
et bondæ, ratione non introitus in nostras et successorum nostrorum
manus cadant et deveniant, usque donec legitimus hæres, vel hæredes
masculi et assignati dicti domini Roberti, legitime intraverint ad
easdem, nos nullo modo volentes vel cogitantes quod dict. baronia et
terræ aliquo tempore cadant in non introitum, nec etiam quod dictus
dominus Robertus suique præscript. beneficio et commodis earund
interea frustrabuntur; IDCIRCO, cum avisamento antedict. pro nobis
et successoribus nostris, dispensavimus, tenoreque præsentis cartæ
nostræ dispensamus cum dicto non-introitu; omnino renunciando
eidem, nec non exonerando, quiete clamando, et liberando præfatum
dominum Robertum, suosque præscript, simpliciter ab eodem non-introitu, quandocunque dict. terræ et baronia in nostras, vel nostrorum
hæredum et successorum, manus ratione non-introitus cadere vel
devenire contigerint, cum censibus, firmis, proficuis, vel divoriis earund.
et omni actione et instantia exinde competen. jure, lite, et causa
simpliciter, quæ desuper sequi poterint. PROVISO nihilominus, quod
hæredes masculi præfati domini Roberti Gordon et sui assignati,
infra spatium septem anuorum post decessum suorum prædeces-
sorum, vel introitum eorum ad possessionem earund. terrarum et
baroniæ, facient homagium, pro eisd. per se ipsos, vel suos legitimos
procuratores, in eum finem constitutos, habentes sufficientem potestatem ad id effectum, nobis et dictæ coronæ et regni Scotiæ nostris

successoribus, et intrentur et recipientur per nos, nostrosque successores, ad easdem terras, baroniam, aliaque supra mentionat. modo
præscript. quo casu hæres, vel hæredes masculi, dicti domini Roberti,
suique assignati, habebunt, possidebunt, gaudebunt, et fruentur
omnibus et singulis beneficiis et privilegiis earundem, una cum
totis et integris eisdem terris et baronia, censibus, firmis, proficuis,
et divoriis earundem, aliisque quibuscunque specialiter et generaliter
supra mentionat. similiter et tam libere quam dictus non introitus
nunquam extitisset, vel in manus nostras revenisset. ET SIMILITER,
quod si contigerit præfatum dominum Robertum, suosque præscript.
in fata decedere ante sasinam, virtute præsentis cartæ nostræ, vel
suorum infeofamentorum desuper sequi captam, nos, cum consensu
antedicto, pro nobis, et successoribus nostris tenore præsentis cartæ
nostræ, volumus, declaramus, et ordinamus, quod, non obstante
dicto decessu similia præcepta de novo ex nostra cancellaria dicti
regni Scotiæ dirigentur, si visum fuerit, pro infeofamento et sasina
præfato domino Roberto, suis hæredibus masculis, et assignatis,
danda juxta priora warranta et præcepta primo directa, vel in eum
sinem dirigenda, de totis et integris prædictis terris, baronia, et aliis
inibi content. eadem vi, forma, et modo quibus infeodari et investiri
in eisdem antea debuerant et poterant.   Ac ETIAM, si contigerit,
(quod Deus prohibeat,) nos, vel nostros successores, morte præ-
venire ante eandem sasinam vel sasinas, per præfatum dominum
Robertum et suos præscript. capiendas; eo casu, cum avisamento
antedict. pro nobis, et nostris successoribus, volumus, et declaramus,
quod non obstante, præcepta de dicta cancellaria dicti regni nostri
dirigentur pro infeofamento et sasina præfato domino Roberto
Gordon, suisque hæredibus masculis et assignatis, de eisdem terris,
baronia, aliisque prædict. danda, eadem forma, vi, et modo quo
præscripta et warranta sasinarum nunc diriguntur, vel dirigentur
antea ad id effectum, eodem et simili modo, ac si infeofamenta et
sasina earundem terrarum, baroniæ, et aliorum supra script. vel
alicujus partis earund. rite, debite, legitime, et via ordinaria, et
tempore expedita, perfecta, et desuper capta fuissent.   ET PRÆ-
TEREA, considerantes virtutem et industriam honoribus et præemi-
nentiis in primis promovendam, et exinde generosos spiritus ad

F

aggrediendum et prosequendum nobiles actiones et intentiones, autem etiam animari et mitigari, et quod omnis honoris et dignitatis splendor, originem et incrementum habeat a rege, tanquam a primo fonte ejusdem, ad cujus altitudinem et praeeminentiam erigere et instituere novos honorum et dignitatum titulos proprie spectat, tanquam ab eo unde primatim honores, originaliter promanarunt et ex eo volentes nobilissimos nostros progenitores, et antecestores, et ejus memoria dignos imitari, qui habuerunt, et in usum redegerunt potestatem creandi, et erigendi novas dignitates et gradus inter subditos hujusmodi honoribus dignos ; NOS ex nostra regia potestate, et authoritate, ereximus, creavimus, locavimus constituimus et ordinavimus tenore praesentis cartae nostrae pro nobis, haeredibus et successoribus nostris, de speciali gratia, favore, certa scientia, proprio motu, et deliberato animo, cum avisamento et consensu antedict. facimus, erigimus, constituimus, creamus, et ordinamus quendam haereditarium statum, gradum nomen, ordinem, dignitatem, et stilum BARONETTI, nunc et omni tempore a futuro, infra dictum regnum nostrum Scotiae et regionem Novae Scotiae, habendum et gaudendum hujusmodi personis quas nos, nostri haeredes vel successores, in incrementum et propagationem dict. plantationis, et aliter, pro dignitate et merito, facturi sumus baronettos et praelaturi hujusmodi gradibus et stylis : ED IDCIRCO, pro auxilio, ope, et assistentia per praefatum Robertum dominum Gordon praefata, et propagatione dict. plantationis hactenus exhibita, proque diversis aliis bonis et gratuitis servitiis, nobis per ipsum praestitis, et diversis aliis justis et gravibus causis et considerationibus nos moven. EREXIMUS, tenoreque praesentis cartae pro nobis, haeredibus et successoribus nostris, ex speciali gratia, favore, certa scientia, mero motu, et deliberato animo, cum avisamento et consilio antedict. erigimus, praeferimus, praeponimus, et creamus praefatum DOMINUM ROBERTUM GORDON, SUOSQUE HAEREDES MASCULOS QUOSCUNQUE, de tempore in tempus omni tempore a futuro, IN ET AD praefatum haereditarium statum, gradum, ordinem, nomen, dignitatem et stilum BARONETTI, cum omnibus et singulis praerogativis, privilegiis, praecedentiis, conditionibus, et aliis specialiter et generaliter sub-

script. Nec non fecimus, constituimus, et creavimus, tenoreque
præsentis cartæ nostræ facimus, constituimus, et creamus memo-
ratum dominum Robertum Gordon, et suos hæredes masculos,
hæreditarie Baronettos in perpetuum, et ut habeant et gaudebunt
omnibus et singulis prærogativis, privilegiis, et titulis et aliis particulariter et generaliter subscript. in eorum favorem conceptis ; et
dedimus, concessimus, voluimus, ordinavimus, et declaravimus,
tenoreque præsentis cartæ nostræ pro nobis, hæredibus et successoribus nostris, ex speciali gratia, favore certa scientia, mero motu,
et deliberato animo, cum avisamento et consensu antedict. Damus,
concedimus, volumus, declaramus, et ordinamus quod dictus dominus
Robertus Gordon, et sui hæredes masculi quicunque, de tempore in
tempus, virtute præsentis cartæ nostræ et dicti status, gradus, ordinis,
dignitatis, et stili Baronetti sibi per præsentis cartæ nostra tenorem
concess. habebunt, tenebunt, capient, et gaudebunt omni tempore
a futuro, diem datæ præsentis cartæ nostræ sequen. et infra dictum
regnum nostrum Scotiæ, et regionem Novæ Scotiæ, et alibi, locum,
prioritatem, præeminentiam, et præcedentiam in omnibus et quibuscunque
commissionibus, brevibus, literis patentibus, appellationibus, nomina-
tionibus, et scriptio quibuscunque; et in omnibus et universis sessionibus,
conventionibus, comitiis, synodis, et omnibus temporibus et occasionibus quibuscunque, ante omnes milites auratos hactenus factos
et creatos, aut quocunque tempore a futuro faciendos et creandos, et
præ omnibus baronibus, lie Lairdis, armigeris lie Esquyris, et
generosis quibuscunque, lie Gentilmen, excepto nostrum locum
tenente, suisque hæredibus nostrum locum tenentibus, dicti regni
Novæ Scotiæ, et non aliter, quorum uxores et liberi habebunt, et
juxta gaudebunt simili loco et præcendentia (et exceptis hujusmodi
militibus, bannerettis quos contigerit fieri, et in milites curatores
designari per nos, nostros hæredes, vel successores, sub nostro vexillo,
et in erecto signo lie standart, et displayit banner, in omnibus
exercitibus regiis, in aperto bello, lie oppen warre, nobismet-ipsis
personaliter præsentibus et non aliter, neque alio modo, et hoc
durante tempore vitæ dictorum militum bannerettorum tantum, et
non diutius) *et ante omnes baronettos quoscunque* aliquo tempore a
futuro per nos, nostros hæredes et successores, faciendos, et ante

suos hæredes et successores, tametsi contigerit alios baronettum vel
baronettos in posterum per nos faciendos, et literas suas patentes
dicti gradus, dignitatis, status, nominis, ordinis, tituli et stili baronetti
sub nostro magno sigillo dicti regni nostri Scotiæ, perficere et
expedire antequam præfatus dominus Robertus, suique hæredes
masculi, absolvent et expedient hanc nostram cartam, nostro sub
magno sigillo, non obstante aliqua lege, consuetudine, vel constitutione quacunque in contrarium. ET SIMILITER voluimus,
concessimus, declaravimus, et ordinavimus, tenoreque præsentis
cartæ nostræ, pro nobis, hæredibus et successoribus nostris, cum
avisamento et consensu antedict. de specialibus nostris gratia, favore,
certa scientia, mero motu, et deliberato animo, volumus, concedimus,
declaramus, constituimus, et ordinamus, quod uxor et nepotes dicti
domini Roberti Gordon suorumque hæredum masculorum præscript.
de tempore in tempus in perpetuum, virtute præsentis cartæ nostræ,
et dicti gradus, status, et dignitatis suorum maritorum, habebunt,
tenebunt, capient, et gaudebunt omni tempore a futuro, *loco, præcedentia, prioritate, et præeminentia, tam durante* vita suorum
maritorum quam ex inde durante sita vita, si contigerit ipsas diutius
superstites, ante uxores omnium personarum quarumcunque pro
quibus præfatus dominus Robertus, vel dicti sui hæredes masculi,
debent vel poterint, virtute præsentis cartæ nostræ, vel dicti gradus,
status, dignitatis, nominis, ordinis, tituli vel stili baronetti, tenore
præsentium concess. habere, tenere, capere, et gaudere loco, prioritate, præcedentia, et præeminentia, et ante uxores dict. militum
bannerettorum prius except. propterea quod dictus gradus baronetti
est hæreditarius gradus sanguinis; NEC NON quod filii et filiæ
respective dicti domini Roberti, et suorum hæredum masculorum,
in perpetuum, virtute præsentis cartæ nostræ, et dict. dignitatis
baronetti præsentibus concess. præfato domino Roberto, suisque
hæredibus masculis, habebunt, tenebunt, capient, et gaudebunt loco,
prioritate, præcedentia, et præeminentia præ filiis et filiabus respective omnium personarum præ quibus præfatus dominus Robertus,
vel sui hæredes masculi, locum capere, et præcedentium poterint,
vel debent, vel virtute præsentis cartæ nostræ, vel dicti gradus, et
stili baronetti ipsis præsentibus concess. præ filiis militum, banneret-

torum prius except. ET SIMILITER, quod uxores, filiorum dicti domini Roberti, suorumque hæredum masculorum, omni tempore a futuro respective habebunt, tenebunt, capient, et gaudebunt loco, prioritate, et præcedentia ante uxores omnium personarum quarumcunque, præ quibus ipsarum mariti locum capere poterint, vel debent; idque tam durante vita ipsorum maritorum quam postea. INSUPER, ex specialibus nostris gratia, favore, certa scientia, mero motu, et animo deliberato, tenore præsentis cartæ nostræ pro nobis, hæredibus, et successoribus nostris, cum avisamento antedict. volumus, concedimus, ordinamus, declamus, et promittimus quod quocunque tempore, et quam primum filius natu maximus, et apparens hæres masculus dicti domini Roberti, vel filius natu proximus, aut hæres apparens masculus quorumcunque hæredum masculorum ipsi succeden. venerint ad ætatem viginti unius annorum, quod ipse, et unusquisque eorum respective, per nos, hæredes et successores nostros, milities lie KNIGHTS inaugurabuntur, quandocunque ipsi, vel eorum aliquis, hujusmodi ordinem requisiverint, absque solutione mercedum et expensarum quarumcunque, et quod dictus dominus Robertus, et sui hæredes masculi præscript. habebunt, et habere et gerere in perpetuum dehinc poterint, vel in paludamentis, vulgo lie canton in thair coit of armis, vel in scutis, vulgo lie scutcheons, pro eorum arbitrio, arma regni Novæ Scotiæ nimirum. Et quod dictus dominus Robertus, hæredesque sui masculi præscript. ex tempore in tempus in perpetuum habebunt locum, omni tempore a futuro, in omnibus exercitibus nostris, hæredum et successorum nostrorum in acie, vulgo lie crosse, prope et juxta vexillum nostrum regium, vulgo neir about our royal standart, nostrorum hæredum et successorum, pro defensione ejusdem, et quod dictus dominus Robertus, suique hæredes masculi præscript. in perpetuum habeant et habebunt omni tempore a futuro, duos assistentes seu asseclas sui corporis, vulgo twa assistents of his body, ad supportandum volamen, lie peill, et principalem lugentem, et sibi quatuor assistentes in suis funeribus. ET QUOD dictus dominus Robertus, suique hæredes masculi respective, in perpetuum omni tempore a futuro, nominabuntur, vocabuntur, et designabuntur, nomine BARONETTI, et quod omni vulgari sermone Scotiæ et scriptis hac additis (SIR) et in omnibus aliis linguis, sermonibus, et scriptis similia signativa verba nominibus respective dicti domini Roberti, et suorum hæredum masculorum respective in perpetuum præmittentur. ET QUOD dictus stilus, et titulus Baronetti fini ipsorum cognominum apponetur et subjicietur in omnibus et singulis nostris, et successorum nostrorum literis patentibus, et in omnibus et singulis aliis literis, scriptis, et cartis quibuscunque, tanquam vera legitima, et necessaria dignitatis additio. ED QUOD inde præfatus dominus Robertus nunc, et omnibus temporibus futuris nominabitur, vocabitur et intitulabitur, DOMINUS ROBERTUS GORDON BARONETTUS; AC ETIAM quod uxor et uxores dicti domini Roberti, suorumque hæredum masculorum respective, in perpetuum habebunt, tenebunt, fruentur, et possidebunt, omni tempore a futuro, stilum, titulum, et appellationem dominæ, vulgo MADAM ET DAME respective, juxta usum et phrasim in sermonibus et scriptis; ET PRÆTEREA, ex nostra speciali gratia, favore, certa scientia, mero motu, animoque deliberato, ordinavimus, et promisimus, tenoreque præsentis cartæ nostræ pro nobis, hæredibus et successoribus nostris, cum avisamento et consensu antedict. damus, concedimus, ordinamus, declaramus, et promittimus præfato domino Roberto, et suis hæredibus masculis respective in perpetuum, quod numerus baronettorum, tam infra regnum nostrum Scotiæ quam regionem Novæ Scotiæ, nunquam pro præsenti, vel aliquo tempore a futuro, excedet, vel augebitur in totum ultra numerum centum et quinquaginta baronettorum: NEC NON ex speciali nostra gratia, favore, certa scientia, mero motu, animoque deliberato, dedimus, concessimus, declaravimus, ordinavimus et promisimus, tenoreque præsentis cartæ nostræ pro nobis, hæredibus et successoribus nostris, cum avisamento et consensu antedict. damus, concedimus, ordinamus, declaramus, et promittimus præfato domino Roberto, hæredibus suis masculis respective in perpetuum, quod neque nos, hæredes vel successores nostri, erigemus, vel nunc, aut aliquo tempore a futuro, erecturi, facturi, creaturi, vel constituturi sumus aliquas alias dignitates, gradus, status, ordines, titulos, vel stilos; nec dabimus, concedemus, permittemus, ordinabimus, vel constituemus locum, prioritatem, vel præcedentiam aliquibus personis quibus-

cunque sub vel infra stilum et gradum domini parliamenti dicti
regni nostri Scotiæ altiorem, priorem, vel parem dicto gradui, ordini,
titulo, vel stilo baronetti per nos præfato domino Roberto, suis
hæredibus masculis respective, tenore præsentis cartæ, dat. concess.
et ordinat. et quod dictus dominus Robertus, suique hæredes masculi
respective habebunt, et omni tempore a futuro libere et quiete
habere, tenere et possidere poterint, omnes et singulas prædictas
suas dignitates, loca, præcedentias, prærogativa, privilegia, ante et
præ omnibus aliis personis quibuscunque factis, vel faciendis, creandis,
vel constituendis, in aliquo tali gradu, gradibus, statibus, ordinibus,
titulis, vel stilis, vel cui aliquis hujusmodi locus vel præcedentia
datur, dabitur, aut concedetur. Et quod uxores, filii, filiæ, filio-
rumque uxores dicti domini Roberti, et sui hæredes masculi,
respective omni tempore a futuro dicta sua loca, prioritates, et
prærogativa juxta et convenienter exinde habebunt, tenebunt, et
possidebunt. Et præterea, si quæ dubitatio vel quæstio, præsentibus
non enodata, oriatur de aliquo loco, præcedentia, vel prærogativa
præfato domino Roberto suisque hæredibus masculis, uxoribus, filiis,
filiabus, vel filiorum uxoribus respective, vel alicui eorum quocunque
tempore a futuro debita, quod hujusmodi dubitationes et quæstiones
determinabuntur et decidentur usu et praxi consuetudinis et legis,
prout aliæ graduum hæreditariæ dignitates ordinantur et diriguntur
de loco, prærogativa, et præcedentia. Et ulterius, quod nulla persona, seu personæ quæcunque, aliquo tempore a futuro fient baronetti
Scotiæ, vel regni Novæ Scotiæ, vel præferentur dicto gradui, statui,
dignitati, nomini, ordini, titulo, vel stilo baronetti per nos, hæredes
vel successores nostros, nisi qui primo perficient et perimplebunt conditiones, per nos pro bono et propagatione plantationis Novæ Scotiæ
constitut. et manifestabunt easdem nobis, et commissionariis per
dictum nostrum locum tenentem constituendis. Et præterea,
quod præsentes sunt et erunt validæ, sufficientes, et efficientes omni
tempore a futuro, omnibus suis punctis, ut præmissum est, præfato
domino Roberto, et suis hæredibus masculis respective, in omne
ævum, et suis uxoribus, filiis, filiabus, et filiorum uxoribus respective,
et eorum singulis de jure, contra nos, hæredes et successores nostros,
et contra omnes alias personas quascunque in omnibus nostris,

hæredum, et successorum nostrorum curiis, et omnibus aliis locis quibuscunque, omnibus temporibus et occasionibus, non obstante quocunque jure, consuetudine, præscriptione, praxi, ordinatione, seu constitutione hactenus fact. ordinat. vel publicat. vel in posterum quocunque tempore faciend. ordinand. et publicand. ordinat. vel proviso. et non obstante aliqua alia materia, causa, vel occasione quacunque. INSUPER, pro munificis et amplis auxiliis, et impensis nobis hactenus præstitis per præfatum dominum Robertum Gordon, pro auxilio et propagatione dictæ plantationis Novæ Scotiæ, ordinavimus hanc cartam nostram, absque aliquo sine vel compositione nobis, vel nostro thesaurario vel deputato solvenda, perficiendam et expediendam. ET PROPTEREA, tenore præsentis cartæ nostræ ordinamus, et declaramus, quod nec nunc, nec aliquo tempore præterito, diem datæ præsentis cartæ nostræ præceden. fecimus, nec creavimus aliquos barones vel baronettos, nec prætulimus aliquam personam, vel personas, dicto statui, gradui, dignitati, nomini, ordini, titulo, vel stilo baronetti, exceptis præfato domino Roberto Gordon, et domino Alexandro Strachan de Thornetoun milite. Et quod dedimus locum, prioritatem, præcedentiam, præeminentiam inter ipsos duos, præfato domino Roberto Gordon militi. ET PRÆTEREA, per præsentis cartæ nostræ tenorem, declaramus, quod nec fecimus, nec creavimus aliquem baronettum, vel baronettos quoscunque, nec prætulimus aliquam personam vel personas quascunque dicto statui, gradui, nomini, ordini, titulo, seu stilo baronetti, præ velante præfatum dominum Robertum Gordon, infra dictum regnum nostrum Scotiæ. POSTREMO, nos, pro nobis, et successoribus nostris, cum avisamento et consensu antedict. volumus, decernimus, declaramus, et ordinamus præsentem hanc nostram cartam, cum omnibus et singulis privilegiis, libertatibus, clausulis, articulis, et conditionibus antedict. in proximo nostro parliamento dicti regni nostri Scotiæ. vel aliquo alio parliamento ejusdem deinceps celebrand. pro arbitrio dicti domini Roberti Gordon, suorumque hæredum masculorum, ratificandum, approbandum, et confirmandam ; et ut habeat robur, vim, et effectum decreti et sententiæ illius supremi et præeminentis judicii, penes quam nos pro nobis, et successoribus nostris, volumus et declaramus hanc nostram cartam et clausulas inibi content.

ad hunc effectum, sufficiens fore warrantum; promittend. in
verbo principis idem fore perficiendum. INSUPER dilectis nostris,
etc., et vestrum cuilibet, conjunctim et divisim, vicecomitatibus
nostris in hac parte specialiter constitutis, salutem. VOBIS præcipimus et mandamus, quatenus præfato domino Roberto Gordon,
vel suo certo actornato, latori præsentium, sasinam totarum et
integrarum prædict. terrarum et baroniæ de GORDOUN,
cum omnibus et singulis partibus, pendiculis, privilegiis, libertatibus, commoditatibus, licentiis, et immunitatibus iisdem spectan.
seu spectare valen. et aliorum quorumcunque specialiter et
generaliter supra mentionat. quam quidem sasinam, cum avisamento et consensu antedict. pro nobis, hæredibus et successoribus
nostris, tenore præsentis cartæ nostræ volumus, declaramus, et
ordinamus tam fore legitimum et sufficientem quam si præcepta
sasina separatim et ordinarie ex nostra cancellaria ad id effectum
super dicta carta fuissent directa; penes quam, cum avisamento
antedict. pro nobis, nostris hæredibus et successoribus, dispensavimus,
tenoreque præsentis cartæ nostræ dispensamus in perpetuum. IN
CUJUS REI TESTIMONIUM huic præsenti cartæ magnum sigillum
nostrum apponi præcipimus, TESTIBUS prædilectis nostris con-
sanguineis et consiliariis, Jacobo marchione de Hamilton, comite
Araniæ et Cambridge, domino Aven et Innerdail, Gulielmo Maris-
chall comite, domino Keyth, regni nostri marescallo, prædilecto
nostro consiliario, domino Georgio Hay de Kinfauns milite, nostro
cancellario, et prædilecto nostro consanguineo et consiliario, Thoma
comite de Melrose nostro secretario, dilectis nostris familiaribus
consiliariis, dominis Ricardo Cockburn de Clerkingtoun, nostri
secreti sigilli custode, Johanne Hamilton de Magdalenis, nostrorum
rotulorum registro ac consilii clerico, Georgio Elphingston de
Blythiswood nostræ justiciariæ clerico, et Johanne Scot de Scottis-
tarvet, nostræ cancellariæ directore, militibus. APUD QUHYTHALL,
vigesimo octavo die mensis Maii, anno Domini millesimo sexcentesimo vigesimo quinto, regnique nostri anno primo.

It will have been observed that in the Patents of which
examples have been given, the dignity has been conferred

on each recipient for life, and to the heirs male of his body lawfully begotten ; but there are many cases of their being granted with special remainders, of which the following are sufficient examples :—

'29th May 1619. Sir William Hervy for life with reversion to his son William Hervy, Esq., and the heirs male of his body ; remainder to any other heirs male of the body of the said William the father, and the heirs male of their bodies.

'9th February 1639. Sir Edward Tyrrell to hold the dignity for life with remainder to his son Tobias Tyrrell, Esq. in tail male, remainder to Francis Tyrrell another son in tail mail remainder to the heirs male of the body of the said Edward in tail male.

'11th August 1660. Sir William Wheeler with remainder to Charles Wheeler Cousin to the said Sir William and the heirs of the said Charles.

'5th May 1670. Sir George Stonehouse for life (having surrendered his former Patent by a fine) with remainder to John Stonehouse his second son and to the heirs male of his body ; and for lack of such issue to James his third son, etc. with precedency to him and his said sons according to the first Patent dated 7 May 1628.

'22nd April 1678. Sir Francis Edwards "and to the heirs male of his body, with remainder to Thomas, Benjamin, Herbert and Jonathan, and the heirs male of their bodies,' etc. and a special clause for precedency before all Baronets created after the year 1644.

'18th May 1678. Sir James Bowyer Grandson and heir to Sir Thomas Bowyer Baronet (created 23 July 3 Car. I.) surrendering his Patent had now a new creation to that dignity, for life only, the remainder to Henry Goring of Highden in the same County, Esquire and to the heirs male of his body with the same precedency as the said Sir Thomas Bowyer enjoyed.

'29th June 1682. Sir Cornelius Gans of the Netherlands, with remainder to Stephen Groubart and his heirs.

'31st January 1700. Sir Nicholas Van-Acker with remainder to his brother John Van-Acker and Sir Jeremy Sambrooke, Knight.

'4th May 1725. Sir Henry Fermor, with remainder to Charles Eversfield, Junior.

'17th January 1748. Sir Edward Lawrence with remainder to his Nephew Isaac Woolaston Esquire.

'3rd May 1774. Sir Richard Clayton. In default of issue-male, to the heirs male of John Clayton Esquire; his late father, deceased, and their heirs male.

'3rd May 1774. Sir Charles Raymond. In default of issue-male to William Burrell Esquire of Beckenham, in Kent, and his heirs-male by Sophia his wife daughter of the said Charles Raymond.'

It will be noticed that in some of the above examples there is also a special clause giving precedency. To these examples may be added the following, which appear to be very special and unusual :—

'22nd June 1631. Sir Charles Vavasor with an especial clause of precedency, viz., to take place next below Sir Thomas Moulson of Carleton in com. Linc. Baronet and next above Sir George Greseley of Drakelow in com. Derb. Baronet created 29 June 1611.

'8th May 1674. Sir Arthur Onslow in reversion after death of his father-in-law Sir Thomas Foote without issue male (who was created 21 November 1660) and with the same precedency.'

The Patent of Sir Benjamin Wright, dated 7th February 1645, was afterwards superseded by the King's Royal Warrant. During the troublous times of Charles I. many of his Patents were dated abroad; for example, that of Sir Richard Browne was dated at St. Germains in France, 1st September 1649, as was also that of Sir Richard Forster, dated 18th September 1649, and others, while that of Sir Arthur Slingsby was dated at Bruges, 19th October 1657.

Two instances are recorded of ladies receiving the dignity. In 1635 Dame Mary Bolles and her heirs whatever were created Baronets of Scotland, and had a grant of eighteen miles square of land in Nova Scotia. Charles I. ordained that she should be designed Lady, Madam, or Dame before her surname ; and that she should have rank amongst the ladies of the Baronets, according to the date of her Patent. Another instance is the mother of General Cornelius Spellman, said to have been created by James II. as a Baronettess of England.

The following instance of the grant of a Baronet's Patent to a Corporation, and the proposed sale of the Patent, taken from the *Gentleman's Magazine*, vol. lix. p. 423, may be of interest :—

'21 May 1789. In the minute books of the Scotish Corporation in Crane-court, occurs the following entry, which I transcribe for you as an historical curiosity ; wishing at the same time to learn whether any and what consequences arose from the grant :—

"Monday, April 16, 1688. At a court of this Corporation then held, Ordered, that the Knights Baronet's patent of England, granted by his Majesty in favour of the Corporation, be exposed to sale at 500 guineas, and not under, the Corporation being at all reasonable charges ; and the two Scots patents at 300 each ; with full power to John Renny, John Alexander, John Hay, and Sir Andrew Forrester, any two of which, with the Master, to be a quorum, to treat and dispose of the same accordingly."'

As the minutes of the Scottish Corporation relating to this period have all been destroyed by a fire, the result of this 'Order' cannot be given.

Sir Maurice Fenton, Knight of Mitchelstowne, whose Patent is dated Dublin, 22nd July 1661, appears to have been previously created by Oliver Cromwell by Privy Seal,

Whitehall, 25th May 1658, Patent, Dublin, 14th July 1658, with this preamble : 'Whereas, we having taken in our consideration the faithful services performed unto us by our trusty and well-beloved Maurice Fenton, esq ; we are now pleased to confer some such especial mark of our favour upon him for the same, as shall not only be an honour to him during his own life, but descending by course of inheritance to his posterity, and that may give them cause seriously to imitate him in those virtuous courses, for which he has found so gracious an acceptance in our sight.'

The following is the Commission of James I. touching the creation of Baronets, the Instructions annexed thereto, and the Commission respecting the Oath to be taken by each Baronet that he had not given any consideration for the acquisition of the Degree beyond the State service required :—

BY THE KING.

'His Majesties Commission to all the Lords, and others of the Privie Councell, touching the Creation of Baronets.

'James by the Grace of God, King of England, Scotland, France, and Ireland, Defender of the Faith, etc.   To Our right trustie, and right well beloved Councellour, Thomas Lord Elles-mere, Lord Chancellour of England, And to Our right trustie, and right well-beloved Cousins and Councellors, Robert Earle of Salisburie, Lord High Treasurer of England, Henry Earle of Northampton, Lord Keeper of our Privie Seale, Ladouike Duke of Lenox, Charles Earle of Nottingham, Our high Admirall of England, Thomas Earle of Suffolke, Lord Chamberlaine of Our Houshold, Gilbert Earl of Shrewsbury, Justice in Eire beyond Trent Northward, Edward Earle of Worcester, Master of Our

Horse, Thomas Earle of Excester, John Earle of Marre, Alexander Earle of Dunfermyline, And to Our right trusty, and right wel-beloved Councellours, Thomas Lord Viscount Fenton, Edward Lord Zouche, William Lord Knolles, Treasurer of Our Houshold, Edward Lord Wotton Comptroller of Our Houshold, John Lord Stanhope, Vice-Chamberlaine of our Houshold, And to Our trustie, and right well beloved Councellours, Sir John Herbert Knight, Our second Secretarie of State, Sir Julius Caesar Knight, Chan-cellour and Under-Treasurer of Our Exchequer, and Sir Thomas Parrie Knight, Chancellour of Our Dutchie of Lancaster, Greeting.

'Whereas divers principall Knights, and Esquires of Sundry parts of this Our Realme, mooved with zeale and affection to further the Plantation of Ulster, and other like Services in our Realme of IRE-LAND, have offered and agreed, every of them to maintaine thirtie Footmen Souldiers in the same Our Realme, at their owne proper costs and charges, after the rate of eightpence apiece by the day sterling, during the space of three yeeres now next ensuing, (By the imitation of which example that good worke, whereupon the establishment of Religion and Civility, in place of blindnesse and barbarisme doeth so much depend, is likely to be so much advanced and supported, as no reasonable meanes would be forborne, that may cherish and encourage such an endeavour) Wee have been pleased, as an Argreement of Our Gracious acceptation of so remarkeable a Service, not only to bestow upon them a dignitie newly erected and created by Us, answerable to their Estate and Merit, (which Wee have stiled by the name of BARONET, with divers Priviledges annexed thereunto, And the same have granted by Letters Patents to them, and the Heirs males of their bodies, to the end the memory thereof may remaine to them and their Posteritie) But are deter-mined to doe the like also to some such other selected persons, as shall concurre in the same intentions, not exceeding a convenient number : And therefore although Wee could not (in reason) forbeare to begin and conclude with some principall Persons of especiall Note and Qualitie, that first discovered their good affections in this kinde, before Wee had made any publique Declaration of Our certaine Resolution to proceed further, yet when We enter into consideration,

that there may be divers other Knights and Esquires of all parts of
this Our Realme, that are capable of this Dignitie (respecting their
Estate and Qualitie) and in whom there would be found a like
affection to the said Service, if they could take notice of this course
so soone as others, that are not so remote in their habitations, We
have thought fit hereby, aswell to notifie our Pleasure to receive
a convenient number of this Dignity, as to Warrant and Authorise
you (when any that are moved with the same Affections to the
Publique good, and are otherwise qualified as is fit, shall repaire
unto you within the time limited for this our Commission) to treat
and conclude with them in manner and forme as you have done
with others, and according to those Instructions, which for your
better direction in a matter of this consequence, Wee have annexed
to this Commission. KNOW yee therefore, that Wee have appointed
you to be our Commissioners, and Wee doe by these Presents give
and grant unto you all, or unto any eight or more of you, (whereof
you the said Lord Chancellor, or Lord Treasurer, to be alwayes
one,   And you the said Lord Privie Seale, Duke of Lenox, Earle
of Nottingham Our Admirall, Earle of Suffolke our Chamberlaine,
and Earle of Worcester Master of Our Horse, to be alwayes two ;
who are so much the more able to judge of mens blood and antiquitie, in regard you are Commissioners in the Office of Earle
Marshall) full, free, and lawfull Power and Authoritie, to commune
and treat with any of Our loving Subjects, whom you shall finde
willing to give such pay and entertainment to such number of
footmen as is aforesaid, to be imployed in the said service, and for
such time as aforesaid, And thereupon to informe your selves of
their family, living, and reputation, And such and so many of the
said persons, as you or any such eight or more of you (as is aforesaid) shall find and approove to bee in all the respects aforesaid
worthy such Degree, (not exceeding the number of two hundred,
which We have covenanted in our Patents shall not be exceeded,
but suffered to diminish as their Issue shall faile) to cause every
one of them for himself to make Payment, or to give good and
sufficient Assurance for the due answering of so much, as shall be
sufficient for maintenance of thirtie Souldiers footmen, after the

rate of eight pence apiece by the day for the terme of three yeeres, as is aforesaid, And thereupon to give Warrant and Direction under any such eight or more of your hands, as is aforesaid, unto our Attourney, or Sollicitor generall, for the drawing up of several Bills and Grants to passe from Us unto all, and every such person and persons, as shall be so approoved by you, or any such eight or more of you, as is aforesaid, for the making and creating of every such person Baronet, with all priviledges of Precedencie, Place, Title, and all other things thereunto belonging, according to the forme hereunto annexed, And these Presents, together with such Warrant & Direction of you, or any such eight or more of you, as is aforesaid, shalbe from time to time to Our said Attourney, and Sollicitor Generall for the time being, sufficient Warrant for the drawing up, and subscribing of every such Bill or Graunt to passe from Us, according to the true meaning of these Presents And our Will and Pleasure is, that Our Attourney, or Sollicitor Generall shall draw, Ingrosse, and subscribe the Bills and Grants to be made of the said dignitie of Baronet, according to the Directions and Warrants by you, or any such eight or more of you as is aforesaid, And the said Bills and Grants so drawen, Ingrossed and subscribed with the hands of Our Attourney or Sollicitor Generall, or either of them, shall be a sufficient Warrant and Discharge to you Our said Commissioners, to subscribe likewise the said Bills or Grants with the hands of any such eight or more of you, as aforesaid.

'And furthermore, for the more easie and speedy passing of the Grants and Letters Patents to be made of the said Dignitie, Wee are pleased and contented, and by these Presents for Us, Our Heires & Successors, Wee doe grant, ordaine and appoint that the Bills for such Patents prepared by our said Attourney, or Sollicitor as aforesaid, and signed with the hands of you, or any such eight or more of you, as is aforesaid, shall be a sufficient and immediate Warrant to the Lord Chancellour of England, or Lord Keeper of the great Seale of England for the time being, to passe the same Grants and Letters Patents under the Greate Seale of England, without any other or further Warrant from Us to be had or obtained in that behalfe. And this Our Commission, Wee have made to continue till the sixt day of July next comming after the date hereof, and then to cease and determine. In witnesse whereof, &c., Witnesse, &c.

'BY THE KING

'THE INSTRUCTIONS within mentioned to be observed by Our Commissioners within named.

'Forasmuch as Wee have bene pleased to authorize you to Treate and conclude with a certaine number of Knights and Esquires, as they shall present themselves unto you with such offers of assistance for the service of Ireland, and under such Conditions as are contained in these Presents, wherein We doe repose great trust and confidence in your discretions and integrities, knowing well that in such cases, there are so many circumstances incident, as require a choice care and consideration. Wee doe hereby require you to take such course as may make known abroad both our purpose, and the Authoritie given unto you, that by the more publique notice thereof those persons who are disposed to advance so good a worke, may in time understand where, and to whom to addresse themselves for the same; For which purpose We require you to appoint some certaine place and times for their Accesse: which We thinke fittest to be at the Councel Chamber at WHITEHALL, upon Wednesdayes and Fridayes in the afternoone, where you shall make knowen to them (as they come) that those who desire to bee admitted into the dignitie of Baronets, must maintaine the number of thirtie foote-Souldiers in Ireland, for three yeeres, after the rate of eightpence sterling Money of ENGLAND by the day; And the wages of one whole yeere to be payed into Our Receipt, upon the passing of the Patent.

'Provided Alwayes, that you proceed with none, except it shall appeare unto you upon good proofe, that they are men for qualitie, state of living, and good reputation worthy of the same; And that they are at the least descended of a grandfather by the fathers side that bare Armes, And have also of certaine yeerely revenue in Lands of inheritance, in possession, one Thousand pounds per Annum de claro; Or lands of the old Rent, as good (in accompt) as one Thousand pounds per Annum of improved Rents, Or at the least two parts in three parts to be divided of Lands, to the said values in possession, and the other third part in reversion, expectant upon one life only, holding by Dower, or in Joynture.

'And for the Order to be observed in ranking those, that shall receive, the dignitie of a Baronet, although it is to be wished that those Knights, which have now place before the Knights (in respect of the time of their Creation) may be ranked before others (Cæteris paribus), yet because this is a Dignitie, which shall bee Hereditarie, wherein divers circumstances are more considerable, then suche a Marke as is but Temporarie, (that is to say of being now a Knight, in time before another) Our pleasure is, you shall not bee so precise, in placing those that shall receive this Dignitie, but than are Esquire of great antiquitie, and extraordinary living, may be ranked in this choise before some Knights. And so (of Knights) a man of greater living, more Remarkeable for his house, yeeres, or calling in the Commonwealth, may bee now preferred in this Degree, before one that was made a Knight before him.

'Next, because there is nothing of Honour, or of value, which is knowen to be sought or desired (bee the Motives never so good) but may receive scandall from some, who (wanting the same good affection to the publique) or being in other considerations incapable can be contented out of envie to those that are so preferred, to cast aspersions, and imputations upon them ; As if they came by this dignitie for any other consideration, but that which concerneth this so publique and memorable a worke, You shall take order, That the party, who shall receive this dignitie, may take his Oath, that neither he (nor any for him) hath directly or indirectly given any more for attayning the degree, or any precedence in it, than that which is necessary for the maintenance of the number of Souldiers, in such sort, as aforesaid, saving the charges of passing his Patent.

'And because We are not ignorant, that in the distribution of all Honours, most men will be desirous to attaine to so high a place as they may, in the Judgement whereof (being matter of dignitie) there cannot be too great caution used to avoyd the interruption, that private partialities may breed in so worthy a Competition.

'Forasmuch as it is well knowen, that it can concerne no other person so much to prevent all such inconveniences, as it must doe Ourselfe, from whom all Honour and dignitie, (either Temporarie, or Hereditarie) hath his only roote and beginning, You shall publish and declare to all, whom it may concerne, That for the better warrant of your owne Actions, in this matter of PRECEDENCIE, (wherein Wee finde you so desirous to avoyd all just exceptions) Wee are determined upon view of all those Patents, which shall be subscribed by you, before the same passe Our great Seale, to take especiall care upon Us, to order and ranke every man in his due place; And therein alwayes to use the particular counsell and advise, that you Our Commissioners shall give Us, of whose integritie and circumspection, Wee have so good experience, and are so well perswaded, as Wee assure Our selfe, you will use all the best meanes you may to enforme your owne Judgements in cases doubtfull, before you deliver Us any such opinion as may leade Us in a case of this Nature, wherein Our intention is (by due consideration of all necessary circumstances) to give every man that satisfaction, which standeth with Honour and Reason.

'Lastly, having now directed you, how, and with what caution you are to entertaine the Offers of such as shall present themselves for this dignitie, Wee doe also require you to observe these two things, The one, That every such person as shalbe admitted, doe enter into sufficient Bond or Recognizance, to Our use, for the payment of that portion, which shall be remayning after the first payment is made, Which you are to see payd, upon delivery of the Letters Patents; The other, That seeing this Contribution for so publique an Action, is the motive of this dignitie, And that the greatest good which may be expected upon this Plantation will depend upon the certaine payment of those Forces, which shall be fit to bee maintained in that Kingdome, untill the same bee well established, the charge whereof will bee borne with the greater difficultie, if We be not eased by some such extraordinary meanes; We require you Our Treasurer of England, so to order this Receipt, as no part thereof bee mixed with Our other Treasure, but kept apart by itselfe, to be wholely converted to that use, to which it is given, and entended; And in regard thereof, that you assigne it to be received, and the Bonds to be kept by some such particular person, as you shall thinke good to appoint, who upon the payment of every severall portion, shall both deliver out the Bonds, and give his Aquittance for the same. For which this shall be yours, and his the said Receivours sufficient Warrant in that behalfe.

'BY THE KING

'HIS MAJESTIES COMMISSION to the Lords, and others of his Privie Councell, for taking the Oath of the Baronets.

'JAMES by the grace of God, King of ENGLAND, SCOTLAND, FRANCE and IRELAND, Defender of the Faith, &c., To Our right trustie, and right well beloved Councellour, THOMAS Lord Ellesemere, Lord Chancellour of ENGLAND, And to Our right trustie, and right well-beloved Cousens and Councellour, ROBERT Earle of Salisburie, Lord High Treasurer of ENGLAND, Henry Earle of Northampton, Lord Keeper of our Privie Seale, Lodouike Duke of Lenox, Charles Earle of Nottingham, Our high Admirall of England, Thomas Earle of Suffolke, Lord Chamberlaine of our Houshold, Gilbert Earle of Shrewsbury Justice in Eire beyond Trent Northward, Edward Earl of Worcester, Master of Our Horse, Thomas Earle of Excester, John Earle of Marre, Alexander Earle of Dunfermyline, And to Our right trusty, and right welbeloved Counsellours, Thomas Lord Viscount Fenton, Edward Lord Zouche, William Lord Knolles, Treasurer of Our Houshold, Edward Lord Wotton Comptroller of Our Houshold, John Lord Stanhope, Vicechamberlaine of Our Houshold, And to Our trustie, and right welbeloved Councellours, Sir John Herbert Knight, Our second Secretarie of State, Sir Julius Cæsar Knight, Chancellour and Under-Treasurer of Our Exchequer, and Sir Thomas Pawe, Knight, Chancellour of Our Dutchie of Lancaster, Greeting. Wheras We have already by Our severall Letters Patents created divers principal Knights and Gentlemen of sundry parts of this Our Realme of England, BARONETS, as by the same Our Letters Pattents may appeare, Know yee that We have authorized you, and by these presents doe authorize you, or any eight or more of you, whereof you the said Lord Chancellour or Lord Treasurer to bee alwayes one,

and you the said Lord Privie Seale, Duke of Lenox, Earle of
Nottingham, Our Admirall, Earl of Suffolke, Our Chamberlaine,
and Earle of Worcester, Master of Our Horse, to be alwayes two, to
take the Oath of all and every of the saide BARONETS, already
created, or to be created severally before his said Patent of his
Creation bee delivered unto him, that he hath not given directly
or indirectly, by himselfe or any other with his privitie, nor is
to give by himselfe or any other with his privitie, any more
for attaining the said degree, or any precedence in it, than that
which is necessary for the maintenance of thirtie footmen souldiers in
Our Realme of Ireland, after the rate of eight pence by the day
sterling, during the space of three yeeres now next insuing, saving
the charges of passing his Patent.

'And because it may so fall out, that some of the said BARONETS
already created, and others hereafter to be created, shall or may by
sicknesse, infirmitie, or other occasion be hindred so as they cannot
be present with you to receive their Patents at your hands ; We
do therfore by these presents, authorize, and commaund you Our
Councellour of England, to award Commissions from time to
time, for any such BARONETS that shall require the same, to such
three, foure, or more discreet Knights or other Gentlemen, as
you shall thinke fit, Commanding them, or any two of them, to
take the like Oath of every such BARONET, and to returne the
same to you.'

Upon the first erection of the Degree there was paid by
each Baronet into the Exchequer the sum of one thousand
and ninety-five pounds, being for the maintenance of thirty
soldiers for three years at the rate of eightpence per day for
each soldier, in addition to twelve hundred pounds, the
charges of passing the patent. It was not necessary that the
whole of the amount should be provided at once, but the
wages of one year had at least to be paid on the passing of
the Patent ; and as regards the balance, the Baronet had to

enter into a sufficient bond and recognisance for the balance
which remained due after the first payment was made.

The following is a form of the Bond :—

'Noverint universi per præsentes me —— —— de —— in Com :
—— : Milit : et Baronett : teneri et firmiter obligari serenissimo
domino nostro Jacobo Dei gratia Anglie, Scotie, Francie, et Hibernie
nunc Regi in Mille marcis legalis monete Anglie solvendis eidem
Domino Regi heredibus et executoribus suis, Ad quam quidem
solicitatione bene et fideliter faciendam, Obligo me, heredes, executores,
et administratores meos firmiter per præsentes Sigillo meo sigillat :
dat : quarto die Junii 1611, Anno Regni Domini nostri Regis
Anglie, Francie, et Hibernie Nono, et Scotie Quadragesimo Quarto.

'The Condition of this Obligacion is such that if the above
bonded Sir —— ——, Knight and Baronett, his heirs, executors,
or administrators, or some of them, doe well and truelie paie or
cause to be paid into the handes of Thomas Wattson, Esquire,
or into the handes of anie other to be by the Lord Treasurer of
England named and appointed Receyvour of the monyes paide & to
be paied by such as his Matie hath or shall create Baronette, to the
use of his Matie his heirs or successors the some of Three Hundred
Three Score & Fyve Pounds of Lawfull money of England, being
one full thirde part of One Thousand Four Score & Fyftene
Pounds, at or within the now office of the saide Thomas Wattson
within his Ma^{tie's} Receipte of the Exchequire in or upon the fyveth
daie of June which shalbe in the yere of our Lord God One
Thousand Six Hundreth & Thirtene without fraude or covyne that
then this Obligacion to be voide & of none effect, or else to stand
in full strength & virtue.

'Recognit xxij° die   —— ——
Junii nono Jacobi
Regis coram me
     EDW. BROMLEY.'

The following is a form of the Receipt given for the
three annual instalments of £365 :—

' In Pelle Recept' in Termino Pasche a°-xj° R. Jacobi,
Sabbi xvto Maii.

'————.———— ————, mil. et Baronett' trescentas Sexagint' quinque libras in plen' solutione M iiij^{xx} xv^l p ips' dno. Regi Jacobo
dat' et concess' ad manutenend' triginta viros in cohortibus suis
pedestribus in regno suo Hibernie pro defensione eiusdem, et p'cipue
p securitate Plantationis Provincie Ultonie ibm p spatium trium
annorum secundum ratam viijd. p quolibet huiusmodi pedite p diem
durante termino predicto solubil' p recognit' suam quinto die Junii
prox' futuro .   .   .   . ccclxv^l—sol'.
' *Exx.   Edw: Wardour.'*

This, however, was by no means the whole amount of the
payments, as is shown by the following long list of Fees
paid by Sir Edward Hussey for the issue of his Patent and
for his release from his Bonds :—

' At Mr Wattsons office in the Receipt.
Quinto Junii 1612   .   .   .   . ccclxv^l.
Quinto Junii 1613   .   .   .   . ccclxv^l.
It^m there was the other third pte paide into thexchequer in hand
before the passing of the patent, viz. ccclxv^l, as may appear by the
Receipt under the Receivours hand plimlary appointed for this
Receipt for the Baronettcy.
Baron Bromley before whom these ij bondes in the nature of re-
cognizances were acknowledged, his man had for his Master xiijs. iiijd.
This man had for enteringe them into the booke   . — iiijd.
' May itt please yor Ldshps. there was paide into my Office this
p'sent day by Sir Edward Hussey, Knight & Baronett, the some of
ccclxv^l in pte of One Thousand Fourscoore & Fifteene poundes by
him given & graunted to his Matie. towardes the maintenaunce of
30 Footemen servinge his Matie. in Ireland for defence of the province of Ulster by the space of iij yeares followinge att the rate of
viijd. per diem to each of them during the same time for which
there is a Talley stricken this p'sent day as appeareth, And ij severall

bondes for ccclxv^l entered into by the said Baronett for the remaine being vii^c xxx^l, & acknowledged before Sir Edward Bromley, Knight, one of the Barons of thExchequer to his M̃atie. accordinge to such directions as I have received for the same   .   .   ccclxv^l.

Witness my hand this xviij day of June, 1611,

Tho: Wattson.'

Watson had for this & striking ye Talley   .   .   .   . xxs.

Watsons man, viz. Poydon, had for him & the rest of his fellows for making the aforesaid ij bondes   .   .   .   .   .   . xvs.

Memd. that this xviij of June, 1611, Sir Edward Hussey in the County of Lincoln hath taken the oath appointed by his M̃atie for the Baronetts in the presence of us.

Jul: Cæsar.

Sir Julio Cæsars clarke had for this   .   .   .   .   . vjs.

Itm. pd. unto Joanes & the rest of his fellows being Mr Coulwerts men for provinge viij of the Lordes Commissioners hand to the patent for warrant unto the great seale   .   .   .   .   . xs.

Itm. unto the doore keepers of the Councell Chamber.   . ijs.

The names of Councellors that subscribed,—*R. Salisbury, H. Northampton, Nottingham, T. Suffolke, Gilbt. Shrewsbury, Edw. Worcester, Edw. Wotton, Julius Cæsar.*

Edw. Bromley.

Given unto Mr Collverts man, which he demanded as a fee dew unto his Mr. who was then Clarke of the Councell attendaunt for the warrant unto Mr Sollicitor, viz. Sir Fr. Bacon, for drawinge the patent   .   .   .   . xxs.

Itm. given unto Mr Collverts man of whome I received the sd. warrant   .   .   .   . xs.

Itm. to the doore keepers of the Councell Chamber   .   . iijs.

Itm. given to Mr Sollicitor for drawinge the patent   . v^l.

Itm. given unto Younge his clarke for writen the same   . xls.

Itm. to Younges man   .   .   .   . ijs.

Itm. to Watsons man, viz. Poydon, for making a bill for payment of some pte. of the money the next morninge that I wanted when I was in payinge the money into thexchequer   .   .   . ijs.

Itm. to Mr Kirkham, one of my Lorde Treasurer's Secretarys xls.

Itm. the Charges to the Crown Office for passinge the pattent which was paid to Sir George Coppin . . . . xiiij^l.

Itm. given unto the Clarkes amongst them . . . xxs.

Itm. to Mr Pinches beinge one of them who specially ingrossed the patent . . . . xs.

Itm. to his boye that brought me word uppon Thursday att night that the patents should be sealed the next day . . . ijs.

Itm. to his boye for writing a copie for me of theire names who hadd theire patents sealed when myne was . . . xxijd.

Itm. given Mr Calvert, the Clarke of the Councell, when Sir Phillipp Woodhouse was with me for to know what Lincolnshire or other men was comed into the roale since I was ranked . xxs.

Itm. given unto Mr Kirkhams man att severall times . . iijs.

Itm. pd. unto Sr. George Coppin, the clarke of the Crowne, att the receit of my Patent under the Seale, witnes his man Mr Pinches who rould the money & delivered itt to his measter . xiiij^l.

Itm. given unto the Clarkes of the Crowne Office amongst them in devident for ingrossinge my patent . . . . . xxs.

Itm. given unto Mr Pinches, one of the clarkes, for his speciall care that itt should be fare written . . . . . xs.

Itm. for the box & lock to lay the patent ynn . . iiijs. vjd.

Itm. to Mr Pinches for a copie of the patent & sight of the instructions before the book came forth in print . . xvijs.

Itm. for ij bookes after they came in print wherein the Commissioners patent & the instructions with a copie of the patent & copie to be granted & taken by the Baronetts are expressed & imprinted.

1612.

Pd. 20 Maij to Mr Watson, one of the tellers in thexchequer, when I payed my second payment, viz. ccclxv^l for my creation of Baronitt for making the bill wheruppon the taylie was stricken ijs.

Itm. to Mr Wardour in office Pellin' for the constat uppon the taylee . . . . ijs.

Itm. to him for registringe & inroulinge of both the bondes in that office, when they were acknowledged . . . . iiijs.

Md. that Mr Watson delivered in my bond without any other fee when I payed the money.

And Lorde Townsend did have inroulmt. of my bond & recognizance erased & crossed over, and a vacato intered in the margent in Mr Wardours office hard by my lord Chauncellors house in the Strand without fee.

So as att the last paymt. I am to pay butt ijs. to Mr Watson his Clarkes for the bill wheruppon the Taylee is to be stricken, and ijs. to Mr Wardour for the constat for that both the bondes are payde for theire inrolmts.'

The following is the Warrant which appointed an Officer in the Court Receiver of the Moneys to be paid by the Baronets on creation :—

' JAMES &c.   To our right trusty and right welbeloved Cousin and Councellor Robert Erle of Salisbury our high Treasurer of England and to our trusty and welbeloved Councellor Sir Julius Cæsar Knight Chauncellor and under-treasurer of our Exchequer. And to our trusty and welbeloved Sir Lawrence Tanfield Knight Cheife Baron of our Exchequer and the rest of the Barons of the said Court greeting : WHEREAS wee have alredy by or speciall Letters Patentes, Created divers principall Knightes and gent. Barronetts as by ye same our Letters Patentes may appeare, and are likewise purposed to Create more Barronetts of like qualitie and Condicion.   And where the Barronetts Created and to be Created are to give for the maintenance of Thirty footemen Soldiers to be imployed in our Realme of Ireland after ye rate of Eight pence by the day sterling a peece during the space of three yeares nowe next ensewing.   A third part of wch money they are to make presente payment of and are to give securitie by Bondes or Recognizances for payment of th' other two partes at Certaine dayes yet to Come ; And because it may fall out that by reason of sicknes, infirmitie or other occasion some of the said Barronetts shall or may be hindered or letted, so as they cannot be present hereabouts to give securitie accordingly, but are to take forth Commissions out of our Court of Chauncery, to be directed to such discreete Knightes or other gentlemen as our Chauncellor of Englande shall in that behalfe

think fitt to be nominated and appointed to receave such Bondes
or Recognizances and to retorne the same into our said Court of
Exchecquer ; Knowe yee nowe that wee for Consideracions us
movinge do Commaund yow our said Treasurer Chauncellor and
Barons and every of yow, so sone as any such Bondes or Recognizances as by vertue of such Commission as aforesaid shal be taken
of or for any Barronett or Barronetts shall be Certified and retourned
into our said Court of Exchecquer, yow and every of yow Cause the
same presently (without any Inrollement or Record at all to be
made of them) to be delivered over to THOMAS WATSON Esq. one
of the Tellors of our Exchecquer (being by yow our said Treasurer
appointed Receavor of such moneys payable by the said Barronetts)
or to such other person or persons as our Treasurer of England for
the time being, shall in that behalfe nominate and appoint That
upon full payment and dischardge of the moneyes due upon such
Bondes or Recognizances, the same shall and may be forthwith, by
such Receavor redelivered to every such Barronett his or their
Executors or Assignes to be Cancelled according to our gratious
intencion in this behalfe   And theise presents shal be aswell to
yow our said Treasurer Chancellor and Barons as also to the said
Receavor, a full & sufficient warraunt and dischardge in that
behalf GIVEN &c. the 27th day of June in the Ninth yeare of
our Raigne of England ffraunce and Ireland, and of Scotland, &c.
44ᵗʰ.'

CHAPTER III

EARLY HISTORY OF THE BARONETAGES
OF ENGLAND AND OF IRELAND

IT was only to be expected that the erection of a new
dignity hereditary like that of the Baronetage should be
viewed with feelings of jealousy by certain of the community. Whether any formal petition was ever made to
the King for the revocation of his first letters patent is not
known, but that such was in contemplation is evidenced by
the following Memorandum contained among the Cotton
Manuscripts in the British Museum (*Faustina*, c. viii.
f. 24) :—

> 'Motiues to induce the Knights Cittizens and Burgesses of the
> Commons howse of Parliament to petition to his Matie for
> the revoking & abolishing of the degree of Baronetts
> lately erected by his hignes letters patents.

'ffirst because this new degree is offensiue to the Nobilitie of this
Realme whose descendants in all reason ought to haue pryme
emynence amongst the gentrie of this Kingdome yet Baronetts by
thease letters Patents are to haue precedence before the descendants
from the younger children of Barons, Earles, Dukes, etc. And to
the order of Knighthood because that degree being a personall
dignitye & springing out of vertue and desert ought to be ranged
next and imediatly vnto Barony. Neuertheles the degree of
Baronetts is interposed betweene Baronie and Knighthood. And
to the gentrye of this Kingdome because many of the Baronetts and

their descendants being meanely descended must haue precedence before gentlemen of auncient families, who by this Innovation wilbe much villified and of smale reckoning in the Comonwealth.

'And vnto the Magistrats of this Kingdome who in respect of their offices & places wherein they serue as also of the grauitie and wisdome of their persons in publick services and assemblies, haue vsed to have precedence before others but now they must giue place vnto Baronetts and their descendants albeit some of them are and many of them in tyme to come may be meane in Birth, poore in estate and of small worth and desert.

'And vnto the whole comynaltie whose descendants by their virtues and good fortunes may hereafter attayne vnto creditt and reputacion in the commonwealth.

'Inconveniences that will arise vnto his Matie and this estate by reason of this new institucion.

'There wilbe allwaies dislike envye and hartburning betweene the gentrie of the Kingdome and the Baronetts.

'The honour of Knighthood wch was wont to encourage generous myndes vnto high exploits will now come into contempt : for be they of never so great prowesse and valour must by this Institucion be inferiour vnto Baronetts of smallest worth.

'Knighthood hath been held a competent reward for forreine and home ymployments But now his Matie must be dryven to seeke new wayes for the recompence and satisfaction of such seruices.

'Gentlemen of great lyvelyhood and estimacion will refraine his Ma^{ts} seruice in publique assemblies for the administration of Justice, and otherwise, because they serue to giue place vnto many of the Baronetts whome they counted their inferiours.

'The reputacion of Knighthood and Antiquitye of descent hath in former tymes much advanced the gentrie soe quallified in preferment of mariages who are very much prejudiced by this hereditorie title.

'Great Noblemen of this Kingdome haue been regarded from their titular dignities for want of meanes to support their honour. But thease Baronetts albeit they shall happen to bee of noe worth, either in estate or desert, must haue precedence before Knights and gentlemen of greatest reputacion.

'Nothing is more commendable then honour springing out of vertue and desert But to purchase honour with money (as Baronetts haue don) is a temporall Simonye and dishonorable to the estate.

'The commonalty of the Kingdome, ever sithence the first institucion therof hath consisted of certaine degrees knowne by legall addicions without change or alteracion by any of his ma^{ties} Progenitours. But this Innovacion may by way of President alter the whole frame of the commonwealth.

'His Matie by his prerogatiue Royall may create Barons, Vicounts, Earles, and any other degrees of Nobilitie as other his Auncestors and Progenitors have don, But the erection of this or any other in the Comminaltie is not warranted by any former President vsage or custome.'

We can imagine that protests resembling the above were made by Earls and Barons when the Degrees of Duke, Marquess, and Viscount were respectively introduced.

The following extract from a long document preserved in the Public Record Office shows that the Officers of the Navy were concerned as to the privileges conferred on the new degree (*State Papers, Domestic Series, James I.*, vol. lxvii. No. 160) :—

A Remonstrance of ye Records heretofore produced in the Councell Chamber concerning the Præcedencie of the offices of the Navie now in question.

. . . .

Præsidents shewinge the Order of the Office not to be inverted by the Dignitie of any other Tytle.

. . . .

To shew that the M^{rs} of Requests have noe præheminence in the office of Marine Causes.

. . . .

To shew that the Priviledges of everie Office are limited within it selfe.

.　　.　　.　　.　　.　　.

To shew that the Patent of a Baronite doth not extend it selfe to take away the Priviledges of Offices.

By these wordes likewise included in our Patents wth all Profits Priviledges and præheminences, we take it as graunted that noe other Patent can seclude us from the præheminencie due unto our severall places, for although the Patent of a Baronite be to take place of other K^{ts}, yet is not included and officers as K^{ts} onely we contend not : for that addeth nothinge to the Dignitie of the office, but as Officer we take our Patents to be of equall force or more, because ye more auncient patents, and if the tenent of our places and Preheminences by Patent be not secure the Tenent of most offices in England will appeare uncertaine, but it is more probable that the priviledges of these two Patents are not contradictorie, and it will appeare that the Patent of a Baronite is not of soe great extent as is pretended.

To shew that the words of a Baronites Patent to take place of all K^{ts} are not universall.

To shew that these words in the Patent of a Baronite are not universall is made plaine by reason they comprehende not at all times, and in all places, for then wee should admitt that a Knight Baronite although ymployed as Rear Admirall, should at all councels and meetings, take ye place of his vice admirall or Admirall, beinge but Knights wch were to adde great confusion to Politicke Government, neither is the Case of officers much different from this of ymployment.

To prove the Præeminencie of the Comp^{tlrs} place from the qualitie of his duties.

Between the 22nd May 1611, the date of the erection of the Degree, and the 31st December following, seventy-five Baronets were created, their general precedency being

clearly established in their Patents, as being before all
Knights, and also before all Bannerets, except those who
should be made by the King or the Prince of Wales on the
field.   Now as, according to various writers, a Banneret
was a knightly person of high consideration, who in earlier
reigns had been summoned to Parliament, who was entitled
to supporters for his Arms, and who claimed rank before
the sons of Barons and the younger sons of Viscounts, these
earliest Baronets were naturally led to suppose that their
place in the chain of precedence was hereditarily just above
that which the Banneret occupied for his life.   They
probably also thought that the King, in creating a sixth
hereditary degree, 'meane in place betwixt the Degree of a
Baron and the Degree of a Knight,' to quote the words
from his final Decree of 1616, intended that the members
of a Baronet's family should be woven into the said chain
of precedence in the natural manner, which would be
(omitting Ladies, Bishops, and Bannerets) as follows :—

First Degree,	. .	DUKE.
Second Degree,	. .	MARQUESS.
		Duke's eldest son.
Third Degree,	. .	EARL.
		Marquess's eldest son.
		Duke's younger son.
Fourth Degree,	. .	VISCOUNT.
		Earl's eldest son.
		Marquess's younger son.

Fifth Degree,	. .	BARON.
		Viscount's eldest son.
		Earl's younger son.
Sixth Degree,	. .	BARONET.
		Baron's eldest son.
		Viscount's younger son.
Non-hereditary Orders,	.	KNIGHT.
		Baronet's eldest son.
		Baron's younger son, etc. etc.

Shortly, however, after the erection of the Degree a dispute arose between the younger sons of the Viscounts and the sons of the Barons on the one hand, and the Baronets on the other, as to precedency, the language of their Patents appearing to the Baronets to justify their taking place and precedence before the younger sons of Viscounts and before all sons of Barons.

The dispute was referred to the Privy Council, who decided against the Baronets, whereupon they appealed to the King. The following is an extract from a letter addressed by Sir John Chamberlain to 'The righte honorable Sir Dudley Carleton Knight his ma^ties Ambassador to the State of Venice,' preserved in the Public Record Office :—

'MY VERY GOODE LORD . . .

'The new Barronetts have a question for place wth Barons younger sonnes, wch is hotly followed by Sir Moyle Finch, Sir William Twisenden, Sir John Wentworth and Sir Robert Cotton. The matter was lately brought to the counsaile table where by the earle of Northampton and other Lords yt was decreed against them, but they have appealed and made petition to the King, who promiseth to reverse yt as they geve out. . . . From London this last of December 1611.

'Yor Lo^{ps} to comaund,

'JOHN CHAMBERLAIN.

(Endorsed)   'The Disputes betwixt Baronets & Barons younger sons for precedency.'

The following Memorandum is contained in the Cotton Manuscripts in the British Museum (*Faustina,* c. viii. f. 23) :—

> 'Certein Questions humbly sought of my Lords the Marshalls to be resolued & declared, touchinge the Baronnetts, arisinge from some doubtfull words in their Patent & in his Maties decree.

'Whereas in the Patent fol. 32. are theis words followinge Atque quod primogenitus filius, ac ceteri omnes filii et eorum uxores, et filiæ ejusdem . . . et heredum suorum prædictorum respective, habeant, et capiant locum et præcedentiam, ante primogenitos filios, ac alios filios et eorum uxores, et filias omnium quorumcunque respective, præ quibus patres hujusmodi filiorum primogenitorum, et aliorum filiorum, et eorum uxores, et filiarum vigore presentium habere debent locum et præcedentiam.

'*Quæ.* 1.—Whether the eldest sonne & his wife & the daughters of a Baronnett ought not to take place & precedence next & imediatly after a K^t Bachelour (as the words seeme to import) & before all other inferior to a K^t Bachelour & the yonger sonnes & their wives next & imediatly after the eldest sonne & his wife & the daughters of a K^t Bachelour. & before all other inferior. And whereas in the decree fol. 4. are theis words. His Matie &c. hath finally sentenced, ajudged, & established, that the yonger sonnes of Viscounts & Baronns, shall take place and precedence before all Baronnetts.

'*Quæ.* 2.—Whether the children of the heyre gennerall to a Baron whose husband was newly reputed or ajudged a Baron, ought to be deemed & taken the sonnes & daughters of a Baron, & so to take place And whereas in the fol. 8. touchinge the precedence of the wives of Baronnetts, are theis words, they shall take and enjoy their place & præcedencie duringe their liues, next vnto, & imediatly after that place that is due. & belongeth vnto the wiues of the yonger sonnes of Viscounts & Baronns, & to the daughters of such Viscounts & Baronns.

'*Quæ.* 3.—Whether the daughter of a Baron maried vnto a Baronnett or K^t ought to take ye place of her husband onely & not otherwise. Wherein we are informed, some sentence hath passed already from yor Lo^{rps}.

'And whereas fol. 10. are theis words. Saueing newly the lesse to his Matie his heyres & successors, full & absolute power & authority to continue or restore to any person or persons from tyme to tyme such place & præcedencie, as at any time heereafter shall be due vnto them, wch by any accidente or occasion whatsoeuer shalbe heereafter changed, any thinge in these points, or other cause or respect whatsoeuer to the contrary notwthstanding.

'*Quæ.* 4.—ffor what purposse the said saueing was inserted & in what casses it shall take place.

'And because his Matie was gratiously pleased to declarre vnto them his princely meanninge to concurre & agree, wth his formo^r ordinance touchinge the quallities of such personns for birth & estate of liueing as should be admitted into the order, they humbly pray yor Lo^{rps} that in yor ho^{ble} fauour towards them, you would be pleased that heereafter his Maties said ordinance & true meaninge touching the said quallities of such personns as are to be admitted into the said order, be truely obserued & kept, that neither his Maties order it selfe be brought into Contempt by the meanenesse of the personns thereinto admitted, nor that the Gentry of bet[ter] quallities doe thereat take a just offence or mislike.

'Lastely there bonds beeing recorded (as they conceaue not by his Maties ordinance) they humbly pray that they may haue a good & sufficient discharge for the same, out of the exchequo^r that there heyres be not heareafter troubled for that there fathers haue so freely giuen.'

In the same volume, folio 28, will be found the following Memorandum :—

'The Baronetts are humble sueto^{rs} to his Matie that now his Matie hath ben pleased (after much dispute) to give the place to the yonger sonnes of Viscounts and Barons before them, Soe his Royall meaneing may be likewyse declared that the Baronetts shall have the very next place vnto them, wthout interposeing any estate place or persons betwene them.

'And that for likewyse the wyves of the Baronetts may be declared to have the very next place to the wyves of Barons yonger sonnes, and the daughters of Barons vnmarryed.

'And that it may likewyse be declared that the daughters of Viscounts and Barons, if they marry knights shall from thenceforth take place not by their byrth but by their husbands.

'They also desyre that his Matie wilbe pleased to graunte for him his heires and successo^{rs}, That neither any person dignity or estate of men vnder the degree of Barons shalbe herafter sett before them.

'And theise things they humbly beseech his Matie may be made parte of his now sentence and decree for avoydeing of new questions; And that they may have ltres patents of them by waye of addition to their former, if they will; wch cleare setling and establishing of their place & priviledges they knowe will invyte others to come up, wch yet stand out as vnsatisfyed.'

The result of his Majesty's decision was communicated to Sir Dudley Carleton by Sir John Chamberlain in a letter (*State Papers, Domestic Series, James I.*, vol. lxviii. No. 18), from which the following is an extract :—

'MY VERY GOODE LORD,

'The same day (Sunday) the new Baronnetts had there (at the "counsaile" table) a second defeat in the cause of precedence wth barons younger sonnes, for yt was told them that howsoever the words of theyre patent might seem to carry a contrarie construction, yet yt was never the K^s intention, wch he would shortly declare by proclamation wherupon they beeing not satisfied, but still urging the words and validitie of theyre patent, and how in that consideration they had payed theyre monie, yt was answered by the L. Treasurer that yf any of them misliked his bargain he shold have his monie again. . . .

'From London this 15th of January 1611.

'Yor Lo^ps to commaund,

'John Chamberlain.

(Endorsed) 'Touching the Precedency of the new Baronets.'

The following extract is from the same volume, No. 60 :—

'My deuty to your ll most humbly remembred.

'Those former points having filled up my paper I thought good to writt the matter of the Baronets by itselfe. This afternoon comming by his ma^ty's appointment to have my byls signed for the pyrates which herewith I send to yor lo. I found with his H. fowre of the Baronets, Sr Tho. Brudenell, Sr William Twisden, Sr George Greisly & Sr Gervase Clifton who had delivered a petition to his ma^ty wth a copie of that which they had presented to your ll. There was much altercation and his ma^ty defended his act very stiffely and stood uppon these termes that in ambiguis ejus est interpretare cujus est condere and he had never intention to give them precedency before noble mens sonnes. Their plea was the wordes of their Patent the right of the place of a Baronett of auncient tyme, their own intentions in taking the degree. His ma^ty replyed with many witty and strong arguments they were as earnest and vehement, the disputation was about an houre And when his ma^ty wold have sent them to your ll of his Councell they refused and prayed to be heard when he was present. So as after his ma^ty was retired and had dismissed them He gave me direction to lett your ll understand That his H. could not refuse to heare them the rather for that they sayd they had not been fully heard before your ll. His ma^ty thought if they had no more to say then they had uttered here he should aunsweare them well enough, but yet could not refuse to heare them. In the mean tyme seing he was so soone to be there

your ll might prepare the proclamation or draught which you had
in hand and at his ma^{tys} comming he wold putt it to a point. . . .

(No signature.)

(Endorsed) 'Feb^r 1611.   Sir Th. Lake to my Lord from Royston
concerning Baronnetts and Ambassadors.'

The appeal of the Baronets was accordingly heard by the
King presiding in his Privy Council, who decided in favour
of the younger sons of the Viscounts and Barons, as appears
by the following letter written on the 29th April 1612 by
Sir John Chamberlain to Sir Dudley Carleton (*State Papers,
Domestic Series, James I.*, vol. lxviii. No. 104) :—

'MY VERY GOODE LORD,

'I make no question but you have understoode from others what
hath passed here in mine absence wch was not much to be related,
one of the greatest matters was that after three or fowre times
audience the K. hath determined that the Baronnetts shall not take
place of Lordes younger sonnes, but in requitall hath geven them
three or fowre additions, that first they shall quarter or beare in a
canton the armes of Ulster wch is a hand in a bloudie feild: but
many thincke this so far from Honor that yt may rather be taken
for a note of disgrace to shew how they came by yt.   The next is
that they shal be Knighted of course at 21 yeare old, the third that
they shall fight in the feild under the K^s standard and neere his
owne person and the fourth that they shall have fowre (or five)
Knights assistants at their funerall.   The cause was argued w^{th}
much vehemencie and contestation insomuch that Sr W. Twisenden
charged the earle of Northampton wth sending Sr Robert Cotton
out of the way who was furnished wth thayre best reasons and
records wch he denieng Sr W. urged Sr Henry Savile to deliver what
annswer he had from him by his man that he sent to him into the
countrie for that purpose wch he did in these wordes, that Sr Robert
Cotton saide his brother Baronnetts must pardon him but yf my L.
privie seale did send for him he wold come wth a tantara : the K.

asked my L. what he could say to this who annswered he could say no more but that he was glad to understand that his frend the antiquarie was become so goode a trumpeter: wch made them all merrie.

'From London this 29th of Aprill, 1612.

'Yor Lo^ps to commaund,

'JOHN CHAMBERLAIN.

(Endorsed)   'Touching the precedency disputed betwixt Baronets & the younger sons of Barons.'

Immediately afterwards the following Decree was passed, which, in addition to settling the question of precedency, entered upon other matters with a view to their explanation and settlement :—

ROYAL DECREE, 28TH MAY 1612.

'JAMES, by the grace of GOD, King of England, Scotland, France and Ireland, Defender of the Faith, &c.

'To all to whome these presents shall come, Greeting.   Know ye that We have made a certaine Ordinance, Establishment, and finall Decree, whereof the tenor followeth in these wordes :—

'The Decree and Establishment of the King's Majestie, upon a controversie of Precedence, betweene the yonger sonnes of Viscounts and Barons, and the Baronets ; And touching some other points also concerning, as well Bannerets, as the said Baronets.

'The King's Most Excellent Majestie, having upon the Petition, and submission of both parts, taken into his Royall audience and censure, a certaine controversie, touching place and Precedence, betweene the yonger sonnes of Viscounts, and Barons, and the Baronets, (being a degree by his Majestie newly created) which controversie did arise upon an inference onely out of some darke words contained in the Letters Patents of the said Baronets : And having in person heard both parts, and their learned Counsell, three severall daies at large after information taken from the Heraults, and due consideration of such proofes as were produced on both sides, hath declared and decreed as followeth.

'His Majestie well weighing that the Letters Patents of the Baronets have no speciall clause or expresse wordes to give unto them the saide Precedence; And beeing a witnesse unto himselfe (which is a testimonie above all exception) that his Princely meaning was onely to grace, and advance this new Dignitie of his Majesties erection; but not therewithall any wayes to wrong tacitely and obscurely a third partie, such as the yonger sonnes of Viscounts and Barons are, in that which is a flower of their fathers Nobilitie :

'And having also had the attestation of the Lords of his Privie Councell, who did declare that the Precedence (after debate and deliberation, while the Patent of the Baronets was in consultation) was with one consent resolved and ordered for the yonger sonnes of the Viscounts and Barons :

'And finding also that the clause whereby the Precedence is challenged by the Baronets, as by a kinde of consequence in regard of place given unto them above some Bannerets, doeth not warrant their claime (forasmuch as the Precedence betweene the Bannerets themselves, and the yonger sonnes of Viscounts and Barons, appeareth not to have bene regular or certaine, but full of confusion and variety, and therefore not sufficient whereupon to ground such their pretence) but being chiefly mooved by the clearenesse of his Majesties Royall intent, and meaning, and the explanation thereof by his Councell, (which his Royall meaning doeth, and ever must leade his Majesties judgement in the interpretation of his owne Actes,) hath finally sentenced, adjudged, and established, that the yonger sonnes of Viscounts, and Barons, shall take place and Precedence before all Baronets.

'And further, the better to settle, and cleare also all question of Precedence that may concerne either Bannerets, or the yonger sonnes of Viscounts and Barons, or the said Baronets, either as they have relation among themselves, or towards others respectively; His Majestie for himselfe, his heires and successours, doeth ordaine and establish, that such Bannerets, as shall be made by the Kings Majestie, his heires and successors under his or their Standard, displayed in an Armie Royall in open warre, and the King personally present, for the terme of the lives of such Bannerets and no longer, (according to the most ancient, and noble institution) shall for ever heereafter in all places, and upon all occasions, take place, and Precedence, aswell before all other Bannerets whatsoever, (no respect being had to the time, and prioritie of their creation) as likewise before the yonger sonnes of Viscounts and Barons, and also before all Baronets.

'And againe, that the yonger sonnes of Viscounts and Barons, and also all Baronets, shall in all places, and upon all occasions, take place and Precedence before all Bannerets whatsoever, other then such as shall bee made by the King himselfe, his heires and successours in person, and in such speciall case, manner and forme as aforesaid.

'Neverthelesse, for a singular honour to the person of the most high and excellent Prince HENRY now Prince of Wales, his Majesties eldest sonne ; aswell the yonger sonnes of the Viscounts, and Barons, as the Baronets, have freely and voluntarily consented and agreed at the hearing of the said cause, in the presence of his Majestie, and his Privy Councell, and all the hearers, to give place and Precedence, to such Bannerets, as shalbe hereafter made by the said most noble HENRY, now Prince of Wales, under the Kings Standard displayed in an Armie Royall in open warre, and the said Prince there personally present.

'Saving the right of the yonger sonnes of Viscounts and Barons, and of the said Baronets, and of the heires males of the bodies of such Baronets, for the time being, in all other cases according to the effect, and true intent and meaning of their Letters Patents, and of these presents.

'And his Majestie doth likewise by these presents, for himselfe, his heires and successours ordeine, that the Knights of the most noble order of the Garter, the Privie Councellours of his Majestie, his heires and successours, the Master of the Court of Wardes and Liveries, the Chancellour and under-Treasourer of the Exchequer, Chancellour of the Duchie, the chiefe Justice of the Court commonly called the Kings Bench, the Master of the Rolls, the chiefe Justice of the Court of Common Pleas, the chiefe Baron

of the Exchequer, and all other the Judges and Barons of the degree
of the Coife of the saide Courts, now, and for the time being, shall
by reason of such their Honourable order, and imployment of State
and Justice, have place and Precedencie in all places, and upon all
occasions before the yonger sonnes of Viscounts and Barons, and
before all Baronets, Any custome, use, ordinance, or other thing to
the contrary notwithstanding. But that no other person or persons
whatsoever, under the degree of Barons of Parliament, shall take
place before the said Baronets, except onely the eldest sonnes of
Viscounts and Barons, and others of higher degree, whereof no
question ever was, or can bee made. And so his Majesties meaning
is, and accordingly he doth by these presents, for him, his heires
and successours, ordeine and decree, that the said Baronets, and the
heires males of their bodies, shall in all places, and upon all occasions
for ever, have, hold, and enjoy their place and Precedencie, next
unto, and immediatly after the yonger sonnes of Viscounts and
Barons, and that no person or persons, nor State or States of men,
shall have or take place betweene them, Any Constitution, Order,
Degree, Office, Service, Place, Imployment, Custome, Use, or
other thing whatsoever, now or heereafter to the contrary notwithstanding.

'And that the wives of the saide Baronets, and of the heires males
of their bodies, shall likewise by vertue of the saide Dignitie of their
said husbands, in all places, and upon all occasions, have, take and
enjoy their place and Precedencie during their lives, next unto, and
immediatly after that place that is due, and belongeth unto the
wives of the yonger sonnes of Viscounts and Barons, and to the
daughters of such Viscounts and Barons, any Constitution, Use,
Custome, Ordinance, or other thing whatsoever, now or heereafter
to the contrary in any wise notwithstanding.

'And further, his Majestie doth by these presents, for him, his
heires and successours, of his certaine knowledge and meere motion,
promise and graunt to the said Baronets, and every of them already
created, and heereafter to be created, and the heires males of their
bodies, That neither his Majestie, nor his heires or successours,
shall or will at any time heereafter erect, ordaine, constitute, or

create any other Degree, Order, Name, Title, Stile, Dignitie or
State, nor will give place, Precedencie or preheminence to any
person or persons whatsoever, under or beneath the Degree, dignitie
or State of Lords of Parliament of this his Realme of England,
which shall or may be, or be taken, used, or accompted to be higher,
before or equall to the Degree, dignitie or place of the said Baronets,
or any of them. AND therefore his Majestie doeth for him, his
heires and successours ordeine, graunt, and appoint by these presents,
that all and every the said Baronets, and their saide heires males, and
the wives sonnes, sonnes wives, and daughters of the said Baronets,
and of their said heires males, shall, and may for ever heereafter,
freely and quietly have, hold, and enjoy their said Dignities, Places,
Precedencie and Priviledges before all other which are or shall be
created of such Decrees (*sic*), States, Dignities, Orders, Names, Stiles,
or Titles, or to whom such place, Precedencie, or Preheminence
shall be so given as aforesaid ; their wives and children respectively,
according to the true intent and meaning of these presents :

'Saving neverthelesse to his Majestie, his heires and successors,
full and absolute power and authoritie to continue or restore to any
person or persons from time to time such place and precedencie, as
at any time heereafter shalbe due unto them, which by any accident
or occasion whatsoever shall be heereafter changed, any thing in
these presents, or other cause or respect whatsoever to the contrarie
notwithstanding.

'And now though this Precedent declaration doth clearly ridde
all questions arising upon the Letters Patents, yet his Majestie
having upon the occasion of this controversie and hearing, and of
some of the Baronets grievances, propounded out of their owne
mouthes, considered more maturely upon the points and latitude of
their said Patents, his Majestie beeing resolved (as out of his owne
royall mouth it pleased him to declare unto them) to ampliate his
favour, especially where it meetes with these so well borne and well
deserving Gentlemen, (this dignitie beeing of his Majesties owne
erection, and the worke of his owne handes,) his Majestie is therefore graciously pleased (not contented with those markes of his
favour, which alreadie they enjoy by the wordes of their Patent,

which layeth such a marke of dignitie and precedence upon them
and their posterity) further to strengthen and adorne his Majesties
gracious favour towards them, with addition of the priviledges, preheminencies, and ornaments ensuing.

'First, his Majestie is pleased to knight the present Baronets,
that are no Knights : And doeth also by these presents of his meere
motion and favour, promise and graunt for him, his heires and successours, that such Baronets, and the heires males of their bodies, as
herafter shalbe no Knights, when they shall attaine, or be of the
age of one and twentie yeares, upon knowledge thereof given to
the Lord Chamberlaine of the houshold, or Vice-chamberlaine for
the time beeing, or in their absence to any other Officer attending
upon his Majesties person, shall be knighted by his Majestie, his
heires and successours.

'His Majestie doth also graunt for him, his heires and successours,
that the Baronets, and their descendants shall and may beare, either
in a Canton in their coate of Armes, or in an Inscutchion, at their
election, the Armes of Ulster, that is, in a field Argent, a hand
Geules, or a bloudy hand.

'And also, that the Baronets, for the time beeing, and the heires males
of their bodies shall have place in the armies of the Kings Majestie,
his heires and successours, in the grosse, neere about the royall Standard
of the King, his heires and successours, for the defence of the same.

'And lastly, that the Baronets, and the heires males of their
bodies shall have two assistants of the bodie to support the Pall, a
principall mourner, and foure assistants to him at their funerals,
being the meane betwixt a Baron and a Knight.

'And to the end that every of the Baronets, and the heires males
of their bodies, may have upon all occasions present, use, and proofe
of these his Majesties favours; His Majestie is graciously pleased,
that as-well the Baronets alreadie created, as hereafter to be created,
shall and may have, and take Letters Patents under the great Seale
of England, to the effect of the said former Letters Pattents of
Creation, and of these presents, either joynt or severall, as they shall
be advised by the learned Councell of his Majestie, his heires and
successours, and according to his Highnesse true intent and meaning.

'In witnesse whereof, We have caused these Our Letters to be made Patents. Witnesse Our selfe at Westminster, the eight and twentieth day of May, in the tenth yeere of our Raigne of England, France, and Ireland, and of Scotland the five and fortieth.'

It is possible that the King, as argued in a document of the present day, had reasons for not offending the Barons of Parliament; but His Majesty's 'Flower of nobilitie' argument in favour of younger sons who had not, at that time, even a generally accepted courtesy title, when addressed to heads of families, whom he had just ennobled by a hereditary title, and who would have Flowers of their own, does not seem convincing.

His Majesty's decision clearly prejudiced the position of the Baronetage, in creating a chasm between five hereditary degrees on the one hand, and the sixth on the other, by which cause alone the latter has lost in distinction.

Again, by giving Cadets such an idea of their importance, he made it next to impossible for his successors to reward meritorious and sufficiently endowed younger sons of peers with a Baronetcy; surely an oversight, considering that such cadets would often be desirable persons to enrol in the sixth Degree Hereditary, and that they themselves might be grateful for such an opportunity to found a family with hereditary distinction. In this way, for example, was rewarded Captain the Hon. Henry Blackwood, who brought home the despatches announcing the victory of Trafalgar.

Besides this, had the King paid less respect to the 'Flowers of nobility' who argued the case against the Baronets, he would probably have realised, with his natural acumen, that in each successive generation a family bearing a hereditary title recovers itself as against the issue of Cadets of all Degrees.

His Majesty, however, did more than violate the canons of precedence.   He bequeathed everlasting unrest to his new Degree, not only by this means, but by his failure to appoint any officer or Court to have cognisance of its affairs, or otherwise to provide it with some defence of its own against the caprice of monarchs and the encroachments of impostors, such as is enjoyed by the nobility of one of the smallest of the British possessions—Malta.

During the following two years, with the exception of those created later in the same year, no one accepted a Baronetcy, which led to the issue on the 18th November 1614 of the following Commission by the King to the Lord Chancellor and others (*State Papers, Domestic Series, James I.*, vol. lxxv. f. 17) :—

'JAMES by the grace of God Kinge of England Scotland ffraunce and Ireland defendor of the faith &c.   To our trustie and right welbeloved Councellor Thomas Lord Ellesmere Lord Chauncellor of England.   And to our right trustie and right welbeloved Cousins and Councellors Henrie Earle of Northampton Lord keeper of our privie Seale Lodovike Duke of Lenox Charles Earle of Notingham our highe Admirall of England Thomas Earle of Suffolke Lord Chamberlaine of our household Gilbert Earle of Shrewsburie Justice in Eyre beyond Trent Northward Edward Earle of Worcester Master of our horse William Earle of Pembrook Lord Warden of the Stanneries Thomas Earle of Exeter Robert Earle of Sommersett John Earle of Marre Alexander Earle of Dunfermiline.   And to our right trustie and right welbeloved Councillors Thomas Lord Viscount ffenton Edwurd Lord Zouche William Lord Knollis Treasurer of our household Edward Lord Wotton Comptroller of

our household John Lord Stanhope vice-chamberlaine of our household And to our trustie and right welbeloved Councellors Sir John
Herbert Knight our Secretarie of State Sir Julius Cesar Knight
Chauncellor and undertreasurer of our Exchequer Sir Thomas Parrie
Knight Chauncellor of our Duchie of Lancaster and Sir Edward
Coke Knight our cheife Justice of our Bench greiting.—WHEREAS
by severall Commissions under our greate Seale of England we did
give power and authoritie unto you to commune and treate with
such Knightes and Gentlemen of this our realme as being moved
with zeale and affection to further the Plantacion of Ulster and
other like services in our Realme of Ireland had offered and agreed
or should offer and agree everie of them to maintaine Thirtie ffoote-
men Souldiers in our said Realme of Ireland at their proper costes
and charges after the rate of Eight Pence a peece by the Daie
sterling during the space of three yeares then next ensuing. In
respect whereof we were pleased in rewarde of soe remarkable a
service to bestowe uppon them a Dignitie newly erected and created
by us annswereable to their State and merritt which we had stiled
by the name of Baronett with divers priviledges annexed thereunto,
and the same to graunte by letters patentes to them and the heires
males of their bodies lawfullye begotten, to the ende the memorie
thereof might remaine to them and their Posteritie. The execucion
of which our purpose in that behalfe we committed to you to be
performed according to certaine Instruccions and a President of
letters patentes in schedules to the said severall Commissions annexed
conteined. As by the said severall Commissions and schedules maie
appeare. By vertue of which severall Commissions you have treated
and concluded with divers principall knightes and Gentlemen of
sondrie partes of this our Realme of England accordinglie which
have both given the said entertainement for Souldiers and received
the said Dignitie and degree as they well deserved which severall
Commissions being nowe expired we are given to understande that
there be manie other Knightes and Gentlemen that being moved
with the like affeccion to the publique service are most willing to
give such Paie and entertainement for Souldiers so to be imploied
as aforesaid if there were the like Commission in force. By meanes

whereof they might have the like proceeding in that behalfe, as the rest have had by vertue of the former Commissions KNOWE YE THEREFORE that we have appointed you to be our Commissioners againe AND doe by these presents give and graunt unto you all or unto any eight or more of you (whereof you the said Lord Chauncellor or lord privie Seale to be alwaies one) and you the said Lord Privie Seale Duke of Lenox, Earle of Notingham our Admirall, Earle of Suffolk our Chamberlaine and Earle of Worster Master of our horse to be alwaies two who are soe much the more able to judge of mens bloud and antiquitie in regard you are Commissioners in the Office of Earle Marshall) full free and lawfull power and authoritie according to the former instruccions annexed to our said former Commissions to commune and treate with any of our loving Subjectes whome in like sorte you shall find willing to give such paie and entertainement to such nomber of footemen as is aforesaid to be imployed in the said service and for such tyme as aforesaid And thereuppon to informe your selves of their familie living and reputacion. And such and so many of the said persons as you or any such eight or more of you as is aforesaid shall finde and approve to be in all the respects aforesaid worthie such degree (not exceeding in the whole with those alreadie created Baronettes the nomber of two hundred which we have covenanted in our former Patentes shall not be exceeded but suffered to dimynisse as their issue shall faile) to cause everie one of them for himselfe to make payment or give good and sufficient assurraunce for the due annswearing of soe muche as shalbe sufficient for maintenaunce of Thirtie Souldiers footemen after the rate of eight pence a peece by the daie for the terme of three yeares as is aforesaid And thereupon to give warrant and direccion under any such eight or more of your handes as is aforesaid unto our Attorney or Sollicitor generall for the drawing upp of severall Bills and grauntes to passe from us to all and everie such person and persons as shalbe soe approved by you or any such eight or more of you as is aforesaid for the making and creating of everie such person Baronett with all priviledges of precedencie place title and all other things thereunto belonging according to the President of the former letters Patentes passed of the same dignitie and with such addicions as are by our declaracion and ordinaunce since graunted and expressed . . . ey shall desire the same. And these presentes together with such warrant and direccion of you or any such eight or more of you as is aforesaid shall be from tyme to tyme to our said Attorney and Sollicitor generall for the tyme being sufficient warrant for the drawing upp and subscribing of everie such Bill or graunt to passe from us according to the true meaning of these presentes AND OUR WILL and pleasure is that our Attorney or Sollicitor generall shall drawe ingrosse and subscribe the bills and grauntes to be made of the said Dignitie of Baronett according to the direccion and warrant of you or any such eight or more of you as is aforesaid. And the Bills and grauntes soe drawne ingrossed and subscribed with the handes of our Attorney or Sollicitor generall or either of them shalbe a sufficient warrant and discharge to you our said Commissioners to subscribe likewise to the said bills or grauntes with the handes of any such eight or more of you as is aforesaid AND FURTHERMORE for the more speedie and easie passing of the grauntes and Letters Patentes to be made of the said Dignitie we are pleased and contented And by these presentes for us our heires and Successors we doe graunt ordaine and appointe that the bills for such Patentes prepared by our said Attorney or Sollicitor as aforesaid and signed with the handes of you or any such eight or more of you as is aforesaid shalbe a sufficient and ymmediate warrant to the lord Chauncellor of England, our lord keeper of our greate Seale of England for the tyme being to passe the same grauntes and letters patentes under the greate Seale of England without any other or further warrant from us to be had or obteined in that behalf. And this our Comission we have made to continewe till the Nyne and twentith daie of September next ensuing the date hereof, and then to cease and determyne IN WITNES whereof we have caused these our letters to be made patentes.—WITNES our selfe at Westminster the eightenth daie of November in the eleaventh yeare of our Raigne of England ffraunce and Ireland and of Scotland the seaven and ffortith

per ipsum Regem.

(Endorsed) 'A Commission unto the Lord Chauncellor of England Lord Privie Seale and others to treate with Baronettes.'

A scheme of Silvanus Skory to raise additional funds for the Treasury by increasing the sum to be paid by Baronets to £3000, and enlarge their privileges as an equivalent, fell through, as evidenced by the following letter (*State Papers, Domestic Series, James I.*, vol. lxxx., No. 115):—

'MY VERY GOODE LORD,

'The project of pardons was on foot again but finally defeated the last weeke, as likewise Silvanus Scories devise for inlarging the priveleges of Baronnets to be no wardes to be justices of peace at 21 yeres of age, deputie lieutenants at 25 that theyre bodies should be free from arrests, wth divers other immunities for wch theyre rate should rise to 3000^{li} a man wherby the K^s wants might be much relieved out of the vanitie and ambition of the Gentrie, he had often accesse to his m^{tie} and pleased himself much wth the invention and hope that he and his heyres (for this service) should be perpetuall chauncellors of that order but after much discussing the busines was overthrowne and he dismissed wth a flowte that argentum ejus versum est in scoriam et aurum in orichalcum wch that yt mighte be the better understood was thus englished, that his silver was turned to drosse and his gold to alchimie.

'From London this 15th of June 1615.

'yor Lo^{ps} to commaund

'JOHN CHAMBERLAIN.'

(Addressed)   To the right honorable Sir Dudley Carleton Kn^t.

On the 13th March 1616 the final Decree of James I. relating to the Baronetage was issued, and is as follows:—

'JAMES, by the grace of God, King of England, Scotland, France, and Ireland, Defender of the Faith, &c.

'To all to whom these presents shall come greeting.   Know yee that whereas We heretofore have ordeined, Erected, Constituted, and created the Degree, State, Dignitie, Name, and Title, of Baronet; to continue for ever within this our Realme of England. And to that end of our speciall Grace, certaine knowledge, and

meere motion have (by our several Letters Pattents, under the great
Seale of England; in that behalfe made) conferred the same State,
Dignitie and Degree of Baronet, upon divers principall Gentlemen
of this our Kingdome. And thereby severally, and accordingly
created them Baronets. To have and to hold the same Dignitie, State
and Degree; to them and their several heires Males of their severall
bodies respectively. Together with such place and Precedency, to
them and to their said heires Males, and to the wives of them, and
of their said heires Males, and to their eldest sonnes, and other their
sonnes, and to the wives of their sonnes, and to their daughters,
with such stile, addition and appellation, to them and to their said
heires Males: And to their wives, and the wives of their said
severall heires Males, and with such other priviledges, advantages,
and covenants, and in such sort, as in and by the said several Letters
Pattents doth appeare. And whereas also of our further Grace and
favour, we have by other our Letters Pattents under our great
Seale of England, bearing date the eight and twentieth day of May,
in the yeere of our Raigne of England, Fraunce, and Ireland, the
tenth, and of Scotland, the five-and-fortieth, farther enlarged our
gracious favour towards the same Baronets, by addition of certaine
priviledges, preheminencies, and ornaments; in and by our said last
recited Letters Pattents made, expressed, and granted; giving also
libertie thereby to such Gentlemen, as then were or should be
created Baronets, to take Letters Pattents accordingly under our
great Seale of England, to the effect of the same Letters Pattents,
and of the said former Letters Pattents of creation, jointly and
severally in such sort, as in and by the same Letters Pattents doth
and may appeare. We of our Princely favour and gracious disposition, upon all occasions to make knowne, and publish the con-
tinuance of our favour and good affection, as well towards the
Gentlemen, whom of our power and grace We have advanced, or
shall heereafter advance, to the said Degree, as to the Degree it selfe
being a matter of our owne erection, doe heereby for us our heires
and successors, not onely ratifie, confirme, allow, and approve of the
said Dignitie, State, and Degree of a Baronet, so erected by Us as
aforesaid. And the particuler and severall Letters Patents made by

Us to the severall Gentlemen, whom We have thereby created Baronets, together with all the benefits, advantages, rights and priviledges of place Precedency: and otherwise by our said severall Letters Pattents, to them severally graunted or mentioned to be granted : and also all other priviledges, benefits, and advantages ; in or by any other our Letters Pattents given, granted, mentioned, or intended to them. But also of our speciall Grace and favour, certaine knowledge, and meere motion, doe for Us our heires and successors, declare heereby that We imitating therein our predecessors and progenitors of famous memory, who have had and put in practice the power of creating new Degrees amongst their Subjects, have of our Regall power and authority erected and ordeined the said Degree of Baronet ; and did then and yet intend and doe heereby appoint and expresse our will and pleasure to be, and doe graunt for Us our heires and successors, that the same Title, Stile, Dignity, and Degree, shall be and continue to such Gentlemen, on whom of our goodnes and favour We have conferred, and shall heereafter con-ferre the same and to every of them, and to the severall heires Males, of their severall bodies, and that the said Title, Stile, Dignitie, and Degree of Baronet, shall be, and shall be reputed and taken to be a Title, Stile, Dignity, and Degree of Dignity Hereditary, meane in place betwixt the Degree of a Baron, and the Degree of a Knight.

And We doe heereby declare that not only such Gentlemen as are or heereafter shall be Baronets, as aforesaid : and the heires Males of their bodies, and their wives, during their husbands lives, shall have and hold such place and Precedency as by our former Letters Pattents are granted, mentioned, or intended to them, but also their wives after the decease of their husbands, shall during their lives have and hold the like place of Precedency, which they had and held in their husbands lives according to the manner and usage in other Degrees. And forasmuch as the Degree of a Baronet, is an Hereditarie Degree in blood, therefore We doe declare ; That the eldest sonnes of the same Baronets and their wives, as well during their husbands lives as after : And the daughters of the same Baronets, the said daughters following next after the said wives of the eldest sonnes of the same Baronets, shall have place and Pre-

cedency before the eldest sonne, and the wife of the eldest sonne of
any Knight of what Degree or order soever : And likewise that the
younger sonnes of the same Baronets and their wives, as well during
their husbands lives as after, shall after the same manner have
place and Precedency next after the eldest sonnes, and the wives
of the eldest sonnes, and before the yonger sonnes, and before
the wives of the younger sonnes of any of the Knights aforesaid.
And our will and pleasure is, and We doe for Us, our heires and
successors, heereby further grant and appoint, that if any doubts or
questions not heereby, nor by any our recited Letters Pattents
cleared and determined doe or shall arise, concerning any place,
Precedency, priviledge, or other matter touching or concerning the
same Baronets, and the heires Males of their bodies, and their wives,
their eldest sonnes and their wives, their daughters, their yonger
sonnes, and their yonger sonnes wives, or any of them ; such doubts
or questions shall be decided and determined, by and according to
such usuall rules, custome, and lawes, for place Precedency, priviledge or other matters concerning them as other Degrees of Dignity,
Hereditary, are ordered and adjudged. And further of our especiall
Grace certaine knowledge and meere motion, We doe heereby
declare and expresse our true intent and meaning to have beene,
and doe heereby promise and graunt for Us, our heires and successors, to and with such Gentlemen as now be, or at any time
heereafter shall be Baronets ; That so soon as they or any of them,
shall attaine to the age of one and twenty yeeres. And likewise so
soone as the eldest sonne or apparant heire Male of the bodies of
them, or any of them, shall during the life of their Father, or Grandfather, attaine to the age of one and twenty yeeres ; and that the
said Baronets, or the said eldest sonnes or apparant heires Males,
shall be presented to Us by the Lord Chamberlaine of our houshold,
or Vice Chamberlaine for the time being, or in their absence by any
other officer attending upon the person of Us, our heires or successors to be made Knights, that they and every of them shall from
time to time be made Knights by Us, our heires and successors
accordingly : Provided neverthelesse that any such eldest sonne of a
Baronet being made Knight, shall not during his fathers life take

place of any auntienter Knight.   And to the end that such as are,
or at any time heereafter shall be Baronets, may have upon all
occasions present use and proofe of these our favours: We are
farther graciously pleased, that as well such as now are, as also such
as at any time heereafter shall be Baronets, and every of them shall
and may at all times heereafter, have and take Letters Patents
under our great Seale of England, to the effect of the said former
recited Letters Patents and of these presents.   As they shall be
advised by the learned Counsell to Us, our heires or successors: And
according to the true intent and meaning heerein, and in our said
severall Letters Pattents expressed.

'In witness whereof, &c.'

The following letter is in the Public Record Office (*State
Papers, Domestic Series, James I.*, vol. cx., No. 26 :—

'My very goode Lord,

'a blunt brother of Secretarie Winwods (one Sir Edward Richard-
son) was knighted this progresse at Sir William Candishes, these and
such like Knights make baronetts begin to come in request again,
as of late we have had three or fowre wherof the first was Sir . . .
Villers eldest brother to the L. of Buckingham a man so careless of
honor or courting as the King saide he wold scant geve them thanks for
yt, and dowbted whether he wold accept it.   another was Sir James
Lee atturny of the court of wards: besides Sir William Harvy that
married the old countesse of Southampton, and younge Hickes sonne
to Sir Michaell Hicks that comes to yt I know not by what title.

'Sir Francis Crane hath three baronetts geven him in consideration of a project he hath in hand of setting up the making of
tapistrie and arras.

'From London the 23rd of August 1619.

'Yor Lo^ps most assuredly at commaund,

'JOHN CHAMBERLAIN.'

On the 22nd December 1622, Thomas Harris of Boreatton,
in Shropshire, a Master in Chancery, son of Roger Harris,
a draper of Shrewsbury, and grandson of William Harris, a

yeoman of Wheathill, Condover, was created a Baronet. This creation was quite contrary to the custom of that period, the baronetage being confined to gentlemen of descent; and Captain Thomas Leeke impleaded Sir Thomas Harris in the Court of Chivalry, as unworthy of the distinction.

The Earl Marshal reported thereon to the King, who thereupon wrote him the following letter (*State Papers, Domestic Series, James I.,* vol. cliii., No. 54) :—

'Right trusty and right welbeloved Cousin & Councellor,

'Wee greete you well : Wee have considered of yor report made unto us in the case of Sir Thomas Harris Baronet, and doe give good allowance unto that which you have allready done, and because wee doe thereby perceive that many particulars alleadged by either party doe rest upon further proofe and that this cause may concerne Sir Thomas Harris in the right of his inheritance, wee cannot but commend your care in proceeding therein with all caution & circumspection and therefore wee doe hould it fitt that if the Petitioner Leeke doth intend to prosecute the same to sentence that he doe formally proceede according to the custome & usage of the Court Marshall as you shall direct, provided that there be respect had to the paynes allready taken, & that such things as have been confessed & agreede upon may not be without fruite, but stand good for directing yor judgment in the sentence, whereunto our pleasure is that you doe juditially proceede if either of the sayd partyes shall require the same at yor hands ; and we doe further signifie unto you that in the institution of Baronets our true intent and meaning was & yett is, that no person whatsoever should be advanced to that degree unless he were a person of undoubted gentrye, and descended at least from a Grandfather who was a Gentleman, & that noe supernumerary person should be admitted to be a Baronett above the number of two hundred mentioned in our Letters Patents : willing and commanding you that whensoever you shall finde any promoted to that place contrary to our intent and meaninge before expressed you doe juditially proceede to their actuall degradation, that soe no well deserving person may have just cause of complaint. Given &c.

(Endorsed) 'October 16 1623.
'His Ma^tes letter to the Earle Marshall concerninge
'Sir Thomas Harris a Barronnett, &c.'

The following letter from Sir George Paul appears in vol. clxxxv. of the same series, No. 91 :—

'Sir,

'Concerning the Complaintes made by Capten Leake unto my Lord Duke & his Graces referrence thereof unto Mr. Comptroller & other his Commissioners wee accordingly mett about the busines & gave warning both to Mr. Harris Sir Thomas his sonne & Capten Leake to be present. The Capten execused himself by a private letter to Mr. Comptroller But Mr. Harris accompanied with one of the Herallds, made good proofe of his fathers pedigree & gentry, aswell by entry in the office of Armes, in a visitacion of Shropshire made in anno 1585 as by diverse deedes with Seales of Armes, Coppies of Courte Rolles & other autentique writinges & proofes from the 13th of Edward the fourthe unto the yeare of our lord God 1623 At what time nine of the Cheife heralds of the Kingdome subscribed their names unto the said pedigree in testimony of the truth thereof which gave us soe good satisfaccion, that wee then resolved what to have done & soe much the rather because it appeared unto us, by the Lord Keepers subscription to a peticion exhibited by Leake against Sir Thomas Harris, that the said peticion was false & scandalous & indiscreete in the highest degrie, as the peticioner himself was reported to bee: But Sir there hath since that tyme of our meetinge bin (as I heare) another stoppe made by Sir Raphe ffreeman to whom for his better satisfaccion I have written at large to the ende hee might also salve the wounde which hee hath made. And soe in hast I take my leave, & rest.

'Yor assured loving frind to Com̃.

'From Lambeth the xx^th   'Geo. Paule.
    of March 1624.'

Sir Thomas Harris ultimately presented the following petition to the King, which sufficiently shows what had taken place in the interval (*State Papers, Domestic Series, James I.*, vol. clxxxv., No. 92) :—

'TO THE KYNGS MOST EXCELLENT MA^tie.

'The humble peticion of Sir Tho. Harris Baronett. Sheweth that whereas about twelve yeres last past it pleased yor ma^tie to graunt a Commission to ye lordes of ye Councell gyving them power to elect to the nomber of 200 Baronettes & to graunt warrantes for the passing of ther patentes under the greate Scale with provision or limitacion thearin that ech of them so to be elected shold be such as had landes of 1000^tl per annum & had taken oath that he gave nothing for the same but what should be expressed in the patent & whose grandfather bare armes which commission was to endure for a certaine time   After the expiracion whearof yor ma^tie by yor highnes letters patentes out of yor highnes prerogative being ye supreame Judge & fountaine of all honor did absolutely graunt the said dignity unto divers persons any statut law ordinance or provision made to ye contrary thearof notwithstandinge and among others it pleased yor ma^tie by yor highnes letters patentes dated in Dec. 1622 to graunt the said dignity unto yor petitioner upon ye humble suite & recommendacion of the Right ho^ble the Erle of Anglesea albeit your petitioner had a certificat from ye heraldes of armes unto the Right ho^ble ye Earle Marshall that yor petitioner was a gent. of 3 discentes & bare for his armes or 3 hedghoggs azure and the said Erle Marshall did certify somuch unto yor ma^tie.

'But so it is may it please yor ma^tie that one Simon Leake gent. whom yor petitioners sonne did imploy & use as an agent in obteyning of the sayd letters patentes and to whom yor said petitioner's sonne did gyve for his paynes thearin 30^tl more then he had agreed to gyve him according to the articles made betweene them ready to be shewed which said Leake alone procured the said Certificates from the Earle Marshall and Herrolds and payed the fees

thearof to each of them yett the sayd Leak contrary to his owne
acte by the procurement of some Knightes yor petitioner's neigh-
bours themselves disdayning the said dignity and yet envying others
soe dignifyed did exhibitt and prosecute a suite in the Cort of
Chivalry against yor petitioner for a supposed undue procuring of
the said Certificate from the sayd Herrolds and for the bearing of the
sayd Armes and also for the Quartering of some other armes In
which suite yor pet^r conceaving some hard measure to be offred
him and also for that he legaly tendring into the sayd Cort certaine
pleas and exhibites the same were disallowed thearuppon yor pet^r by
the advise of his Councell did appeale from the said Cort according
to 'the ancient presidentes thearof unto yor Matie in yor highnes
Cort of Chauncery, and exhibited his peticion unto the Right ho^{ble}
the Lord Keeper for a Comission of Appeale   The consideration of
which petition the Lord Keeper referred unto yor Highnes Attorney
and Solicitor who uppon long serch of recordes and presidentes in
the Tower made theyr Certificat unto the Lord Keeper for the
approving of the said appeale to be just and lawfull but the same is
not yet granted depending which appeale the sayd Leake did exhibit
a scandelous peticion unto the sayd Lord Keeper to impugne the
granting of the said Comission of appeale for which his Lordship
severely reproving him as may appeare by the Answere unto the
said peticion yet the sayd Leake before the validity of the said
appeale was decided (being a president for future ages) and also well
knowing that yf yor petitioner his Councell or Proctor did appeare
or speak in the said cause in the Cort of Chivalry during the tyme
of the sayd appeale that then he should utterly overthrowe the
same and loose the benifitt thearof did notwithstanding proceede
in the sayd Cort of Chivalry and procured a sentence in the sayd
Cort of Chivalry by default against yor pet^r who cold not appeare
or make any defence thearunto howbeit yor pet^r doth not doubt
but to make sufficient proof of his gentry whensoever he shall be
legally called thearunto both by Charters of yor highnes ancestors
and diverse deeds records and Cort Rolles from the 13 of Edward
the 4th as also by severall bookes in the office of armes all which
were truly drawne out and extracted by the 3 Kings and six others

of the officers of armes as may appear by yor pet^{rs} pedegree ready
to be shewed and subscrybed by them under their handes which
they are ready to justify and mainteyne to be good and sufficient
either before yor Maties or any others indifferent judges whom yor
Matie shall please to nominate or appoint.

> 'Thearfore yor petitioners humble suite unto yor Matie is that
> yor Matie wold be pleased to suffer the Lord Keeper to
> graunt the sayd Comission of appeale according to the
> sayd Certificat of yor highnes Attorney and sollicitor in
> that behalfe made whearby yor pet^{r} may reverse the said
> sentence pronounced against him in the sayd suite against
> him by the sayd Leak. In which suite uppon full open-
> ing thearof as yor pet^{r} is assured by his Councell yor pet^{rs}
> gentry will not come in question although yor pet^{r} will
> endeavour the same And yor pet^{r} as in duty bound shall
> ever pray for yor excellent Matie.

(Endorsed) 'R. 27° Martii 1625. A Draught of Mr. Harris
pet^{n} to his Matie concerning the busines between him &
Capt. Leake.'

As a result the Baronetcy remained in the family, Sir
Thomas transmitting the honour to his son and heir, Sir
Paul, who served the office of High Sheriff of Shropshire
in 1637. The Baronetcy became extinct in 1685.

The dispute over the creation of this Baronetcy is a
further proof, if any were needed, of the social position
demanded of those on whom the dignity was conferred, and
how shocked were the feelings of the age when it imagined
that it had been given to a person not possessed of the
essential attributes of a gentleman by birth; namely, the
being descended at the least from a grandfather who bore
hereditary coat armour, as well as being the owner of a
considerable income derived from his own broad acres.

The Baronetage received a great accession to its numbers from Charles II., which was only natural, considering the events which had taken place between the death of his royal father and his own restoration. About this time the payment of the fees, commonly called the Ulster fees, and other charges necessarily incident to the passing of Patents began to cease. In many instances the heads of some of the most distinguished families in the kingdom received the degree as a reward for the losses and sufferings they had gone through and for their services rendered during the rebellion. This remission of fees was made by special warrant from the King, expressed in honourable terms. The warrant was issued by the King, directed to the Treasurer, Chancellor, Under-Treasurer, and Barons of the Exchequer, to cause a tally to be struck in the Exchequer purporting the payment thereof (the ancient form being still retained in the Patent) as if it had actually been paid, and then the officials had their *quietus* out of the Exchequer for the same.

CHAPTER IV

THE EARLY HISTORY OF THE BARONETAGE OF
SCOTLAND AND NOVA SCOTIA

On the 5th March 1496, John Caboto, a Venetian resident in Bristol, and his three sons obtained from Henry VII. letters patent for a voyage of discovery, as a result of which they reached the Island of Newfoundland on the 24th June 1497. Nearly a century later, Sir Humphrey Gilbert, under a patent granted by Queen Elizabeth, took possession of Newfoundland; and various settlements were subsequently attempted.

Early in 1621, Sir William Alexander of Menstrie, Viscount, and afterwards Earl of Stirling, who followed James the Sixth of Scotland to London, and who, after holding various offices, had been made Master of Requests for Scotland, became interested in the English settlements in Virginia or New England, and resolved to embark in colonial adventure on his own account.

He accordingly obtained from James I. the grant of a large and extensive territory on the mainland, to the east of the river St. Croix, and south of the St. Lawrence, 'lying between our Colonies of New England and Newfoundland' as a foreign plantation.

On the 5th August 1621, the King addressed a letter

from Beauvoir on this subject to the Lord Chancellor and the other members of the Privy Council of Scotland, and accordingly the Royal Warrant or signature for a Charter was prepared and signed by the King at Windsor on the 10th September 1621, and on the 29th of the same month the Charter under the Great Seal was duly passed and registered.

In this Charter Sir William Alexander had almost unlimited privileges and liberties conferred on him as the King's hereditary Lieutenant-General, the lands of New Brunswick, Nova Scotia, Cape Breton, Prince Edward's Island, Gaspe, Anticosti, and all the adjacent islands being erected into one whole and free lordship and regality in favour of Sir William.

A similar Charter was granted on the 8th November 1621 to Sir Robert Gordon of Lochinvar and his second son Robert, with the view of promoting colonisation.

Late in 1622, Sir William Alexander, after considerable trouble in persuading suitable persons to set out for unknown lands, came within sight of the shore near Cape Breton ; but owing to storms, some of the company passed the winter in St. John's Harbour, Newfoundland, sending the vessel home for new supplies. The following year no better success was obtained, and the proposed establishment of a Colony was postponed, and the company returned to England.

The following year Sir William Alexander published a tract called ' An Encouragement to Colonies,' which, in 1630, six years later, was reissued under the title of ' The

Mapp and Description of New England ; together with A
Discourse of Plantation, and Collonies also A relation of
the nature of the Climate, and how it agrees with our owne
Country England.' At the conclusion of this tract Sir
William stated that no one man could accomplish such an
undertaking by his own private fortunes ; but that ' if it
shall please his Majestie (as he hath ever beene disposed
for the furthering of all good Works more for the benefit
of his Subjects, then for his owne particular) to give his
helpe accustomed for matters of lesse moment hereunto,
making it appeare to be a Worke of his own, that others
of his subjects may be induced to concurre in such a
common cause, no man could have had my charge that
with more affection and sinceritie should have used his
endevours for discharging of the same, but I must trust
to be supplyed by some publike helps, such as hath beene
had in other parts, for the like cause whereunto, as I doubt
not, but many will be willing out of the noblenesse of their
disposition, for the advancing of so worthy a Worke, So
I hope will some others, the rather out of their private
respect to me, who shall continue as I have heretofore
done, both to doe and write in so farre, so meane an
abilitie as mine may reach, what (I conceive) may prove
for the credit or benefit of my Nation, to whom I wish all
happinesse.'

The personal influence of Sir William with the King
caused him to approve of the scheme of creating in Scotland
an hereditary dignity under the title of Knights Baronets of
Nova Scotia, by means of a scheme similar to that which

had proved successful for colonising the districts in the
province of Ulster.   James, in fact, was so pleased with the
idea that he addressed the following letter to the Privy
Council of Scotland :—

'FROM HIS MAJESTIE ANENT BARONETTIS.

'[JAMES R.],
                        Right trustie and welbeloved Counsellour Richt
trustie and welbeloved Cosens and Counsello^{rs.} and trustie and weilbeloved Counsellours We greate you weill The Letter ye sent
giving us thankes for renueing of the name of that our ancient Kingdome within AMERICA intreateing our favour for the furthering of
a Plantatioun ther, was verie acceptable unto us and reposeing upoun
the experience of uthers of oure subjects in the like kinde We ar
so hopefull of that enterprise that We purpose to make it a worke
of oure Owne And as We wer pleased to erect the honour of
KNICHT BARRONETTS within this oure Kingdome for advancement
of the Plantatioun of Ireland, So We doe desire to conferr the like
honour within that our Kingdome upoun suche as wer worthie of
that degree and will agree for some proportioun of ground within
NEW SCOTLAND furnisheing furth such a number of persones as salbe
condiscended upoun to inhabite there Thus sall both these of the
cheife sorte (avoydeing the usuall contentions at publick meetings)
being by this Heredetarie honour preferred to others of meaner
qualitie know ther owne places at home and likwyse sall have ther
due abroad from the subjects of our other countreyis accordeing to
the course apointed for that our ancient Kingdome   And the
mentioning of so noble a cause within ther Pattents sall both serve
the more by suche a singular merite to honour them and by so
goode a ground to justifie our judgement with the posteritie   But
thouch the conferring of honour be meerely Regall and to be done
by Us as We please yet We would proceed in no matter of such
moment without youre advyse OUR PLEASURE is haveing considered
of this purpose if ye find it as We conceive it to be both fitt for the
credit of that Our Kingdome and for the furtherance of that

intended Plantatioun that ye certifie us your opinione concerning
the forme and conveniencis thairof, togither withe your further
advyce what may best advaunce this so worthie worke which We
doe verie muche affect but will use no meanes to induce onie man
thereunto further then the goodnes of the busines and his awne
generous dispositione shall perswade Neither doe We desire that
onie man salbe sent for or travelled with by you for being Barronet,
but after it is founde fitt will leave it to their owne voluntarie
choise, not doubteing (howsoever some for want of knowledge
may be averse) but that ther wilbe a greater nomber than we
inttend to make of the best sorte to imbrace so noble a purpose
whereby bothe they in particular and the whole Natione generally
may have honour and profite And We wishe you rather to thinke
how remedies may be provyded against any inconveniencies that
may happin to occure then by conjecturing difficulties to loose so
faire and unrecoverable occasioun whiche other Nations at this
instant are so earnest to undertake. And for the better directinge
of your judgement We have appointed ane printed copie of that
Order quhiche was taken concerning the Barronettis of this our
Kingdome to be sent unto you as it was published by authoritie
from Us. So desireing you to haste back your ansueire that We
may signifie our further pleasure for this purpose We bid you
Fairweill. From Our Courte at Roystoun the 18 day of October
1624.'

It is doubtful whether the Order referred to in the latter
part of this letter was 'His Majestie's Commission as
touching the creation of Baronetts' published in 1611, or
'Three Patents concerning the Honourable Degree and
Dignitie of Baronets' published in 1617, the contents of
which have previously been referred to.

This letter of the King was taken into consideration by
the Privy Council of Scotland, who, under date of the
23rd November 1624, sent the following reply :—

'To His Majestie anent the Baronettis.

'Most sacred Soverane,

'We have considerit of your Majesties letter concerning the Barronettis and doe therby persave your Majesties great affectioun towards this your ancient Kingdome and your Majesties most judicious consideratioun in makeing choise of so excellent meanes both noble and fitt for the goode of the same, wherein seeing your Majestie micht have proceidit without our advyce, and unacquenting us with your Majesties royall resolutioun therein, we ar so muche the more boundin to rander unto your Majestie our most humble thankes for your gracious respect unto us not onlie in this but in all uther thinges importeing this estate outher in credite or profit. And we humblie wisse that this honour of Barronet sould be conferrit upoun none but upon Knichtis and Gentlemen of chiefe respect for their birth, place or fortounes, and we have taken a course by Proclamatioun to mak this your Majesties gracious intentione to be publicklie knowen that non heirafter prætending ignorance take occasion inwardlie to compleyne as being neglected bot may accuse thameselffis for neglecting of so fair ane opportunitie And whereas we ar given to understand that the country of New Scotland being dividit in twa Provinces and eache province in severall Dioceises or Bishoprikis, and eache diocese in thrie Counteyis, and eache countey into ten Baronyis, everie baronie being thrie myle long upon the coast and ten myle up into the countrie, dividit into sex parocheis and eache paroche contening sax thousand aikars of land and that everie Baronett is to be ane Barone of some one or other of the saids Barroneis and is to haif therein ten thowsand aikars of propertie besydis his sax thousand aikars belongeing to his bur^t (burgh) of baronie To be holdin free blanshe and in a free baronie of Your Majestie as the barronies of this Kingdome ffor the onlie setting furth of sex men towardis your Majesties Royall Colonie armed, apparelld, and victuald for two yeares And everie Baronet paying Sir William Alexander Knicht ane thousand merkis Scottis money only towards his past charges and endevouris Thairfore our humble desire unto your Majestie is that care be taken by suirtie actit in the bookis of Secreit Counsall, as was in the Plantatioun of

Ulster that the said nomber of men may be dewlie transported thither with all provisions necessar and that no Baronet be maid but onlie for that cause And by some such one particular course onlie as your Majestie sall appointe And that Articles of Plantatioun may be set furth for encourageing and induceing all others who hes habilitie and resolutioun to transport themselffis hence for so noble a purpose.

'Last we consave that if some of the Englishe who ar best acquainted with such forrayn enterpreises wald joyne with the saids Baronetts heir (as it is liklie the lyker conditioun and proportioun of ground wald induce thame to doe) That it wald be ane grite encouragement to the furtherance of that Royall worke quhilk is worth[ie] of your Majesties care And we doubte not sindrie will contribute their help heirunto. So exspecting your Majesties forder directioun and humblie submitting our opinione to your Majesties incomparable judgement We humblie tak our leave prayeing the Almichtie God to blisse your Majestie with long and happie Reigne. From Edinbrugh the 23 of November 1624.'

This letter is signed by twelve Members of the Privy Council, and a week later was issued a Proclamation of the Council announcing the King's resolution on the 1st of April the following year to proceed to the creating and ranking of the one hundred Baronets referred to, and the Knights and Esquires who were to receive the honour were directed to appear previously to that day and have their names enrolled in the Books of the Privy Council. The following is the text of the Proclamation :—

'PROCLAMATIOUN ANENT BARONETIS.
'Apud Edinburgh ultimo die mensis Novembris 1624.
'At Edinburgh the last day of November The yeir of God 1600 Tuentie four yearis Our Soverane Lord being formarlie gratiouslie pleased to erect the heritable honnour and title of ane Baronet as ane degree, state and place nixt and immediatlie following the

younger sones of Vicounts and Lordis Baronis of Parliament as ane
new honnour whairwith to rewaird new meritis   Haveing conferrit
the same honnour place and dignitie upoun sundrie of the Knights
and Esquhyris of Ingland and Ireland to thame and thair airis maill
for ever   In consideratioun of thair help and assistance toward that
happie and successfull plantatioun of ULSTER IN IRELAND   To the
grite strenth of that his Majesties Kingdome, incresse of his Hienes
revenues and help to manie of his Majesties goode subjects   And
quhairas our said Soverane Lord being no les hopefull the plantatioun
of NEW SCOTLAND in the narrest pairt of America alreadie discovered
and surveyed be some of the subjects of his Majesties Kingdome of
Scotland joyning unto NEW INGLAND quhairin a grite pairt of his
Hienes nobilitie, gentrie, and burrowis of Ingland ar particularlie
interessed and hes actuallie begun thair severall Plantations thairof
And for that conceaving that manie his Majesties subjects of this
his ancient Kingdome emulating the vertews and industrious inter-
pryssis of utheris   And being of bodies and constitutionis most able
and fitt to undergo the Plantatioun thairof and propagatioun of
Christiane relligioun will not be deficient in anie thing quhilk may
ather advance his Majesties Royall intentioun towards that Plantatioun or be beneficiall and honnourable to this his Hienes ancient
Kingdome in generall or to thameselfis in particular   The samyn
being ane fitt, warrandable and convenient means to disburding this
his Majesties said ancient Kingdome of all such younger brether and
meane gentlemen quhois moyens ar short of thair birth worth or
myndis who otherwayes most be troublesome to the houses and
freindis from whence they ar descendit (the common ruynes of
most of the ancient families)   Or betak thameselfis to forren warke
or baisser chifts to the discredite of thair ancestouris and cuntrey
And to the grite losse of manie of his Majesties goode subjects who
may be better preservit to his Hienes use, honnour of thair freindis,
and thair awne comfort and subsistance   Gif transplantit to the said
cuntrey of NEW SCOTLAND, most worthie and most easie to be
plantit with christiane people and most habill by the fertilitie and
multitude of commodities of sea and land, to furnish all things
necessarie to manteine thair estaitis and dignitie as Landislordis

thairof and subjects to his Majestie to be governed by the Lawis of
this his ancient Kingdome of Scotland And our said Soverane Lord
being most willing and desyreous that this his said ancient Kingdome
participate of all such otheris honnouris and dignities as ar erected in
anie of his Majesties others Kingdomes To the effect that the
Gentrie of this his Hienes said ancient Kingdome of Scotland may
both haif thair dew abroad amonge the subjects of utheris his
Majesties Kingdomes and at home amonge thameselffis according to
thair degree and dignitie As alsua his Majestie being most graciouslie
pleasit to confer the said honnour of heretable Baronet as ane
speciall mark of his Heighnes princelie favour upoun the Knights
and Esquyris of principall respect ffor thair birth worth and fortouns
Togidder with large proportionis of Landis within the said cuntrey
of NEW SCOTLAND who sall be generouslie pleasit to set furth some
men in his Hienes Royal Colonie nixt going thither for that plantatioun. THAIRFORE his Majestie ordanis his Hienes lettres to be direct
chargeing Herauldis Pursevantis and Messengeris of Armes to pas to
the mercat Cros of Edinburgh and utheris placeis neidfull and thair
be oppin proclamatioun to mak publicatioun of the premises And
that it is his Majesties princelie pleasure and expres resolutioun, to
mak and creat the nomber of Ane hundreth heretable Baronettis of
this his Hienes Kingdome of Scotland be patentis under his Majesties
grite seale thairof Who and thair airis maill sall haif place and precedencie nixt and immediatlie after the youngest sones of the
Vicounts and Lordis Barrounis of Parliament and the addition of the
word SIR to be prefixed to thair propper name and the style and the
title of BARONETT subjoyned to the surname of everie ane of them
and thair airis maill Togither with the appellatioun of Ladie,
Madame, and Dame, to thair Wyffis in all tyme comeing with precedencie befoir all others Knights alsweill of the Bath, as Knights
Bachelouris and Bannarettis (except these onlie that beis Knighted
be his Majestie his airis and successouris in proper persone, in ane
oppin feild with banner displayed with new additioun to thair armes
and haill utheris prærogatives formarlie grantit be oure said Soverane
Lord to the saidis Barronettis of Ingland and Ireland Conforme to
the printed patent thairof in all poynts And that no persone or

personis whatsumevir sall be created and maid Barronetts bot onlie
such principall Knights and Esquyris as will be generouslie pleasit to
be Undertakeris of the said Plantatioun of NEW SCOTLAND And for
that effect to act thameselfis or some sufficient cautioneris for thame
in the buikis of Secreit Counsaill befoir the first day of Apryll nixt
to come in this insueing year of God 1600 Tuentie fyve yearis To
sett furth sex sufficient men artificeris or laboureris sufficientlie
armeit apparrelit and victuallit for tua yeiris towards his Majesties
Royall Colonie to be established God willing thair for his Hienes
use dureing that space And that within the space of yeir and day
efter the dait of the said Actis under the pane of tua thowsand
merkis usuall money of this realme As also to pay to SIR WILLIAM
ALEXANDER Knight Maister of Requests of this Kingdome and
Lieutenant to his Majestie in the said Cuntrey of NEW SCOTLAND
the sowme also of ane thowsand merkis money foirsaid for
his past chargeis in discoverie of the said Cuntrey and for surrendering and resigning his interest to the saidis Landis and
Barronies quhilks ar to be grantit be our said Soverane Lord
to the saidis Barronettis and everie one of thame To be halden
in frie blensh of his Majestie his airis and successouris as frie
Barronies of Scotland in all tyme comeing And as of the Crowne
of the samyne Kingdome and under his Hienes grite seale thairof
without onie other fyne or compositioun to be payit to his Majestie
or his hienes thesaurar for the tyme thairfore. Quhilkis barronies
and everie one of thame sal be callit be suche names as seemes
meetest to the saids Barronetts And sall border on the sea coast or
some portative river of the said Cuntrey and conteine threttie thowsand aikers quhairof sextene thowsand aikers is intendit for everie
one of the saidis Baronetis thair airis and assignayis quhatsumevir
with ane Burgh of Barronie thairupoun And the remanent four-
tene thowsand aikeris for such other publick use and uses as for the
Crowne, Bishops, Universities, Colledge of Justice, Hospitals, Clargie,
Phisitiounis, Schools, Souldiouris and utheris at lenth mentionat in
the Articles and Plattforme of the said Plantatioun And forder
that his Majesties will and pleasure is That publict intimatioun be
maid as afoirsaid To all the saidis Knights and Esquyris who desyris

to accept the said dignitie of Baronett and Baronie of Land upoun the conditionis above exprest that betuix and the first day of Apryle nixt to come they repair in persoun or by some Agent sufficientlie instructed to the Lordis of his Majesties privie Counsall or to suche as sal be nominat be his Hienes and intimat to thame be the saidis Lordis to inroll thair names and ressave forder informatioun fra thame concerning the said plantatioun and for passing of thair infeftmentis and patents accordinglie   And sicklyk that all otheris personis who intendeth not to be Barronetts and that hath suche affectioun to his Majesties service as they will also be Undertakers of some proportionis of Land in New Scotland (as the nobilitie gentrie and burrowis of Ingland hath done in New Ingland) may herafter tak notice of the printed Articles of the Plantatioun of New Scotland and informe thameselfis by all laughfull wayes and meanis thairof With certificatioun to all his Majesties lieges and subjects that immediatlie after the said first day of Apryle nixt to come Our said Soverane Lord will proceid to the creatioun and ranking of the saidis Barronettis, and passing of thair patents and infeftments without respect to ony that sall happin to neglect to cum in before the said day who ar heirby requyrit to tak notice heirof and inroll thair names that thair neglect may be rather imput unto thameselfis then to his Majestie who is so graciouslie pleasit to make offer to thame of so fair ane occasioun of heretable preferment honnour and benefite.'

No copy of the printed Articles of the Plantation of New Scotland referred to in the above proclamation has ever been discovered.

On the 17th March 1625, Prince Charles addressed to the Privy Council the following letter :—

'ANENT BARONETTIS

'CHARLES P.,

'Right trustie and right welbeloued Cosens and Counsellouris and right trustie and welbeloued Counsellouris, Whereas it hath pleased the Kingis Majestie in favour of the Plantatioun of NOVA

SCOTIA to honnour the Undertakeris being of the ancientest gentrie of Scotland with the honnour of Barronetts and thairin haif trusted and recommendit SIR WILLIAM ALEXANDER of Menstrie to his Counsell to assist him by all laughfull meanis and to countenance the bussienes by their authoritie.   In like maner We do recommend the said Sir William and the bussines to your best assistance hereby declairing that we favour bothe the bussines and the persone that followeth it in suche sort That your willingness to further it in all you can sall be unto us very acceptable service So We bid you hartelie farewell.   From the Court at Theobalds, the 17 of Marche 1625.'

On the 23rd March 1625, the King addressed another letter to the Privy Council, of which the following is a copy :—

'ANENT BARONETTIS

'JAMES R.,

'Right trustie and welbeloued Counsellour Right trustie and welbeloued Cosens and Counsellours and trustie and welbeloued Counsellours We greete you weele We persave by your letters directit unto us what care you haif had of that bussienes which We recommendit unto you concerning the creatting of KNIGHT BARONETTIS within that our Kingdome for the Plantatioun of New Scotland, and ar not onlie weele satisfied with the course that you haif taikin thairin but likewayis it doeth exceidinglie content ws that We haif so happielie fund a meanis for expressing of our affectioun towards that our ancient Kingdome as we find by the consent of you all so much tending to the honnour and proffite thairof, and as we haif begun so we will continue requireing you in like maner to persevere for the furthering of this Royall work that it may be brought to a full perfectioun   And as you haif done weele to warne the auncient Gentrie by Proclamatioun assigneing thame a day for comeing in and that you are carefull to secure that which they sould performe Our pleasure is to this end that this bussienes may be carried with the lesse noice and trouble that everie ane of them that doeth intend to be Baronet give in his name to our trustie and wel-

beloued Sir William Alexander Knight our Lieutennant for that
enterprise or in cais of his absence to our trustie and welbeloued
Counsellour Sir John Scott Knight that one of thame after the
tyme appoyntit by the Proclamatioun is expyred may present the
names of the whole nomber that ar to be created unto thame
whome We sall appoynt Commissionaris for marshalling of them in
due ordour And becaus it is to be the fundatioun of so grite a
work bothe for the good of the Kingdome in generall and for the
particular enterest of everie Baronet who after this first protec-
tionarie Colony is seatled for secureing of the cuntrey may the
rather thairefter adventure for the planting of their awne proportioun whiche by this meanis may be maid the more hopefull That
the sinceritie of our intentioun may be seen Our further pleasure
is that if any of the Baronettis sall chuse rather to pay two thowsand
merkis than to furnishe furth sex men as is intendit that then the
whole Baronettis mak chois of some certaine persones of thair
nomber to concurr with our said Lieutennant taking a strict course
that all the said monie be onlie applied for setting furth of the
nomber intendit or at the least of so many as it can convenientlie
furnishe And as we will esteeme the better of suche as ar willing
to imbrace this course so if any do neglect this samine and sue for
any other degree of honnour hereafter We will think that they
deserve it the lesse since this degree of Baronet is the next steppe
unto a further And so desiring you all to further this purpose als
far as convenientlie you can We bid you Farewell, from our Court
at Theobaldes, the 23 of Marche 1625.'

On the 27th of March, four days after the date of this
letter, James i. died at Theobalds. At the close of the
Charter or original Patent granted to Sir William Alexander,
dated the 10th September 1621, already referred to, the
King had engaged that all the privileges and liberties it so
bountifully conferred should be ratified, approved, and confirmed by the following Scottish Parliament. Parliament,
however, did not meet again during the lifetime of the King.

It was clear, however, from his letter of the 27th March, the date of his Royal father's death, that Charles I. was not likely to let the scheme drop; and on the 28th of May following he raised Sir Robert Gordon, the second son of the Earl of Sutherland, to the dignity of a Baronet of Scotland and Nova Scotia.   Sir Robert thus became the premier Baronet of this branch of the dignity ; and on the resignation of Sir William Alexander, his grant of sixteen thousand acres of land in Nova Scotia was erected upon the Free Barony and Regality of Sir Robert Gordon, in favour of himself, his heirs male, and assignees whomsoever.

This Royal Charter, which was twice ratified and confirmed by Acts of the Parliament of Scotland, namely, on the 31st July 1630 and the 28th June 1633, which was recognised as valid by William III. under a Royal Warrant in 1698, and which is secured under the clause in the Act of Union in 1707, by which it is irrevocably settled and declared, that ' No alteration shall be made in the laws which concern private rights in Scotland, except for the evident utility of the subject within Scotland,' was made, by subsequent instruments under the Great Seal, the regulating Charter for the Baronets of Scotland and Nova Scotia. Although it is printed at length in Chapter II., yet as it is in Latin, it may be convenient to give an abstract in English of the rights, privileges, and immunities conferred by the Charter.

1st. Territorial.—A grant of 16,000 acres of land in the Royal Province of Nova Scotia, as anciently bounded, which comprehends Nova Scotia proper, Cape Breton, Anticosti,

Gaspe, Prince Edward's Island, and New Brunswick, to be incorporated into a full, entire, and free Barony and Regality for ever, to be held of the Kingdom of Scotland in blench-farm for payment yearly of one penny, if asked only ; the said free Barony and Regality to extend three miles in length along the sea coast, and six in length inland, with gifts of benefices, patronage of churches, fisheries, huntings, minerals, mines, pearls, jewels, offices, jurisdictions, and power of pit and gallows, as plenary as had ever formerly been enjoyed by whatsoever nobleman under the Crown of Scotland ; also with express power of planting the said free Barony and Regality, and of removing thence from Scot-land, or any other country, persons, goods and chattels ; with liberty to such persons, their children and posterity, to have, hold, acquire, enjoy, and possess, all, and whatso-ever, the liberties, privileges, and immunities of children and natural-born subjects of the Kingdom of Scotland, and the other dominion thereunto belonging, as if they had been born in the said kingdom or dominions.

2*nd. Seigneurial.*—The right and liberty to erect cities, towns, corporations, burghs of barony, etc. ; of nominating provosts, baillies, justices of the peace, and other municipal officers, etc. ; of making such particular laws, ordinances, and constitutions as should be deemed expedient for the good order and police of the free Barony and Regality, with the heritable justiciary and sheriffship of the same ; the power of judging and discerning in all causes, as well civil as criminal, within the bounds ; of holding Courts of Justi-ciary, Sheriff Courts, Baron and Barony Courts, and Courts of Free Regality ; of appointing their officers, and of exacting and appropriating all escheats, amercements, etc. ; also of imposing and levying tolls, customs, anchorages, etc. etc.

3rd. Commercial.—The right of erecting free ports, harbours, naval stations, etc. ; of building ships, craft, vessels, etc., as well for war as merchandise ; of importing and exporting from and to Scotland, or any other country, wares, merchandise, and commodities of whatever description, for payment of the sum of five pounds Scots money of custom for every hundred pounds only, without payment of any other custom, impost, or duty of any kind ; also, of imposing and exacting five pounds for every hundred, on all goods imported into Nova Scotia by the Colonists, and ten per cent. on all imported by foreigners.

4th. Legislative.—The right, either personally or by deputy, of a suffrage and vote in framing all and sundry the laws to be made concerning the public state, good, and government of the Royal Province of Nova Scotia, in all assemblies, parliaments, synods, councils, and conventions, to be called together, convened, or held for that end ; and that no person or persons whatsover, who should not be heirs of the said free Baronies of Regality, should have vote or suffrage in framing whatsoever laws concerning the said Province, without the advice, counsel, and consent of the Baronets.

5th. Dignitorial.—The hereditary style and title of Baronet, with precedency between the degree of free Baron and the degree of Lord, and privilege to resolve all questions concerning their place and prerogative by the use and practice of custom and law, as the other hereditary degrees of dignity, are ordained and directed concerning place, prerogative, and precedency ; their wives to have and enjoy as Baronetesses precedence above the wives of all Knights ; and their eldest sons to possess in perpetual succession the right, on coming of age, to demand inauguration as Knights of the reigning Sovereign, without payment of fees or charges of any kind.

In addition to these rights and privileges, the Charters of the Baronets of Scotland, *firstly*, contain a clause empowering them to sit in the Scottish Parliament by deputy, when they may be furth of the kingdom ; *secondly*, they grant that the Baronets, and those who colonise their free Baronies and Regalities in Nova Scotia, shall be judged, ruled, and governed, in all time coming, in all cases, civil and criminal, by the laws of the said Province of Nova Scotia only, and not by others ; *thirdly*, they provide that the Baronets shall participate in all the privileges, liberties, immunities, profits, and casualties whatsoever, that are specified in the Charters and infeftments granted to Sir William Alexander, afterwards Earl of Stirling, and his heirs, and that in as full, free, and ample manner and form as if the said privileges, prerogatives, immunities, etc., with all the clauses and conditions relating to them, had been inserted at full length in their patents ; *fourthly*, they dispense with non-entry, and taking seisin in Nova Scotia, and grant authority to have seisin and instruments of possession taken on the Castlehill of Edinburgh, because the said Province of Nova Scotia, and original infeftment thereof, is holden of the ancient

Kingdom of Scotland, and forms part of the county of
Edinburgh; *fifthly*, they promise for King Charles I., his
heirs and successors, in *verbo principis*, that the said Charters,
with all and sundry the privileges, liberties, clauses, articles,
and conditions, as specified, should be ratified, approved, and
confirmed by the Parliament of Scotland, in order that they
might have the strength, force, and effect of a decree and
sentence of that supreme and pre-eminent tribunal; and,
sixthly, they stipulate and declare, that no lapse of time,
prescription, non-user, or any adverse circumstance whatsoever, shall ever bar the enjoyment of the rights which they
convey.

It should here be mentioned that the reason of Sir Robert
Gordon being selected for the first recipient of the honour
was that he, like Sir William Alexander, had been interested
in the object of colonisation; and that on the 8th November
1621 a Charter similar to the one granted to Sir William
on the 10th September had been granted to Sir Robert and
his second son Robert.

Sir William Alexander, who was appointed in 1626 one
of the principal Secretaries of State for Scotland, was raised
to the Peerage on the 4th September 1630 by the title of
Viscount of Stirling and Lord Alexander, and three years later
at the King's coronation at Holyrood was raised to the
dignity of Earl of Stirling, Viscount of Canada, etc.

The following precept may serve as an example of the
form or warrant issued for preparing a Charter under the
Great Seal, to convey, with the grant of lands, the title and
honours of a Nova Scotia Baronet :—

'Precept of a Charter to William, Earl Marischal.

'Preceptum Carte fact. per S. D. N. Regem predilecto suo consanguineo Willielmo Mariscalli Comiti Dno. Keith et Altrie &c.
Regni Scotie Mariscallo heredibus suis masculis et assignatis quibuscunque hric [hereditarie] super tota et integra illa parte seu portione
regionis et dominii Nove Scotie ut sequitur bondat. et limitat, viz.
incipien. a maxima meridionali parte terre ex orientali latere fluvii
nunc Tweid appelat. prius autem Sancti Crucis et exinde pergendo
orientaliter sex miliaria per maris et littus et exinde pergendo bore-
aliter a maris littore in terra firma ex orien. latere ejusdem fluvii
observando semper sex milliaria in latitudine a dicto fluvio orientaliter donec extendat. ad numerum quadraginta octo millium acrarum
terre cum castris turribus fortaliciis &c. Quequidem terre aliaque
in dict. carta ad Dominum Gulielmum Allexander de Menstrie
hereditarie pertinuerunt et resignate fuerunt per ipsum in manibus
dict. S. D. N. Regis pro hac Nova Carta et infeodatione Prefato
predicto suo consanguineo Willielmo Mariscalli Comiti &c. desuper
conficienda Preterea cum clausula unionis in unam integram et
liberam baroniam et regalitatem omni tempore futuro Baroniam de
Keith Marschell nuncupand. tenen. de dict. S. D. N. Rege et successoribus suis de corona et regno Scotie in libera alba firma pro
annua solutione unius denarii usualis monete dicti regni Scotie super
solum et fundum dictarum terrarum nomine albe firme si petatur
tantum vel alicujus earundem partis in die festo nativitatis Domini
nomine albe firme si petatur tantum Et quod unica sasina apud
Castellum de Edinburgh capienda et erit sufficiens pro omnibus et
singulis terris aliisque particulariter et generaliter suprascript. in
dicta carta content. et cetera in communi forma cartarum Baronetis
concess. Apud Aulam de Quhythall vigesimo octavo die mensis
Maii Anno Dni. Millesimo sexcentesimo vigesimo quinto.

'*Per Signetum.*'

The form of Charter or Patent issued in accordance with
the foregoing Precept has already been set out.

On the 12th July following, Charles 1. by a Charter of
Novodamus ratified and renewed his father's grant in fee

of Nova Scotia to Sir William Alexander, his heirs and assignees, with extensive additional powers and privileges.

His Majesty having appointed the Castle of Edinburgh as the place for giving sasine by infeftment, that ceremony was performed and correctly implemented within the Castle-gate, on the 29th September 1625. The instrument of sasine bears that it was taken 'intra exteriorem portam,' and was duly recorded in the general Register of Sasines kept at Edinburgh, on the 1st October following. This Charter and sasine form effectual instruments, and constitute a complete feudal right, title, and investment of the property.

It is material to mark its being specially declared in *verbo principis*, that the Charters conveying these grants 'shall be valid, sufficient, and effectual, in all time coming, in all points as set forth, against the crown, its heirs, and successors '—' nor shall be lawfully impugned or called in question,' for ever acquitting and renouncing ' all title, action, instance, and interest heretofore competent, or that may be competent to us and our heirs and successors, renouncing the same simpliciter jure lite et causa, cum pacto de non petendo, etc.'

Between the 28th May 1625—on which day the Premier Baronet of Scotland, Sir Robert Gordon, was created—and the 19th July following, nine other grants of land of sixteen thousand acres each, in Nova Scotia, were erected into free Baronies and Regalities, and, with the hereditary title of Baronet, were conferred upon Sir Alexander Strachan of Strachan ; Sir William Keith, Earl Marshall ; Sir Duncan Campbell of Glenorchy Campbell (now Marquess of Bread-

albane); Sir Robert Innes of New Innes (now Duke of
Roxburgh); Sir John Wemyss of New Wemyss (now Earl
of Wemyss and March); Sir David Livingston of Dunipace
Livingston; Sir William Douglas of Douglas; Sir Donald
Macdonald of Macdonald (now Lord Macdonald); and Sir
Richard Murray of Cockpool (now Earl of Mansfield).

On the 19th July 1625, Charles I. acquainted the Lords
of the Privy Council of Scotland that he had created the
above Baronets in the following letter :—

'To the Privy Council of Scotland anent Baronettis

'Charles R.,
'Right trustie and right welbeloued counsellour, right trustie
and right welbeloued cosens and counsellouris, and trustie and
welbeloued counsellouris, We greete you wele. Understanding that our late deare Father, after due deliberatioun, for furthering
the Plantatioun of New Scotland, and for sindrie other goode
consideratiounis, did determine the creatting of Knight Baronettis
thair; and that a proclamatioun wes maid at the mercatt croce of
Edinburgh, to gif notice of this his Royall intentioun, that those
of the best sort knowing the same might haif tyme to begin first,
and be preferred unto otheris, or than want the said honnour in
their awne default : And understanding likewayes, that the tyme
appoyntit by the Counsell for that purpois is expyred, We being
willing to accomplishe that whiche wes begun by our said deare
Father, haif preferred some to be Knight Baronettis, and haif grantit
unto thame signatouris of the said honnour, togither with thrie mylis
in breadth and six in lenth of landis within New Scotland, for thair
severall proportiounes : And now that the saidis Plantatiounes
intendit thair, tending so much to the honnour and benefite of that
our Kingdome, may be advanced with diligence, and that pre-
paratiounes be maid in due tyme for setting furthe a Colonie at the
next Spring, to the end that those who are to be Baronettis, and to
help thairunto, may not be hinderit by comeing unto us for pro-

L

cureing thair grantis of the saidis landis and dignitie, bot may haif
thame there with lesse trouble to themselffis and unto us, We haif
sent a Commissioun unto you for accepting surrenderis of landis,
and for conferring the dignitie of Baronet upon suche as salbe fund
of qualitie fitt for the samine, till the nomber appoynted within the
said commissioun be perfited : AND THEREFORE OUR PLEASURE IS,
That you exped the commissioun through the sealis with all
diligence, and that you, and all otheris of our Privie Counsell thair,
give all the lawfull assistance, that you can convenientlie affoord for
accomplisheing the said worke, whereby Colonies sould be sett
furth ; and certifie from us, that as we will respect thame the more
who imbrace the said dignitie and further the said plantatioun, so if
ony Knight who is not a Baronet presoome to tak place of one who
is Baronet, or if ony who is not Knight stryve to tak place of one
who hes the honnour from us to be a Knight, inverting the order
usuall in all civile pairtis, WE WILL that you censure the pairty
transgressing in that kynd, as a manifest contempnar of oure
authoritie, geving occasioun to disturbe the publict peace.   So
recommending this earnestlie to your care, We bid you farewell.
Windsore, the 19th of July 1625.'

The Commission referred to in this letter was passed
under the Great Seal of Scotland, 25th July 1625; and it
empowered the Commissioners, or any six members of the
Privy Council, with ' full authority and commission to meet
at such days, and places, as they shall think expedient, and
there to hear the petitions of his Majesty's subjects who
intend the said plantation, and are willing to embrace the
same, and to confer, make, and thereupon conclude with
them to receive resignation of all lands lying within the
country of New Scotland, which shall happen to be resigned
in their hands as his Majesty's Commissioners by Sir
William Alexander, or his lawful procurators in his name,

in favour of any person or persons, and to give and grant
new heritable infeftments under the Great Seal of his
Majesty's said Kingdom (viz. of Scotland) to those to
whom the said resignations are granted of the said Lands,
and of the degree, state, order, dignity, name, honour, title,
and style of Knight Baronet, with such like privileges,
prerogatives, immunities, liberties, and others, whatsoever,
which are granted, and to be granted, in the Charters already
passed to the Baronets of the said Kingdom, made by his
Majesty to be enjoyed and possessed heritably as an especial
token of his royal favour.'

The following Royal Proclamation was issued in August
1625 :—

'Proclamatioun concerning Baronnettis.

'Apud Edinburgh penultimo die mensis Augusti 1625.

'Forsameikle as our Souerane Lordis umquhile dearest Father of
blissed memorie for diverse goode ressonis and considderationis
moveing his Matie and speciallie for the better encouragement of
his Hienes subjectis of this his ancient Kingdome of Scotland
towardis the plantatioun of New Scotland in America being
graciouslie pleased to erect the heretable dignitie and title of
Baronet as a degree of honour within the said kingdome (as
formerlie he had done in England for the plantatioun of Ulster in
Ireland) And being of intention to confer the said title and
honnour of Barronet onlie upoun suche his Ma^{ts} subjectis of the
said ancient Kingdome of Scotland as wald be undertakeris and
furtheraris of the Plantatioun of New Scotland and performe the
conditionis appoyntit for that effect Causit publict proclamatioun
to be maid at the Mercat Croce of Edinburgh be advise of his
Ma^{s} Counsell of the said Kingdome geving notice to the cheiff
gentrie and all his Maties subjectis of that Kingdome of his Royall
intention concerning the creating of Barronettis there, and that

after a certain day now of a long tyme bypast prescryved be the said proclamatioun his Matie wald proceid to the creating of Barronettis and conferring the said title and honnour upoun suche personis as his Matie sould think expedient having performed the conditionis appoyntit for the said Plantatioun   To the effect the cheifest Knightis and Gentlemen of the Kingdome haveing notice of his Maties princelie resolutioun might (if thay pleasit be Undertakeris in the said Plantatioun and performe the appoyntit conditionis) be first preferred be his Matie and have the said heretable honnour and title conferred upoun thame and there aires maill for ever or otherwayes be there awne neglect and default want the same   And now our Souerane Lord being most carefull and desireous that his said umquhile deerest Fatheris resolution tak effect for the weele of this his said Kingdome and the better furtherance of the said Plantatioun and otheris good considerationis moveing his Hienes, His Matie hathe already conferred the said heretable honnour and title of Barronet upoun diverse his Ma^{s} subjectis of this his said kingdome, of goode parentage, meanis and qualitie and grantit chartouris to thame and there airis maill for evir under the Grite Seale of the said kingdome conteining his Ma^{s} grant unto thame of the said dignitie and of the particular landis and boundis of New Scotland designit unto thame and diverse liberties and priviledgeis contenit in there saidis patentis and is of the intention to grant the like to otheris   And for the better furtherance of the said Plantatioun and performe the conditionis appoyntit for that effect and to haif the said honnour and title conferred upoun thame may not be hinderit nor delayit be going to Court to procure from his Matie there severall patentis and grantis of the said dignity and landis in New Scotland to be grantit to thame but may haif the same heir in Scotland with lesse truble to his Matie and chargis and expenssis to thameselffis   His Matie of his royall and princelie power and speciall favour hathe geven and grantit a commission and full power to a select nomber of the Nobilitie and Counsell of this Kingdome whose names are particularlie therein insert or ony five of thame the Chancellair Thesaurair and Secretair being thrie of the five to ressave resignationis of all landis within New Scotland whilk sal

happin to be resignit be Sir William Alexander knight Maister of
Requestis to his Matie for the said kingdome and his Ma^s Lieutennant
of New Scotland in favouris of whatsomevir personis and to grant
patentis and infeftmentis thairof againe to thame Together with the
said heretable honnour and title thay haveing alwayes first performed
to the said Sir William Alexander his aires or assignayis or thair
laughfull commissionaris or procuratouris haveing there powers the
Conditionis appoyntit for the furtherance of the said Plantatioun
and bringing thame a certificat thairof in write under the handis
of the said Sir Williame or his foresaidis to be shewn and producit
before the saidis commissionaris   And his Matie haveing likewayes
gevin informatioun to the Lordis of his Secreit Counsell of this
kingdome to certifie his subjectis thereof concerning his princelie
will and pleasure anent the place due to the Barronettis and Knightis
of the said Kingdome   THAIRFORE the saidis Lordis of Secreit
Counsell to the effect that nane pretend ignorance Ordanis letteris
to be direct chargeing herauldis and officiaris of armeis to pas to the
mercat croce of Edinburgh and all otheris placeis neidfull and mak
publict intimatioun to all his Ma^s leiges and subjectis of this
kingdome   That all suche as intend to be Barronettis and Undertakeris in the said Plantatioun and to performe to the said Sir
Williame or his foresaidis the Conditionis appoyntit for the furtherance of the said Plantatioun and haveing a certificat under his hand
as said is may repair and resort to the saidis Commissionaris at all
tymes convenient and ressave grantis and patentis from thame under
the Grite Seale of this Kingdome of the landis of New Scotland to
be resignit in there favouris to the said Sir Williame or his foirsaidis
with the like liberties and priviledgeis and otheris whatsoevir as ar
grantit to the Barronettis alreadie maid in thair patentis alreadie
past under the said Grite Seale, and of the said heretable title and
honnour of Barronett to thame and there aires maill for ever and
tak place and precedence according to the dates of their severall
patentis to be grantit to thame and no otherwayes   And in like
maner to mak publicatioun that his Ma^s princelie will and pleasure
is That the Barronettis of this Kingdome maid and to be maid, haif,
hald, tak, and enjoy in all tyme comeing freelie but ony impediment

the place prioritie and precedence in all respectis grantit to thame in thair severall patentis under the said Grite Seale and that no Knight, Laird, Esquire, or Gentleman whatsoevir who is not a Barronett presoome in ony conventioun or meeting or at ony tyme place or occasioun whatsoevir to tak place præcedence or præeminince befoir ony who is or sal heirafter be maid a Baronet neyther ony who is not a Knight tak place befoir ony who hathe the honnour to be a Knight thereby inverting the ordour used in all civile pairtis Certifieing all his Ma^s leiges and subjectis of this his kingdome and everie ane of them who sall præsoome to do in the contrair heirof That they sall be most seveirlie punist be his Matie and the saidis Lordis of his Counsell as manifest contempnaris of his Maties royall power and prærogative and thereby geving occasioun to disturb the publict peace.

Subscribitur ut supra.

[GEO. CANCELL.	ROXBURGH
MORTOUN	MELROS
WINTOUN	LAUDERDAILL]
BUGCLEUGH	

As a result of the special precedency given to the Baronets, the Scottish Gentry who had not been raised to the dignity early complained, as will be seen from the following Memorandum :—

'CONVENTIOUN OF ESTATES :—ANENT BARONETTIS.

'Apud Edinburgh secundo die mensis Novembris 1625.

'Anent the Petitioun gevin in be the small Barronis proporting that thay sustenit verie grite prejudice by this new erectit Ordour of Barronettis and the præcedencie grantit to thame befoir all the small Baronis and Freehalderis of this kingdome whairin thay pretendit grit præjudice in thair priviledgeis and dignityis possest be thame and thair prædecessouris in all præceding aiges and thairfoir thay desyrit that the Estaittis wald joyne with thame in thair humble petitioun that his Matie might be intreatted to suspend the præcedencie grantit to thir Barronettis untill the tyme that the Plantatioun for the whilk this dignitie is conferred be first performed be the Undertakeris Whairupon Sir William Alexander cheiff undertaker of this Plantatioun being hard and he having objectit unto thame his Ma⁸ royall prærogative in conferring of honnouris and titles of dignitie in matteris of this kynd importing so far the honnour and credite of the cuntrey and that his Ma⁸ prærogative wald not admitt ony sort of opposition, and that this suspensioun of the Undertakeris præcedencie wald frustratt the whole Plantatioun After that the small Barronis had most humblie protestit that the least derogation to his Ma⁸ royall prærogative sould never enter in thair hairtis and that thair Petitioun was in no sort contrair to the same, and that thay acknawledged that the conferring of honnouris did properlie belong to his Matie as a poynt of his royall prærogative. And thay undertooke that if it wer fund meete be his Matie and the Estaittis that this Plantatioun sould be maid that thay upoun thair awin chairgis wald undertak the same without ony retributioun of honnour to be gevin thairfoir. The Estaittis haveing at lenth hard both the partyis It was fund be pluralitie of voittis that the Estaittis sould joyne with thame in thair petitioun foirsaid.'

On the 27th October 1625, a Convention was held at Edinburgh. The Petition of the Scottish gentry was taken into consideration, with the result as shown in the following extract from the communication addressed by the Privy Council to the King :—

'MOST SACRED SOVERANE,

'The Convention of your Majesties Estaittis, which, by your Ma⁸ direction wes callit to the tuentie sevent day of October last being that day verie solemnlie and with a frequent and famous nomber of the Nobilitie Clergy and Commissionaris for the Shyres and Burrowis præceislie keept, and the Taxatioun grantit, as our former letter to your Majestie did signifie.

'Upon the first second and thrid day of this moneth the Estattis having proceided to the considderatioun of the Propositions and Articles sende downe be your Matie &c.

.   .   .   .

'After that all thir Articles wer propouned hard discussit and answeirit be the Estaittis in maner foirsaid Thair wes some petitions gevin in be the small Baronis and Burrowis whairin thay craved that the Estaittis wald joyne with thame in thair humble Petitioun to your Matie for obtaining your allowance thairof.

.   .   .   .

'Thay had ane other Petitioun and greevance foundit upon the præjudice alledged sustenit be thame by this new erectit Ordour of Barronettis and the præcedencie grantit to thame befoir all the small Barronis and Friebalderis of this Kingdome whairin thay prætendit grite præjudice in thair priviledgeis and dignityis possest be thame and thair prædecessouris in all præceiding aiges.   And thairfore thair desire wes that the Estaittis wald joyne with thame in thair humble Petitioun   That your Matie might be intreatted to suspend the præcedencie grantit to thir Barronettis untill the tyme that the Plantatioun for the whilk this dignitie is conferred be first performed be the undertakeris   Whairupon Sir William Alexander cheif undertaker in this Plantatioun being hard and he haveing objectit unto thame your Ma^s royall prærogative in conferring of honnouris and titlis of dignitye in matteris of this kynd importeing so far the honnour and credite of the cuntrey   And that your Ma^s prærogative wald not admit ony sort of oppositioun and that this suspensioun of the undertakeris præcedencie wald frustratt the whole Plantatioun   After that the Small Baronis had most humblie protestit that the least derogatioun to your Ma^s prærogative sould never enter into thair hairtis and that thair petitioun wes in no sort contrair to the same bot that thay acknowledged that the conferring of honnouris did properly belong to your Matie as a poynt of your royall prærogative   And thay undertooke that if it wer fund meete by your Matie and the Estaittis that this Plantatioun sould be maid That thay upoun thair awne chargeis wald undertak the same without ony retributioun of honnour to be gevin thairfoir.   The Estaittis haveing at lenth hard both partyis   It wes fund be pluralitie

of voitis that the Estaittis sould joyne with thame in thair Petitioun
foirsaid to your Majestie

(*Sic Subscribitur*)

	GEO. HAY	ROXBURGH
' Edinburgh	MAR	MELROS
Octavo Novembris 1625	MORTOUN	B. DUMBLANE
	WYNTOUN	ARC^D NAPER
	LINLITHGOW	

Notwithstanding the support accorded to the Petition by
the Convention, the King was determined that the new
Degree erected by his royal father, and supported by himself, should not be shorn of any dignity. He therefore not
only refused the prayer of the Petition, but intimated his
intention of conferring the additional honour of knighthood
on each Baronet's eldest son, on his attaining the age of one-
and-twenty, in the following letter addressed to his Privy
Council :—

'To THE COUNSALL

'[CHARLES R.]

' Right trustie and weilbeloued Counsellour Right trustie and
weilbelovit Cousines and Counsellours Right trustie and weilbeloved
Counsellours and trustie and weilbeloved Counsellours We Greet
you weill Wheras our late dear Father did determyne the Creating
of Knyghts Barronetts within that our Kingdome haveing first had
the advyse of his privie Counsall therunto whoise congratulatorie
approbation may appear by a letter of thanks sent unto him thairefter And sieing the whole gentrie war adverteised of this his
Royall resolutioun by publict proclamationis that these of the best
sort knowing the same might have tyme to begin first and be
preferred unto uthers or then want the said honour in ther awin
default a competent tyme being appoynted unto them by the said
Counsall that they might the more advysedlie resolve with them
selffis therein. In consideratioun whairof we wer pleased to give a

commission under our great seall wherby the saidis Knights Barronetts might be created according to the conditions formerlie condescendit upoun   And heirefter hearing that sindrie gentlemen of the best sort wer admitted to the said dignitie we never haveing heard of aney complaynt against the same till the work efter this maner was broght to perfection it could not bot seame strange unto ws that aney therefter should have presented such a petition as was gevin to the last Conventioun so much derogatorie to our Royall prerogative and to the hindering of so worthie a work or that the samyne should have bene countenanced or suffered to have bene further prosecuted Now to the effect that the said work may have no hinderance heirefter our pleasur is that the course so advysedlie prescryved by ws to the effect foresaid may be made publictlie knowen of new wairning the said gentrie that they may ather procure the said dignitie for them selffis or not repyne at others for doeing the same And that you have a speciall care that none of the saidis Knyghts Barronetts be wronged in ther priviledges by punisching aney persone who dar presum to doe any thing contrarie to ther grants as a manifest contemner of our authoritie and disturbours of the publict peace   And if it shall happin heirefter that the said Commission by the death or change of any persones appoynted Commissioneris to this effect shall neid be renewed   Our further pleasur is that at the desyre of our trustie and weilbelovit Counsellour Sir William Alexander knyt our Secretarie or his aires the same be gevin of new to the Commissioneris of our Excheker the Chancellour Thesaurer or Thesaurer deputie or any tuo of them being alwyse of the number giveing them such power in all respects as is conteyned in the former Commission with this addition onlie that we doe heirby authorize our Chancellour for the tyme being to knyght the eldest sones of the saidis Knyghts Baronets being of perfyte aige of 21 zeires he being requyred to that effect   And we will that a clause bearing the lyk power be particularlie insert in the said new Commission if upoun the caussis forsaid it be renewed And that the samyne by our said Chancellour be accordinglie performed, So we bid, &c.

'Whythall Feb. 12, 1626.'

In accordance with the intimation contained in this letter
of the King's intention to renew the Commission for the
creation of Baronets of Scotland, and to knight their eldest
sons on their attaining the age of twenty-one years, the
King wrote the following letter to the Chancellor :—

'[CHARLES R.]
'Right, &c. Wheras we have gevin Ordour by a former letter
that the Commission formerlie grantit by ws for creating of knyght
Barronettis in that our kingdome might be renewed at the desyre
of Sir William Alexander our Livetenent of New Scotland or his
Heynes whensoever they should desyre the samyne geving the power
in tyme comeing to the Commissioners of our Excheker which the
persones nominated in the preceiding Commission formerlie had and
that the eldest sones of all Baronettis might be knyghted being of
perfite aige of 21 yeirs whensoever they shall desyre the same
according to ther patents under our greit seall give power to yow or
our Chancellour thar for the tyme being to doe the same both for
frieing ws from trouble and saveing them from charges which ther
repairing thither for that purpois might procure Our pleasur is
that yow caus renew and expeid the said Commission under our great
seall as said is And in the meane tyme that yow knyght the eldest
sones of all and everie ane of such Baronettis who being of 21 yeres
of aige shall desyre the same without putting of them to aney
charges or expenssis For doeing whairof, &c. So we bid, &c.
Whythall 24 March 1626.'

On the 30th March 1626, the following Royal Proclamation was issued from Holyrood :—

'Apud Halyrudhous penultimo Martii 1626.
'Forsamekle as our Soverane Lordis umquhile darrest Father of
blissed and famous memorie out of his princelie and tender regaird
of the honnour and credite of this his ancient kingdome of Scotland
And for the better encourageing of the gentrie of the said kingdome
In imitation of the verteous projectis and enterprises of others to

undertak the Plantatioun of New Scotland in America determined
with advise of the Lordis of his privie Counsell the creating of ane
new heretable title of dignitie within the said kingdome callit Knight
Barronet and to confer the same upoun suche personis of goode
parentage meanis and qualitie as wald be undertakeris in the said
Plantatioun   And of this his Royall and princelie resolution
Importing so far the honnour and credite of the Kingdome publicatioun and intimatioun wes maid be opin proclamatioun with all
solempnitie requisite to the intent those of the best not knawing the
same might haif had time first to begin and to haif bene preferrit to
otheris   And then thrugh thair awne default or negligence the
want of the said honnour to haif bene imputt to thameselffis   Like
as a competent tyme wes appoyntit and assignit be the saidis Lordis
unto thame for that effect whairthrow they might the more advisedlie
haif resolved thairin   And oure Souerane Lord following his said
darrest Fatheris resolutionis in this poynt causit not onlie renew the
said Proclamatioun   Bot for the ease of his Ma^s subjectis and
saulfing of thame from neidles and unnecessair travell chairgeis and
expenssis grantit ane commissioun under his Grite Seale whairby the
saidis Knightis Barronettis might be created and thair patentis exped
in this kingdome   Like as accordinglie sundrie Gentlemen of the
best sort embraced the conditioun of the Plantatioun wer admittit to
the said dignitie of Barronet and no question or objection wes moved
aganis the same till the worke wes brought to a perfectioun then
some of the gentrie repynning at the precedencie done to thir
Barronettis whilk proceidit upon thair awin sleughe and negligence
in not tymous imbraceing the conditionis of the said Plantatioun
They maid some publick oppositioun aganis the precedencie done to
thir Barronettis and so did what in thame lay to haif hinderit the
Plantatioun foirsaid, whairof informatioun being maid to his Matie
and his Matie considdering the goode and necessar groundis whairby
first his said darrest Father and then himself wer moved to creat the
dignitie and ordour foirsaid of Barronettis and his Matie continewing
in a firme and constant purpois and resolutioun that the worke
foirsaid sall yett go fordward and no hindrance maid thairunto
Thairfore his Matie with advyse of the Lordis of his Secreit Counsell

Ordanis letters to be direct chargeing Officieris of armes to pas to
the Mercat Croce of Edinburgh and otheris places neidfull and thair
be opin publicatioun mak said publicatioun and intimatioun of his
Ma^s royall will and pleasur that the course so advysedlie prescryved
be his Matie to the effect foirsaid salbe yitt followit oute   And
thairfore to wairne all and sundrie the gentric of this kingdome
That thay either procure the said dignitie for thameselffis   Or not
repyne at otheris for doing of the same   And to command, charge
and inhibite all and sindrie his Ma^s leiges and subjects that nane
of thame presoome nor tak upoun hand to wrong the saidis Knightis
Barronettis in ony of thair priviledgeis nor to doe nor attempt ony
thing contrair to thair grantis and patentis Certifieing thame that
sall failzie or doe in the contrair   That thay salbe punist as contempnaris of his Matie inclination and disturbaris of the publick
peace.

'[Followis His Majesties Missive for Warrand of the Act above
writtin.]

'Right trustie and welbeloved Councellour, &c.   (See *supra*,
p. 144.)

'So We bid you farewell Frome our Courte at Whythall the
12 of Februar 1626.'

It was only natural that the Heralds and other Officials
should expect the payment to them of fees by the newly
created Baronets; but Charles i., on having the matter
brought to his attention, and having made inquiry of the
practice prevailing in England, directed that no fees should
be demanded, although he raised no objection to their being
voluntarily tendered.

'[CHARLES R.]

'Right, &c.   Haveing considered your letter concerning the fees
that ar clamed from the knyght Barronets thogh at the first it did
appear unto ws that none could justlie challenge fees of them by
vertew of any grant that was gevin befor that ordour was erected

yet befoir we would resolve what was to be done heirin we caused
enquyre of the cheff heraulds and other officers within this our
kingdome wher the said dignitie of Barronet was first instituted by
our late dear Father   And doe find that the baronetts ar bund to
pay no feyis nor did pay ever any thing at all save that which they
did voluntarlie to the heraulds of whom they had present use   And
therfor sieing ther creation within that our kingdome is for so good
a caus wherby a Colony is making readie for setting furth this
next spring to begin a work that may tend so much to the honour
and benefite of that kingdome we would have them everie way to be
encouraged and not as we wryt befoir putt to neidles charges and
our pleasur is that none as Baronetts to be made be bund to pay
feys bot what they shalbe pleased to doe out of ther owin discretion
to the heraulds or to any such officiers of whom they shall have use
And as for ther eldest sones whensoever any of them is cum to
perfyte aige and desyrs to be knighted let them pay the feyis allowed
hertofor to be payed by other knights   For doeing whereof We, &c.
Oatlandis 28 July 1626.'

'KNIGHTIS BARONNETTIS AND THE HERAULDIS.

'Apud Halyrudhous vigesimo Septembris 1626.

'The whilk day the Letter underwritten signed be the Kingis
Matie conteneing a declaration of his Royall Will and pleasure anent
the fees acclamed be the Herauldis and otheris from the Knyghtis
Barronettis and thair eldest sones being presentit to the Lordis of
Secreit Counsell and red in an audience   They allowit of his Maties
will and pleasure thairanent   And Sir Jerome Lindsay knight Lyon
King at armes being callit upon and he compeirand personalie and
his Ma^s will and pleasure in this matter being intimat unto him he
with all humble and deutifull respect promeist that obedience suld be
given thairanent.   Of the whilk Letter the tennour followis

'Charles R.

'Right trustie, etc. (See *supra*, p. 173.)

'And so We bid you farewell From our Courte at Oatlandis the
28 of Julij 1626.'

In 1628, Sir William Alexander obtained an additional

grant from Charles I. of a very extensive district in Canada, on both sides of the river St. Lawrence, with all the rights of property, powers, and privileges which had been granted and confirmed to him, his heirs and assignees, in Nova Scotia. In the preamble of Charles I.'s Charter of 2nd February 1628, granting Canada to Sir William Alexander, it is stated that his Majesty was perfectly mindful of his 'having sustained great charges and expenses in his various undertakings in the providing of ships, engines of war, ordinance and munitions in the conducting of Colonies; as also in exploring, settling, and taking possession of the country,'—and 'for exciring the more earnest resolutions of the said Sir William Alexander, his heirs and assignees, portioners and associates, to further progress in so great an enterprise,' he had Canada added to his grants. Thus showing the high sense and satisfaction entertained by Charles I. and his Government of the progress made by Sir William Alexander in colonising Nova Scotia.

In the succeeding year Charles I. addressed the following letters, both bearing date the 17th November 1629:—

'TO THE CONTRACTERS FOR BARRONETTS.

'[CHARLES R.]

'Right, etc. Whareas wee understand that out of your regard to our service, and the honor of that our antient kingdome, for fothering the plantatione of New Scotland, soe, oftentimes recommendit by our late dear Father, and by our selff, you have agreet with our trustie, etc. Sir Williame Alexander, oure secretarie for Scotland, for advancing great soumes of money for that purpos, taking the benefitt that may arrise by the erectione of Barronettis of the number granted vnto him, as yet to be made for your releef, Wee do heartlie thank you for the same, and doe accept it as a most singulare service done unto ws, wishing you to proceed with confidence and diligence, that the nixt supplie may go out in time, ffor wee wilbe werie sorie and loath to sie you suffer for soe generous ane actione, which may tend soe much to our honour, and the good of that our kingdome; and for your better encouragement, and more speedie repayment, whersoever any persone of qualitie fitt for the dignitie of Barronet hath any particulare favor to crave of ws, wee will and allow yow, according to the severall charge that any of yow hath from ws, to require them first to accept of the said dignitie, according to the conditiones formerlie condiscendit upon, with others which shall mak ws the more willing to gratiefie them, ffor wee desire much to have that work brought to perfectione. Soe willing that this our letter be recorded in the books of our Counsell and Exchecq^r, We, &c. Whitehall, the 17 No^v 1629.'

'To the Counsell.

'[Charles R.]

'Right trustie and right well-beloued Cousin and Counsellour, right trustie and well-beloued Cousins and Counsellouris, and right trustie and well-beloued Counsellouris, We Greete you well.

'Whareas, upon good consideration, and for the better advancement of the plantatione of New Scotland, which may much import the good of our service, and the honor and benefeitt of that our ancient kingdome, oure royall Father did intend, and we since have erected the order and titill of Baronet, in our said ancient Kingdome, which wee have since estabillished, and conferred the same upon divers gentlemen of good qualitie; and sieing our trustie and weilbeloued counsellor Sir Williame Alexander knight, our principall secretarie of that our ancient kingdome of Scotland, and our Leiwetennant of New Scotland, whoe these many yeirs bygone has been at great charges for the discoverie thareof, hath now in end setled a Colonie thare, where his sone, Sir Williame, is now resident; and we being most willing to afford all possible means of encouragement that convenientlie wee can to the Barronettis of that our ancient kingdome, for the furtherance of soe good a wark, and to the effect they may be honored, and have place in all respectis, according to their patents from ws, we have been pleased to authorise and allow, as be theis presents for ws and our successors we authorise and allow, the said Lewetennent and Baronettis, and everie one of them, and thare heirs male, to weare and carry about their neckis in all time coming, ane orange tauney-silk ribbane, whairon shall hing pendant in a scutchion argent a saltoire azeuer, thairon ane inscutcheeine of the armes of Scotland, with ane imperiall croune above the scutchone, and incircled with this motto, FAX MENTIS HONESTÆ GLORIA: Which cognoissance oure said present Leivetennent shall deliver now to them from ws, that they may be the better knowen and distinguished from other persones: And that none pretend ignorance of the respect due unto them, Oure pleasure therefore is, that, by oppen proclamatione at the markett crosse of Edinburgh, and all other head borrows of our kingdome, and such other places as you shall think necessarie, you caus intimat our Royal pleasor and intentione herin to all our subjectis: And if any persone, out of neglect or contempt, shall presume to tak place or precedence of the said barronnettis, thare wiffes or childring, which is due unto them by thare Patents, or to wear thare cognoissance, wee will that, upon notice thareof given to you, you caus punish such offendars, by prisoning and fyning of them, as you shall think fitting, that others may be terriefied from attempting the like: And We ordane that, from tyme to tyme, as occasione of granting and renewing thair patents, or thair heirs succeiding to the said dignitie, shall offer, That the said poware to them to carie the said ribbine, and cognoissance, shalbe tharein particularlie granted and inserted; And Wee likewayis ordaine these presents to be insert and registrat in the books of our Counsell and Excheq^r, and that you caus registrat the same in the books of the Lyone King at armes, and heraulds, thare to remain ad futurum rei memoriam; and that all parties having entres [interest] may have autentick copies and extractis thareof: And for your soe doing, These our lettres shalbe unto you, and everie one of you, from tyme to tyme your sufficient warrant and discharge in that behalf. Given at our Court of Whythall, the sevinteinthe of November 1629.

M

'To our right trustie and right well-beloued cousin and counsellour ; to our right well-beloued cousins and counsellouris ; to our
right trustie and well-beloued counsellouris ; and trustie and well-
beloued counsellouris, the Viscount of Dupleine, our Chanceilor of
Scotland, the Earle of Monteith, the President, and to the remanent
Earls, Lords, and otheris of our Privie Counsell of our said kingdome.'

The preceding letter was presented to the Privy Council
of Scotland on the 24th December 1629, who thereupon
framed the following Act:—

'ACT ANENT THE COGNOISSANCE OF THE KNIGHT BARONNETS.

'Apud Halyrudhous 24 die mensis Decembris 1629.

'THE whilk day the missive underwrittin signed be the Kingis
Matie being presented to the Lords of Secreit Counsell and read in
thair audience   The saids Lords according to the directioun of the
said missive Ordanes the same to be insert and registrat in the Bookes
of Privie Counsell and Exchecker   And siclyke thay ordaned the
same to be registrat in the Bookes of the Lyoun King at Armes
and Heraulds thairin to remaine *ad futuram rei memoriam*   And that
all parteis having interesse may have authentick copeis and extracts
thairof.   Of the whilk missive the tennour followes.

'CHARLES R.
'Right trustie and right &c.   (See *supra*, p. 176.)
Whitehall, the 17 of November 1629.'

In February 1630, Baronets and others sent out a fleet of
fourteen ships, furnished with men, women, children, and
all necessaries, to commence a Colony, which they did at
Port Royal, now called Annapolis.   The Estates of Scotland, on the 31st July 1630, ratified and confirmed the
rights and privileges of the Nova Scotia Baronets, having
'dulie considered the benefit arising to the Kingdom by the

accession of New Scotland, and the successful Plantation alreadie made there by the Baronets.'

On the 31st July 1630, the Charters of James I. and Charles I. erecting the Baronets of Scotland and Nova Scotia, and all the acts and proceedings of the Privy Council thereanent, were approved and confirmed by the Parliament of Scotland. The following is a copy of the Act :—

'Apud Halyrudhous, ultimo die mensis Julij, 1630.

'The Estates presentlie conveened, all in one voice, ratifies, allowes, approves, and confirmes the Dignitie and Order of Knight Barounets, erected be his Matie, and his lait deere Father of blessed memorie, and confered by thame upon sindrie Gentlemen of good qualitie, for thair better encouragement and retributioun of thair undertakings in the Plantatioun of New Scotland ; with all the acts of Secreit Counsell and proclamatiouns following thairupon, made for maintening of the said dignitie, place, and precedencie thairof, and ordains the same dignitie place and precedence dew thairto, to continew and stand in force in all tyme comming ; and that intimatioun be made heirof to all His Ma^{teis} leiges be opin proclamatioun at the mercat croce of Edinburgh, and other places neidfull.

'The Estaites presentlie conveened, having dewlie considderit the benefite arysing to this Kingdome by the accessioun of New Scotland, and of the successfull plantatioun alreadie made there by the gentlemen undertakers of the same. In regarde whairof, and that the saids lands and territoreis of New Scotland, ar by the patent thairof made in favours of Sr Williame Alexander of Menstric Knight His Ma^{teis} Secretarie, annexed to the Crowne Thairfoir the saids Estaits all in one voice hes concluded and agreed, that His Matie sall be petitioned to maintcane his right of New Scotland And to protect his subjects undertakers of the said plantatioun in the peaceable possessioun of the same As being a purpose highlie concerning his Ma^{teis} honnour and the good and credite of this his ancient Kingdome.'

On the 5th May 1631, Charles I. issued the following :—

'SIGNATURE OF COMMISSION FOR THE BARRONETTS

'These conteyne ane Ratificatioun of the two former Commissions of Barronetts and all Patents and Infeftments granted conforme thairto, preceiding the date heirof, with ane new commission gevin power to certane Commissioners above nominat or any fyve of them to receave resignation of lands lyand within the countrie of New Scotland, upoun the resignation of your Ma^{teis} Secretarie Sir William Alexander Lieutennent of Nova Scotia ; and to grant infeftments thairupon of the saids lands to the persones in whois favours the samyne is made, togidder with the title and dignitie of Barronett : And also conteynes ane Ratificatioun of the Seall and Armes of New Scotland, with power to the saids Commissioners, with advyse of the said Sir William Alexander, to change the samyne : And last, conteynes ane Ratificatioun of ane warrant gevin by your Matie to the saids Barronetts for bearing and wearing of ane badge, and cognoscence, with a new warrant for bearing and wearing of the samyne in maner above specifeit, dischergeing the use of the saids former commissions efter the date heirof; and this to indure without revocation ay and whill the full number of ANE HUNDRETH AND FYFTIE BARRONETTS be made and compleit. Greenwich, 5 May 1631.'

The Lords of the Privy Council of Scotland subsequently received the following letter from the King, dated at Greenwich, the 12th July 1631 :—

'[CHARLES R.]

'Right trustie and right weilbelouit Cousine and Counsellour, &c. Seeing we have sene, by a letter from yow, the ordour of Barronets erected by our late dear Father and ws, for furthering the Plantation of New Scotland, was approved by the whole Estats of our kingdome at the last Convention ; And that we understand, both by ther reports that cam from thence, and by the sensible consideration and notice taken therof by our nyghbour cuntreyis, how well that work is begun, Our right trustie and weilbeloued counsellour Sir

William Alexander our Leivtennent ther haveing fullie performed
what was expected from him, for the benefite which was intendit for
him by these Barronets, being verie desyreous that he should not
suffer therin, bot that both he and others may be encouraged to prosecute the good begining that is made, as we hartelie thank all such
as hath contribute ther ayde by contracting with him for advanceing
of the said work alreadie, Our pleasur is that yow seriouslie consider,
either amongst yow all, or by a Committie of such as ar best
affectionat towards that work, how it may be best brought to perfection ; for we are so far (whatever contraversie be about it) from
quyting our title to New Scotland and Canada, that we wilbe verie
carefull to manteane all our good subjects who doe plant themselffis
there, and lett none of the Barronets anyway be prejudged in the
honour and priviledges conteynit in ther Patents by punisching of
all that dare to presume to wrong them therin, that others may be
encouraged to tak the lyk course, as the more acceptable unto ws
and the nearer to a title of Nobilitie, wherunto that of Barronets
is the next degrie : And if the said Sir William as our Livetennent
of New Scotland shall convene the Barronetts to consult togidder
concerneing that Plantation, we herby authorise him, and will yow
to authorise him as far as is requisit for that effect, willing that
Proclamatioun be made of what we have signifeid, or of what yow
shall determine for furthering that work, wherof we recomend the
care to yow, as a matter importing speciallie our honor and the good
of that our ancient kingdome. From our Mannour at Greenwiche,
the twelfe day of Julij 1631.'

On the 28th of the same month the following Proclamation was issued from Holyrood :—

'Apud Halyrudhous, 28 Julij 1631.

'Forsamekle as the order of Barronnets erected by our Soucrane
Lord and his lait dear Father of blessed memorie for fordering
the plantatioun of New Scotland wes approvin be the whole Estaits
of this kingdome at the last Conventioun and his Majesties understanding by many reports that come from hence, and by the sensible

consideratioun and notice taken thairof by nighbour countreis how weill that work is begun, His Majesteis right traist cousine and counseller the Viscount of Stirline his Majesteis lieutennent there haueing fullie performed what wes expected from him for the benefite whilk wes intendit by these Baronnets : And His Majestie being verie desirous that he sould not suffer thairin but that both he and others may be encouraged to prosecute the good beginning that is made His Majestie for this effect is so farre (what ever con-traversie be anent it) from quitting his title to New Scotland and Cannada that his Majestie will be verie carefull to mainteane all his good subjects who doe plant thameselfes there and will lett none of the Baronnets be anie waye prejudged in the honnour and priviledges conteanit in thair Patents, bot will punische all that darre presoome to wrong thame thairin, for encourageing of others to take the lyke course as the more acceptable to his Majestie and the nearer to ane title of nobilitie whairunto that of Baronnet is the nixt degree And Ordanis letters to be direct chargeing officiaris of armes to pas and make publicatioun heirof be opin proclamatioun at the Mercat Croces of the heid Burrowes of this kingdome and uther places neidfull, quhairthrow nane pretend ignorance of the same.'

At a meeting of the Privy Council held at Holyrood the same day, the following Commission was granted :—

'COMMISSION ANENT BARONNETS

'The Lords of Secreit Counsell for the better furderance and advancement of the plantatioun of New Scotland, Gives and grants Commission be thir presents to Thomas Erle of Hadinton Lord Privie Seale, George Erle of Wintoun, Alexander Erle of Lin-lithgow, Robert Lord Melvill, Johne Lord Tracquair, Archibald Lord Naper, David Bishop of Rosse, Sir Archibald Achesone Secretarie, Sir Johne Hamiltoun of Magdalens Clerk of Register, Sir Thomas Hope of Craighall knicht baronnet Advocat, Sir George Elphinstoun Justice Clerk, Sir Johne Scot of Scotistarvet, and Sir James Baillie, Or anie fyve of thame without excluding of anie others of the Counsell who sall be present To conveene and meit with William Viscount of Stirline and the Knights Baronnets at such tyme and place as the said Viscount of Stirline sall appoint And to conferre with thame upoun the best meanis for the furdering of the said Plantatioun   And to make and sett doun Overtures thereanent   And to present and exhibit thame to the saids Lords to the intent they may allowe or rectifie the same as they sall thinke expedient

'Followes his Majesteis missive for Warrand of the Act above writtin.

'CHARLES R.

'Right trustie and weilbelouit Cousine and Counsellour . . . (See *supra*, p. 180.)

'From our Mannour at Greenwiche, the twelf day of Julij 1631.'

On the 14th of June 1632, Charles addressed a letter to the Lord Advocate requiring him 'to draw up a sufficient warrant for our hand, to pass under our great seal, to our right trustie the Viscount of Stirling, to go on with the work of planting Nova Scotia'; and on the 15th of August following he addressed a letter to the Baronets of Scotland, both of which letters show his anxiety that the Baronetage of Scotland and Nova Scotia should realise the objects for which it was created.

On the 24th of April 1633, the King wrote to the Lords of Council signifying his pleasure that, whensoever any of his subjects of England or Ireland should take lands holden of him in New Scotland, their Patents should be passed at as easy a rate as if they were natural subjects of Scotland, and that there was no truth in the report that he had totally lost his intention of planting in Nova Scotia, and that he intended to prosecute the work, and complete the intended number of Knight Baronets.

The King being in Scotland the following June, the Parliament on the 28th of that month passed an Act containing the following clauses:—

'Our Sovereign Lord, and Estates of this present Parliament, ratifies and approves the Act of General Convention of Estates at Holy-rude House the sixth day of July, in the year of God 1630, whereby the said Estates have ratified and approved of the Dignities and Order of Knight Baronet, with all the acts of Secret Council and proclamations following thereupon, made for the maintaining of the said dignity, place, and precedencie thereof.'

'And His Majestie and Estates aforesaid will, statute, and ordain, that the said letters patent charters and infeftments, and the said dignity, title, and order of Baronets, and all letters patent and infeftments of land and dignities granted therewith to any persons whatsoever, shall stand and continue in force, with all liberties, privileges, and precedencies thereof, according to the tenor of the same, and in as ample manner as if the bodies of the said letters patent, infeftments, &c., were herein particularly ingrost and exprest, and ordain intimation to be made thereof by open proclamation to all his Majestie's liegis at the Market Crosse of Edinburgh, and other places needful, that none pretend ignorance thereof.'

The effect of this Act was to give to the Charters of the Stirling family and of the Baronets the force and effects of Acts of Parliament, and by the Charters referred to in the statute the province of Nova Scotia was annexed, and incorporated with the kingdom of Scotland, and made an integral part and portion of that realm.

On the 14th September 1633, Charles issued a Commission for the purpose of passing infeftments to lands in Nova Scotia, which Commission the Lords of the Privy Council took upon them on the 15th of February following.

At this sederunt the Council ordered letters to be issued

charging officers of arms to pass and make publication by
open proclamation at the market crosses of the head burghs
of the kingdom and other places, an Act embodying the
letters of Charles I. already quoted, expressing his Majesty's
intention of continuing the plantation of Nova Scotia, and
to encourage it by all lawful helps thereunto, as well by
completing the intended number of Baronets as otherways.

From this date until Charles's death in 1649, the creation
of Baronets continued; and during his reign, from the erection of the dignity in Scotland in 1625 until his death, one
hundred and twenty-two Baronets appear to have been
created, of whom about one hundred and eleven had grants
of 16,000 acres each, which were erected into free baronies
and regalities.

Owing to the state of the Stirling family, and the civil
war, the Baronets of Nova Scotia created from 1638 to the
Union in 1707 did not receive the stipulated territorial
qualification of 16,000 acres of land with their titles. As,
however, by the original arrangement no Baronet was to be
created in Scotland except for the purpose of planting Nova
Scotia, and as the Commission to the Privy Council authorised the creation of a hundred and fifty Baronets, the
members created after 1638 were equally entitled to have
grants of land with those created before that date.

The Earl of Stirling, on the 29th January 1640, executed
a deed constituting two Writers to the Signet his procurators
for receiving the composition and sums of money for dis-
posing and resigning certain proportions of land in Nova
Scotia, and procuring to sundry persons the infeftments of

the same from his Majesty, with the honour and dignity of Baronet. This was the last act of the Earl of Stirling with reference to the creation of Baronets, he dying shortly afterwards.

There is evidence in existence that at this period Long Island, or, as it was then called, Stirling Island, was a flourishing colony; and from that time to the Union a series of official records exists, showing that the rights of the Stirling family and of the Baronets were allowed. In 1656, Sir Charles St. Estienne, created a Baronet 30th November 1629, who had built a fort called La Tour on the east side of the St. John's river, and had made good his occupation for several years against the French, came over to England, and made good his title under Sir William Alexander, when his right was restored by Oliver Cromwell.

In 1691, William and Mary granted a Charter to the colony of Massachusetts Bay, in which Acadia, or Nova Scotia, is mentioned, and reservation made of the lands and hereditaments of any person or persons, bodies public or corporate, to whom, by virtue of any previous grant, they might belong; and seven years later, in 1698, the Charter of Sir Robert Gordon, the premier Baronet, was officially recognised and confirmed by William III. by the following sign-manual :—

'These contain your Majesty's warrant for a Charter to be passed under your Great Seal of Scotland, in favour of Sir William Gordon, of the title and dignity of Baronet, and the lands and barony of Gordon in Nova Scotia, in America, annexed thereto.'

The Great Seal Record of Scotland accordingly bears that

upon the 27th June 1698 a Charter of Novodamus passed upon this Royal Warrant, and infeftment was taken as authorised by the Charter at the Castle of Edinburgh, and duly recorded in the Register of Sasines. Various other Baronets resigned their grants and titles into the hands of the Crown during the same reign, and procured patents of Novodamus.

By the Act of Union in 1707, nine years after the date of this Charter of Novodamus to the premier Baronet, it is stipulated, declared, and irrevocably settled, that 'whilst the laws which concern public right, policy, and civil government may be made the same throughout the United Kingdom of Scotland and England, no alteration shall be made in the laws which concern private rights, except for the evident utility of the subjects within Scotland.'

Two years after the Union there was a restitution by the French of the possessions of the Scottish Crown, but whether the Baronets took any steps at the time for the recovery of their estates in Nova Scotia does not appear.

CHAPTER V

THE covenanted privileges conferred on the Baronetage are :—

Under the first Letters Patent :—

    I. The dignity, state, and degree of Baronet.

    II. Precedency for themselves, their wives, children, and others.

    III. Style and title.

    IV. Only two hundred Baronets of England to exist at one time.

    V. No degree, order, name, title, dignity, or state under the degree, dignity, or state of Barons of England to be ever created which would or could be superior or equal to the degree and dignity of Baronet.

    VI. If any Baronet of the said two hundred should die without heirs male, no other Baronets of England to be created, but the number of two hundred to diminish accordingly.

Under the second Letters Patent the privileges are :—

    VII. A newly defined precedency.

188

VIII. A repetition of privilege No. V., with the addition
that no person or persons beneath the degree of
Lords of Parliament of England, except the
persons enumerated, should ever have place, precedence, or pre-eminence over, or equality with,
Baronets ; and that no person or persons should
have or take place between Baronets and the
younger sons of Viscounts and Barons [hereditary,
of course].

And, as an ampliation of the King's favour—

IX. Rights of knighthood for Baronets and their eldest
sons.

X. Addition of the Arms of Ulster in armorial bearings.

XI. A place near the Royal Standard in battle.

XII. A funeral ceremony ' meane betwixt that of a Baron
and a Knight.'

XIII. The right for all Baronets, then and in future, to
have Letters Patent under the Great Seal of
England to the effect of the former and present
Letters Patent of creation.

The Third Letters Patent, ratifying and confirming, with
more particularity, the above privileges, adds :—

XIV. The Degree of Baronet to be, and be reputed to be,
a Degree of Dignity Hereditary, mean in place
betwixt the Degree of a Baron and the Degree of
a Knight.

XV. Eldest sons of Baronets to precede eldest sons of all
Knights, whatever their Order ; with similar
provisions respecting other sons, etc.

XVI. Doubts or questions arising in future concerning precedency, privilege, or other matter touching Baronets to be decided according to the rules, custom, and laws of other Degrees of Dignity Hereditary.

The Baronets of Ireland enjoy all the rights and privileges confirmed in the Letters Patent last recited ; and the same were continued to Baronets of Great Britain and to Baronets of the United Kingdom.

The Baronets of Scotland enjoy the same privileges, except the Ulster augmentation ; and the following were conferred upon them in addition, all being confirmed by the Scottish Parliament :—

XVII. Grants of land in Nova Scotia, with plenary baronial rights and jurisdiction, and legislative powers, in that plantation.

XVIII. Precedency above lesser Barons in Scotland.

XIX. Addition of the Arms of Nova Scotia in armorial bearings.

XX. Power to Members thereof to sit and vote by deputy in the Scottish Parliament when absent from the Kingdom.

And, by virtue of King Charles's further Ordinance, dated 17th November 1629—

XXI. Right to wear about the neck the badge of Nova Scotia, suspended by an orange-tawny ribbon.

Having enumerated the privileges in chronological order, they can now be referred to at greater length.

1. *The dignity, state, and degree of Baronet.*—The preceding chapters have dealt very fully with this subject; but the following memorandum, preserved in the Public Record Office, is interesting (*State Papers, Domestic Series, James I.,* vol. lxxxix. No. 6) :—

'BARONET. AR. A HAND *g.*

'Baronet is a new created & distinct title of Knighthood under K. James, who for certaine disbursments towards the Plantacion in Ulster in Ireland, created divers into this dignity & made it hereditary. The particulars of the Patent shall instruct you. Ordinamus (saith the King) ereximus Constituimus et creavimus quendam statum gradum dignitatem nomen et Titulum Baronetti (Anglice of a Baronet) infra hoc regnum Anglie perpetuis temporibus duraturum, & then gives the title to the Created, to him and his heires male of his body.

' And that he shall have precedency in all writing sessions and salutacions before all Kn^{ts} as well of the Bath as Kn^{ts} Bachelors, and also before all Bannerets created or hereafter to be created excepted only illis Militibus Banerettis quos sub vexillis regiis in exercitu Regali, in aperto bello, et ipso Rege personaliter presente explicatis, et non aliter creari contigeret. And that their wivis and eldest sones respectively have precedence.

' That they should be impleaded and sue by the adicion of Baronet.

' That to the name of them and the heirs males of ther bodies in sermone Anglicano et omnibus scriptis Anglicanis preponatur hac adicio viz. Anglice Sir and that their wives have the titles of Lady Madam & Dame : with a grant quod nec nos nec heredes vel successores nostri de cætero in posterum erigemus, ordinabimus constituemus aut creabimus infra hoc Regnum nostrum Angliæ, aliquem alium gradum ordinem nomen titulum dignitatem sive statum sub vel infra gradum dignitatem sive statum Baronum hujus Regni nostri Angliæ, qui erit vel esse possit superior vel æqualis gradui vel dignitati Baronettorum predictorum ; and further that after the proposed number of 2 hundred made, quod tunc nos non creabimus vel preficiemus aliquas aliam personum vel personas in

Baronettum vel Baronettes regni nostri Anglie, sed quod numerus dictorum 200 Baronettorum ea racione de tempore in tempus minuetur et in minorem numerum cedet et redigetur.

'Upon point of precedency a great controversy grew afterwards between these new Baronets and the yonger sonnes of Viscounts and Barons, and after the Councell on both parts 3 severall dayes at larg heard, by his Matie in person it was decreed adjudged and established that the yonger sons of Viscounts & Barons shall take place and precedency before all Baronets. And that such Banerets as shal be made by the K. Matie his heirs and successors under his or their Standard, displayed in an Army Royall in open warre, and the K. personally present for the terme of the lives of such Banerets and no longer (according to the most auntient institucion) shall for ever hereafter in all places and upon all occasions take place & precedence as well before all other Banerets whatsoever (no respect being had to the tyme and priority of their Creacion) as likewyse before the yonger Sonnes of Viscounts and Barons and also before all Baronets. And againe that the yonger sonnes of Viscounts and Barons and allso all Baronettes shall in all places and upon all occasions take place and precedence before all Banerettes whatsoever other then such as shal be made by the K. himself his heires and successors in person and in such speciall case manner and forme as aforesaid. And that the Kn^{ts} of the most ho^{ble} order of the Garter, the privy Councellors of his Matie his heires and Successors, the Master of the Court of Wards and Liveries: the Chancellor and Under Treasurer of the Exchequer, Chancellor of the Duchy, the Chief Justice of the Kings Bench, M^{r} of the Rolls, Chief Justice of the Common Pleas, the Chief Baron of the Exchequer, and all other the Judges and Barons of the degree of the Coife of the said Court now and for the tyme being shall by reason of their ho^{ble} order and imployment of State and Justice have place and precedence in all places and upon all occasions before the yonger Sonnes of Viscounts and Barons, and before all Baronettes, any custome use ordinance or other thing to the contrary notwithstanding.

'And that no other person or persons whatsoever under the degree of Barons of the Parliament shall take place before the said

Baronets, except only the eldest sonnes of Viscounts and Barons and others of higher degree whereof no question ever was or can be made.

'And in the same decree his Matie further granted to Kn^t the present Baronets, which were then no Kn^{ts}, and that the heirs male of the body of every Baronet hereafter when he shal be of 21 yeares upon knowledge thereof given to the Lo. Chamberlyn of the howshould or Vice chamberleyn for the tyme being or in their absence to any other officer attending upon his Ma^{tes} person shal be knighted by his Matie his heirs and successors.

'And that the Baronettes and their descendants shall and may beare either in a Canton in their Armes or in an Inscothean at their election, the armes of Ulster, that is Argent a hand gueules.

'And also that the Baronettes for the tyme being and the heires males of their bodies shall have places in the armies of the K's Ma^{ty} his heirs and successors in the gross neer about the Royal Standard of the K. his heires & successors for the defence of the same.

'And lastly that the Baronets and the heirs males of their bodyes shall have 2 assistants of the body to support the Pall, a principall mourner and 4 assistants to him at their funeralles, being the meane betwixt a Baron & a Kn^t.'

In further support of the assertion that Baronets are members of the Nobiles Majores, the following particulars taken from an old writer show the similarity between Baronets and Barons, Lords of Parliament :—

'(1) In the manner of their creation, which is by the King himself, by letters patent under the great seal of the kingdom and in much the same form and words as barons are, with a mero motu speciali gratia, &c., and an eo quod expressa mentio de vero valore annuo, vel de certitudine præmissorum.

'(2) It is likewise, as Lord Coke observes, a local title.

'(3) It is hereditary, which no degree below a parliamentary baron but this is.

'(4) As the sons and their wives, and the daughters of such

N

barons have an established rank and precedency, so likewise have all the sons and their wives, and the daughters of baronets.

'(5) No title or dignity between Barons, lords of parliament of England, and baronets is ever to be created which shall be higher, or equal to Baronets.

'(6) The place of baronets of a foreign kingdom is regulated in the same manner as that of the greater nobility or Nobiles Majores, and not as that of Knights, who have in all countries place and pre- cedency according to their priority of Knighthood, whereas the greater nobility, be they ever so ancient, shall go below, as puisnes, those of the same degree in the nation in which they may be resident, as barons of Ireland residing in England, give place to all of the same degree of this Kingdom; so in Scotland, before the Union, the Scottish barons, dukes etc., took place before the English, and *vice versa* in conformity to the law of nations. Thus all baronets of Great Britain here take place of Baronets of Ireland or Nova Scotia, and were so placed in the cavalcade of the late King George 1. an incontestable proof of their being considered not as a species of Knighthood, but of the nobiles majores, or, as some have styled them, a middle degree of nobility.

'And thus from the manifest likeness this order bore, and the nearness of its situation unto barons, lords of parliament, it was with much propriety and significancy denominated and styled Baronettus, *i.e.* baro minor, a lesser or inferior baron: But not because, as some have fancied, they take place next to barons' younger sons; a grosser error surely than that of those who have esteemed them Knights, and so called them as Knights baronets, which is sufficiently refuted by this determination alone, which we find in our law books : " That if the heir of a tenant in Knight's service, who was under age at his father's death, and so in ward was made a baronet by the King, it did not discharge such heir from being in ward, or if he were made a knight any more than if he had been made a baron or an earl" (Coke's *Rep.*, par. 12, p. 81). And it is no less clear that between barons' younger sons and baronets (who are here considered as in a distinct degree of men) in respect of their several degrees there is no manner of similitude, the former having by no law any higher name than that of esquire, which is not peculiar or appropriate to them, but common to many others.'

In Selden's *Titles of Honor* is printed a Baron's Patent of James I., passed about the time of the erection of the Baronetage, in which the operative words are the following :—

'Sciatis *igitur* quod nos, *etc. præfatum A. B.* ad statum, gradum, dignitatem *et honorem Baronis B. de C. in Comitatu N.* ereximus præfecimus et creavimus, *ipsumque A. B. Baronem B. de C. prædicto, tenore præsentium* præficimus, constituimus et creamus eidemque A. B. Statum, gradum, dignitatem, *stilum,* titulum, nomen *et honorem Baronis B. de C. etc.* Habendum et tenendum, etc., volentes et per præsentes insuper concedentes, pro nobis hæredibus et successoribus nostris quod prædictus A. B. et heraedes sui masculi prædicti nomen, statum, gradum, stilum, dignitatem, titulum *et honorem* prædictum successive gerant et habeant et eorum quilibet habeat, et gerat *et per nomen Baronis B. de C. vocentur et nuncupentur et quilibet eorum vocetur et nuncupetur,* quodque idem A. B. et heraedes sui masculi prædicti successivé *Barones B. de C.* in omnibus teneantur et ut *Barones* tractentur, *teneantur,* et reputentur, *et eorum quilibet tractetur teneatur, et reputetur,* habeantque teneant, etc.'

[The words not in italics are identically the same with those adopted in the early Patents of the Baronets.]

II. *Precedency for themselves, their wives, children, and others.*—The exact precedency of Baronets as regards Peers and their children and Knights was fixed distinctly by their Patents, and the royal founder's decrees of 1612 and 1616, already set out ; but their precedency in connection with State functionaries was not so easily settled, and has naturally been of gradual growth.

The Patents of the first created Baronets clearly stated

that their precedency was before all Knights as well of the
Bath as of Knights Bachelors, and also before all Knights
Bannerets already created or hereafter to be created, except
those made under the royal standards in open war, the King
himself being personally present.

As a result of the dispute between the younger sons of
the Viscounts and of the Barons on the one hand, and the
Baronets on the other, already referred to, the Decree of
James I., of the 28th May 1612, ordained that the younger
sons of Viscounts and of Barons should take place and precedency before the Baronets, the Decree also ordained that
in addition to Bannerets made by the King, his heirs and
successors, those made by his son, Henry Prince of Wales,
under similar conditions, also Knights of the Garter, and
certain officials by reason of their honourable orders and
employment of State and justice, should have precedence
before the younger sons of Viscounts and of Barons and the
Baronets, any custom, use, ordinance, or other thing to the
contrary notwithstanding.

As the creation of Knights Banneret is now practically
obsolete, and as the honour of election to the Order of the
Garter has not been conferred on any person below the rank
of a Peer since Sir Henry Lee (or Lea) was installed on the
24th May 1597, special mention in this Decree of Knights
Banneret and Knights of the Most Noble Order does not
now concern the Baronetage, whilst for centuries before the
erection of the Degree it had been customary to confer
special precedence on high Judicial, Ecclesiastical, State, and
Court functionaries.

Many of the official positions referred to in this Decree have ceased to exist, but others have been created, to the holders of each of which a special precedence has been assigned, necessitating from time to time a rearrangement of the scale of precedence.   This scale is set out at length, as regards the precedence of the members of the Royal family and of the Peers and gentry of the United Kingdom, in the principal *Peerages* and *Baronetages* published annually, and it has in the past shown Baronets in the place next after the cadets of a Baron's family, where James decided to place them in perpetuity.

The statutes, therefore, 53 Geo. III. c. 24, s. 4, and 5 Vict. c. 5, s. 25, which allowed the Vice-Chancellors of the Court of Chancery to rank before Baronets, infringed the prerogative of the Baronets.   Although they have been repealed, further attempts to interpose new Judicial officers between the Peerage and the Baronetage should be watched and resisted.

According, however, to a well-known legal authority, another not uninteresting question concerning the precedence of Baronets will doubtless occur some day.   In an article in *The Law Magazine and Review* for February 1898, he writes as follows :—

'By the terms of the Letters Patent constituting the older Baronets of England and Great Britain, it is directed that the following Judges shall take precedence of the Order, viz., the Chief Justice of the King's Bench, the Master of the Rolls, the Chief Justice of the Common Pleas, the Chief Baron of the Exchequer, "and all and singular the Judges and Justices of either Bench and the Barons of the Exchequer, of the Degree of the Coif, for the

time being." Of the Degree of the Coif signifies one who has
been created a Serjeant; the Degree of Serjeant, when joined to
the Judicial appointment, being deemed to be entitled by virtue of
its high honour to rank above the Order of Baronets, but only, be
it observed, when those two honourable distinctions are united. The
Judge of the Court of Admiralty, for instance, although a judge of
a superior court, had not the Coif, and therefore always ranked
after, and not before, Baronets.

'In 1873, on the passing of the Supreme Court of Judicature
Act, it was enacted (sect. 8) that no person appointed a Judge of
the High Court of Justice, or of the Court of Appeal, should thenceforth be required to take or to have taken the Degree of Serjeant-
at-Law. The result of this new law is well known. No Judge
has since it has been passed applied for the Coif, and the ancient
Order of Serjeants has practically ceased to exist. For all purposes
of common law and equity, for all purposes of procedure and practice, a Judge without the Coif is as good a Judge as one with the
Coif. It is for social purpose that a difference exists: and umbrage
might properly be taken by a Baronet if not accorded his due
precedence before those Judges who are not of the Coif, on State
occasions, or in the presence of the Sovereign. The present Lord
Chief Justice of England has not the Coif, but independently of
that he takes precedence as a Peer, so his case is not in point. But
Mr. Justice Hawkins is not a peer, nor has he the Coif, and the
same is the case with the other Judges of the Queen's Bench
Division, viz. Justices Mathew, Day, Wills, Grantham, and others
more recently appointed. Nor would it, we submit, be in the
power of Her Majesty to confer the lost pre-eminence on Judges
who have failed to attain the Degree of the Coif; for the Letters
Patent emphatically declare that, "neither we nor our heirs or
successors will hereafter create within our Kingdom of England
any other Degree, Order, Name, Title, Style, Dignity, or State,
nor give or grant place, precedence, or pre-eminence, to any person
under or below the degree, dignity, or state of a Baron of Parliament, who shall be superior or equal to the dignity of a Baronet,
nor shall any person under the degree of a Baron (except those

previously excepted by the Letters Patent) by reason of any constitution, dignity, office, or other thing whatsoever, now or hereafter, have, hold, or enjoy place, precedence, or pre-eminence before
a Baronet."

'The Judicature Acts of 1873 and 1875 have been fertile in
creating new Judicial officers ; but the fact that the Lords of
Appeal in Ordinary are constituted Barons for life, saves the appointment from being *de jure* that which it is *de facto*, viz. a new and
dangerous attack on the precedence of the Order ; for it is, as above
pointed out, prejudicial to the grant of the dignity of a Baronet
that new degrees or titles should be interposed between his Order
and the Peerage.'

Amongst themselves, the Baronets of the five classes of
creation take precedence according to the date of their
respective Patents, as do also their wives and children.

The scale of precedence prevailing since 1612 places the
sons of Baronets as follows :—

Eldest sons of the younger sons of Peers.
Eldest sons of Baronets.
Eldest sons of Knights of the Garter.
Eldest sons of Bannerets not made by the King in person.
Eldest sons of Knights.
Younger sons of Baronets.
Younger sons of Knights.

The younger sons of a deceased Baronet take place of the
younger sons of the present holder of the title.

A protest must here be recorded against the practice of
editors of *Peerages* in placing in their scale of precedence
numerous persons above the eldest sons of Baronets, all of
whom created before December 1827 are entitled to be

created knights, without any proper warrant having been issued giving these persons such precedence.

The sons of Baronets are 'Esquires,' and the eldest sons of such Baronets of Scotland as are also Barons are styled 'Masters' of their family barony.

The wives of Baronets and of their eldest sons have the same 'place and precedency during their lives, next unto, and immediately after that place that is due, and belongeth unto the wives of the younger sons of Viscounts and Barons and to the daughters of such Viscounts and Barons.' A Dowager-Baronetess while a widow has precedence over the living Baronet's wife.

The scale of precedency for ladies hitherto prevailing is therefore as follows :—

Wives of the younger sons of Barons.
Wives of Baronets.
Wives of Bannerets not made by the King in person.
Wives of Knights.
Wives of the eldest sons of the younger sons of Peers.
Daughters of the younger sons of Peers.
Wives of the eldest sons of Baronets.
Daughters of Baronets.
Wives of the eldest sons of Knights of the Garter.
　　　　"　　　　　"　　　　Knights Banneret.
　　　　"　　　　　"　　　　Knights.
Daughters of Knights.
Wives of the younger sons of Baronets.

The daughters of Baronets have each the rank of their

eldest brother, they are therefore ladies by blood ; and if they marry inferior persons, they still retain their rank, it being *character indelebilis.* They take precedence above the wives of Archbishops, Bishops, Judges, and other personages filling high offices in the State.

In 1788 a dispute took place as to the precedency of the daughters of Baronets and the granddaughters of Peers, which was referred to the Earl-Marshal, who decided in favour of the latter in accordance with the above scale of precedency, as recorded in the following letter of the Earl-Marshal and the Report of the College of Arms :—

'Norfolk House,
'25th May 1789.

'My Lord,
'In Obedience to his Majesty's Commands signified to me by your Lordship's Letter of the 20th of June 1788, directing me to take into Consideration a Memorial presented to his Majesty from the Baronets of England and Great Britain, and to report to your Lordship for his Majesty's Information my Opinion upon the Claim stated in the said Memorial, I have considered of the same, and having directed search to be made in the College of Arms for Orders and Precedents relative thereto, I transmit to your Lordship the Report I received from the Kings, Heralds and Pursuivants of Arms.

'I beg the favour of your Lordship to lay the same before his Majesty, and to represent to his Majesty my humble opinion that as the Claim stated in the said Memorial rests solely upon a decision alleged to have been made by his Majesty in 1761, by which such of her Majesty's Maids of Honor as were daughters of Baronets were ranked before such as were granddaughters of Peers, but of which decision there is no official Record, a Patent declaring the Right of Precedence to such of the Parties as his Majesty in his

great Wisdom shall deem intitled to it would be the most effectual
means of obviating all future doubts upon the subject.

'I have the honor to be,

'My Lord,

'Your Lordship's most humble Servant,

'NORFOLK, E. M.

'To the Right Honble Lord Sidney,
  one of his Majesty's principal
  Secretaries of State, &c. &c. &c.'

'To THE MOST NOBLE CHARLES DUKE OF NORFOLK,
  'Earl-Marshal and Hereditary Marshal of England.

'The King's Heralds and Pursuivants of the College of Arms in
Chapter assembled in obedience to your Grace's commands to take
into consideration the Memorial of the Baronets of Great Britain
claiming precedency for their daughters before the granddaughters
of Peers, most respectfully report to your Grace :

'1. That by a Decree made in the 10th year of King James
the First, the younger sons of Viscounts & Barons have precedence
before all Baronets.

'2. That in the patent of every Baronet it is declared "That if
any doubts or Questions as to any place, precedence, privilege, or
other thing touching or concerning the said Baronet and his said
Heirs Male and their Wives, and the first born sons of the Wives,
the younger sons, daughters and wives of the younger sons or any
of them shall hereafter arise which neither by these our Letters
Patent nor by other Letters Patent heretofore made in this behalf,
are determined, such doubts or questions shall be determined and
adjudged by and according to such other Rules Customs and Laws
(as to place, precedence or other things concerning them) as other
Degrees of hereditary Dignity are ordered governed and adjudged."
And they submit to your Grace whether the present Question may
not be determined by another Clause in the same Patent, which
runs thus :—

"And in regard that the said Degree of a Baronet is a Degree
    of hereditary Dignity, the first-born son or Heir-male

apparent and all the rest of the sons and their wives and the daughters of the said Baronet & of his said Heirs-male *respectively* shall have and hold place and precedence before the first-born sons and other sons and their wives and the daughters of all Knights of whatsoever Degree or Order *respectively*. And also before the first-born sons and other sons and their Wives, and the daughters of all persons *respectively* before whom the *fathers* of such first-born sons and sons and daughters by force of these presents ought to have place and precedence."

'From which they infer that the sons and daughters of Baronets are to give place and precedence to the sons and daughters of all persons to whom their fathers give place and precedence.

'That in a Manuscript in the College of Arms intitled " Motives to induce the Knights Citizens and Burgesses of the Commons House of Parliament to petition his Majesty for the revoking and abolishing of the Degree of Baronets lately erected by his Highness' Letters Patent," it is stated as the first and principal Grievance " That Baronets by these Letters Patents are to have precedence before the Descendants from the younger children of Barons, Earls, Dukes, &c."—By which it appears that the *sons and daughters* of Baronets were not at that time considered as intitled to such precedence, for if they were, it would certainly have been so stated as a greater Grievance.

'That at the Coronation of King Chas. ii., Sr. Chas. Stanley, Sr. Francis Fane, and Sr. Henry Fane were ranked according to their blood as *grand-children* of Earls by the Lord High Steward, the Lord High Chamberlain, the Lord High Constable, the Earl-Marshal, and the Lord Chamberlain, above *all* Baronets but having been created Knights of the Bath (whose rank is below that of Baronets) a doubt seems to have arisen as to their place, and therefore the King confirmed to them, their said Rank of Blood by a Warrant under His Royal Sign-Manual, of which a copy is inclosed.

'That in the Tables of precedency transmitted from Garter to Garter, the daughters of Peers' younger sons are placed above the daughters of Baronets, as will appear by the following extract :—

'Wives of Viscounts' younger Sons.

'Wives of Barons' younger Sons.

'Wives of Baronets.

'Wives of Bannerets.

'Wives of Knights of the Bath.

'Wives of Knights Bachelors.

'Wives of the eldest sons of the younger sons of Peers.

'*Daughters* of the younger sons of Peers.

'Wives of the eldest sons of Baronets.

'*Daughters* of Baronets.

'Wives of the eldest sons of Knights.

'Daughters of Knights.

'Wives of Baronets' younger sons.

'From all which the Officers of Arms would think themselves warranted in the opinion, that the daughters of Peers' younger sons should have place and precedence before the Daughters of Baronets.

'But it being alleged in the said Memorial, that in the appointment of the Maids of Honor at the Establishment of her Majesty's Household, this question had received a contrary decision, application was made to Lady Warren (daughter of Sir Cecil Bishopp, Bar^t.), and to Miss Beauclerk (daughter of Lord Henry Beauclerk, a younger son of the Duke of St. Albans), and the following account received in a letter from Lady Warren, viz. :—

"In the year 1761, when her Majesty Queen Charlotte's Household was established, and I was appointed one of her Majesty's Maids of Honor, there was a dispute which of the six was to take place, & consequently *a Reference made to his* Majesty, who was pleased to determine that the *daughters of Baronets* should take place; in confirmation of which her Majesty's Maids of Honor were appointed to take place as follows, Miss Bishopp, Miss Wrottesley, Miss Beauclerk, &c. By this determination I likewise had the first choice of the appartments allotted to us, &c."

'Her Ladyship added by way of conversation, but did not think

fit to give it under her hand, that the Duke of Manchester, when
Lord Chamberlain, told her, that the above determination was
afterwards *altered*, and that the daughters of Peers' younger sons
were placed above the daughters of Baronets at Court Balls, &c.

'If the Determination mentioned in her Ladyship's Letter were
officially signified to your Grace in the usual manner, it would be
the duty of the Office to pay Obedience thereto. If standing upon
its present Authority it should be thought to oppose their opinion
and the matter be yet considered in any degree doubtful, the Officers
of Arms beg leave to suggest to your Grace their idea.

'That as the precedence between Peers' younger sons and
Baronets (Fathers of the parties to the Parties to the present
dispute) was heretofore settled by a Declaratory Patent under the
Great Seal, as above-mentioned, they humbly conceive that a
similar Patent would be an effectual means of adjusting the present
Question.

'All which is most respectfully submitted.

> 'Isaac Heard, Garter.
> 'Thos. Lock, Clarenceux.
> 'George Harrison, Norroy.
> 'Jno. C. Brooke, Somerset.
> 'Ralph Bigland, Richmond.
> 'Francis Townsend, Windsor.
> 'Benjn. Pingo, York.
> 'Edmd. Lodge, Bluemantle.
> 'John Atkinson, Rouge Croix.'

Appeals were made at different times to the Heralds'
College relative to the precedence which ought to be allowed
to the Baronets of Scotland in English assemblies, etc. This,
however, is not a point of ceremonial within their cognisance,
it being in fact a point of law arising out of the 4th
article of the Act of Union, in these words :—'And that
there be a communication of all other rights, privileges, and

advantages, which do or may belong to the subjects of either kingdom, except where it is otherwise expressly agreed in these articles.'

The exception referred to is the 23rd article of the Act of Union, which continues the distinction between the peers of the two kingdoms ; but as no such exception was made in regard to the Baronets of Scotland, they became entitled to a full and unqualified community of rights, privileges, and advantages with the Baronets of England, and rank according to the dates of their respective patents under the authority of the 4th article, in like manner as the peers would have done if it had not been otherwise provided by the 23rd article.

In *Heraldic Anomalies*, a work published early in the century, it is stated that 'the wives of Baronets have as Baronetesses a higher rank than their husbands, for they take place of all Knights' Ladies ; whereas Baronets have not precedency of Knights of the Garter, or of Knights Bannerets created by the King himself in person under his banner displayed in a Royal army in open war.

'The same may be said of the wives of Baronets' sons, and of the daughters of Baronets. They precede the wives of the sons and daughters of all Knights whatsoever.'

At the funeral of H.R.H. Princess Amelia Sophia Eleanora, second daughter of George II., in Henry VII.'s Chapel, on the 11th November 1786, the chief mourner's (a Duchess) train was borne by a Baronet's wife.

At the funeral of H.R.H. Princess Amelia, in St. George's Chapel, Windsor, on the 13th November 1810, the train of the Countess of Chesterfield, chief mourner, was borne by Lady Halford, a Baronet's wife.

The precedency of the eldest sons of Baronets was acknowledged in the nomination and placing of the Knights of the Bath at the Restoration, previous to the coronation of Charles II., when, after the Baronets, their eldest sons immediately followed. Sir Charles Cornwallis, Sir John Monson, and Sir Bourchier Wrey, eldest sons of Baronets of England, were placed above Sir John Coventry, grandson of Lord Coventry, and Sir John Bramston and Sir Edward Heath, sons of the Lords Chief-Justices Bramston and Heath, and many other Knights of the Bath.

On the re-establishment of the Order of the Bath in 1725, immediately after the Baronets, who followed the Privy Councillors, in the appointment of the stalls for the Knights, Robert Clifton, Michael Newton, William Yonge, and John Monson, esquires (eldest sons of Baronets), occur, and are placed above the other Knights elected.

It is worthy of note that Sir Charles Stanley, also Francis and Henry Fane, grandchildren of Earls, were placed amongst the Knights of the Bath, before Baronets of the same order, at the coronation of Charles II.; yet, elsewhere, they could not retain this rank above Baronets, without a special warrant from the King, which extraordinary favour they obtained (14 *June* 13, *Car. II., Earl Marshal's book, J.* 25, *fo.* 88, *in College of Arms*) : ' This seems to be an act of mere power, in favour of these gentlemen, if we reflect on the decree concerning Baronets' precedence, which runs thus : That no degree is to be created, nor place given, to any others (than

what are therein mentioned) which shall be equal to or above
them, under lords of Parliament of England ; how, then,
can they who are below such lords (and not their sons), nor
above their eldest sons, if not above Viscounts' eldest sons
(who are immediately after Lords ; as Baronets' eldest sons
are next after Earls' younger sons) precede Baronets ? '

III. *Style and Title.*—Until the erection of the Baronetage,
the possessors of hereditary titles bore the distinctive style
of their rank, whether territorial or family, before their name ;
for example, ' Duke of Norfolk,' 'Earl Percy ' ; but when
conferring on his new hereditary dignity the designation of
Baronet, the Royal founder ordained that it should be borne
after the family name of the holders, the word ' Sir ' being
placed before the first Christian name.

The latter word, which in England for many centuries
had been prefixed to the Christian names of Knights, is
derived from Cyr, Κυρ, the abbreviation of the Greek
word κύριος; and, as a legal addition, is part of the names
of Baronets and Knights, and may never be omitted. Selden,
in his *Titles of Honour*, observes that the Jews retained this
native word, as given to Knights, in their Hebrew instruments, not presuming, for its peculiar signification, to give
it any translation. The word was much used to the Greek
emperors, and in France was for a long time peculiarly
appropriated to their monarchs. In feudal days there was ·
something very courtly in the formal address ' Sir Knight.'

It is evident, from a perusal of the Decrees of James I.,
that at the time he was contemplating the erection of the

Baronetage he had in his mind a dignity akin to Knighthood, but to be vastly superior to it by reason of its being a dignity hereditary. It was therefore natural, though surely to be regretted, that he ordained that the Knightly title should be assumed, coupled with an addition, after the surname, to denote the hereditary distinction.

The placing of the word 'Baronet' before the surname or territorial title would now doubtless sound for a week or two peculiar to ears not accustomed; but had it been adopted in the first instance, it would in those days have been accepted as the natural sequence of the creation of the dignity. Certainly it would have conduced to simplicity and correctness. The identical prefix of a Baronet and a Knight is, however, on a par with the ridiculous custom which has gradually grown in social intercourse, of describing every Peer, with the exception of the Dukes, by the title of 'Lord.' The Continental aristocracy find no difficulty in making use of their proper title, although Monsieur le Marquis, Monsieur le Comte, Monsieur le Vicomte, Monsieur le Baron is more cumbersome than would be our equivalent of Marquis, Earl, Viscount, and Baron.

While referring to this subject, an even more ridiculous custom has arisen in English society of losing sight of, to a great extent, the courtesy title of 'Honourable' borne by the younger sons of Earls, Viscounts, and Barons, and also by their eldest sons where their father does not possess a second title. Two hundred years ago, when all possessing actual or courtesy titles were known to each other, the failure to call their friends by their proper designation was of little

o

if any consequence; but in the present day, with its numerous social sets, in many of which those I am referring to mingle, at public dinners and other ceremonials, the practice of announcing and calling one entitled to bear the courtesy title of Honourable as Mr., or by a simple naval or military rank, causes endless mistakes and confusion which might easily be avoided. A few years ago an attempt was made to induce those bearing the courtesy title of 'Honourable' to agree amongst themselves to use it on their visiting cards and when being formally announced, but unfortunately it was not successful.

'The Baronets hold a mean or middle degree between Lords and Knights, it being the only hereditary degree of honour the Commons of England have. The word "Commons," in its largest sense, by common law, comprehends all persons who are not Peers of the realm, from the highest to the lowest, so that Dukes' sons, considered in this sense, are alike Commoners with others who are not Peers; and as such are gentlemen without title. For (by whatever titles they are commonly called) by law they enjoy no higher names than Esquires, and are so called in legal proceedings, as writs, etc., which is no name of dignity; whereas Baronets by law enjoy a title of honour and legal dignity, and must be so called in legal proceedings, as writs, etc.'

The Baronets have no fixed and unchangeable title-name. All that they can transmit to posterity is merely the prefix 'Sir' and suffix 'Baronet.' There is no provision whatever in the Letters Patent that the same surname and local title shall always appear between the prefix and suffix, and

accordingly names are unfortunately changed and added to at
pleasure until all identity in this respect is lost between an
old family and its existing representative. This is strangely
unsuited to a Degree Hereditary ; and it would be much
to its interest that Her Majesty should decree that in
the creation of Baronets in future, a clause shall be added
to their Patents, providing that the surname and local title
under which each is raised to the dignity shall for ever
belong to his Baronetcy, and the surname be used on all
occasions as the proper and lawful and perpetual surname
of himself and his successors.

As a courtesy designation, Baronets, upon the erection of
the degree, and until about the end of the eighteenth century, were styled 'The Honourable.' This was only natural,
having regard to the hereditary character of what was
called in King James's time 'the honourable degree and
dignitie of Baronet.' A Duke being styled 'Most Noble,'
a Marquess 'Most Honourable,' Earls, Viscounts, and Barons
'Right Honourable,' it followed that the style of 'Honourable' should be prefixed by the courtesy of society at large
to the newly created hereditary degree.

Instances of this courtesy style are numerous throughout
England, Scotland, and Ireland, some being on tombs, others
in deeds, letters, and other writings. Some Baronets were so
addressed by Oliver Cromwell.

Looking to analogies, it would not be inappropriate were
Baronets to be designated as 'Very Honourable,' leaving
'Honourable' to be used solely for the younger sons of
Peers. The style of 'Honourable,' however, does not

interfere with the courtesy title of the younger sons of Peers, as it is always conjoined with a Baronet's title.

In a book in the library of the College of Arms (J. 9 p. 192), it is recorded that Sir William Segar, when Garter King of Arms, in a declaratory Patent relative to the old arms, quarterings, etc., of Sir Edward Dering, styled this Baronet 'honorabili viro domino Edwardo Dering, militi et baronetto.' He so styled him *quatenus* a Baronet, Sir Edward not being in any office which would of itself entitle him to be called 'The Honourable.'

In the Universities, by the statutes, Baronets enjoy much the same privileges (whilst there) as the highest nobility, and are accordingly styled noblemen in the old and proper fashion.

Although the Patents decree 'that the style and addition of Baronet shall be put at the end of the name' of all Baronets, yet it was only natural that an abbreviation of a word of three syllables, coming after two names prefixed by 'Sir,' should come to be adopted. The simplest and most natural abbreviation is B^t, which was frequently employed, as was also Bar^t, by those who may have thought the former not sufficiently explicit. Among the lazy and illiterate, however, the latter abbreviation was made into a word of one syllable—'Bart,' which unfortunately has become adopted even by some Baronets themselves.

The attention of members of the Degree having been lately called to the advisability of discontinuing this abbreviation, many Baronets at once recognised its unsuitability, and have adopted the word in full when describing themselves in deeds

and official notices, and either append the word in full after
their signature, or use the abbreviation Bᵗ.

The Patents enact that a Baronet 'shall be named,
nominated, called, plead, and be impleaded by the name
of ——— ——— Baronet, and that the style and addition of
Baronet shall be put at the end of the name of the said
——— ——— and of his said Heirs male in all our Letters
Patent, Commissions, and Writs and in all other Charters,
Deeds, and Letters by virtue of these presents, as a true,
lawful, and *necessary* addition of dignity'; hence many
Baronets now print the word 'Baronet' in full or the
abbreviation Bᵗ. on their visiting cards.

The following extract from Hawkins' *Pleas of the Crown*,
vol. ii. cap. 23, § 104, is interesting :—

'Sec. 104. It seems that the common law in no case requires any
other description of an appellant or appellee, but by their name of
baptism and surname, unless they be of the degree of a Knight or
of some higher dignity ; in which cases, whether the name or dignity
be ancient, or (as some say) of a new creation, as that of baronet,
&c., it ought to be added to the name of baptism and surname ; and
if it be of the degree of nobility, it ought to supply the place of the
surname.   And it seems that the law was so curious in this particular, that if a plaintiff, in any action, gained a new name of
dignity hanging a writ, he made it abateable ; but this inconvenience
is remedied by 1 Edw. vi. c. 7, s. 3, by which it is enacted "That
if any plaintiff in any manner of action shall be made a duke,
archbishop, marquis, earl, viscount, baron, bishop, knight, justice of
either bench, or serjeant-at-law, depending the same action, that
such action for such cause shall not be abateable or abated."   But
it hath been holden (1 Sid. 40, Lit. Rep. 81) that the dignity of a
baronet is not within this statute because there was no such dignity
at the time of the making of it.'

The following is the case referred to, and is contained in Thomas Siderfin's *Reports*, 1657-1670, page 40 :—

'Sir . . . . . . Heath *versus* Pagget.

'En Aff le tenant plead que le Defendant fuit fait Miles Balnei pendant le breve & le Defendant monstre que per Lestatute E. 6, cap. 7, est provide que le breve ne abatera lou le Plaintiff est fait Chevalier, Et le doubt fuit si un Chevalier del Bath soit deins ceo Statute. Et tenetur que cy, Et issint touts auter Chevaliers. Mes un Baronet nest deins ceo Stat si non que il soit auxy un Chevalier.'

In the State Trial of George Edmonds and others for seditious conspiracy in 1821, it was shown to have been the invariable course to place Baronets at the head of the list in nominating a special jury. Chief Justice Abbott (afterwards Lord Tenterden) after mentioning this added :—

'Whatever form may be adopted, they will not necessarily be found there. It might be matter of accident in whatever way the selection is made. But in point of rank, they have a right to be placed first, and, therefore, they are and have a right to be—and may have enjoy hold and take place and precedence by virtue of the dignity of a Baronet aforesaid and by force of these presents as well as in all commissions writs letters patent writings appellations nominations and directions in all sessions meetings assemblies and places whatsoever next and immediately after the younger sons of Viscounts and Barons—these Letters Patent give him a right to be first named upon the list. There are no Letters Patent in respect of a Knight; but he has precedence before Esquires. It has been customary to place him, therefore, before them.'

IV. *Only two hundred Baronets of England to exist at one time.*—As already stated, James 1. proposed to limit the number of Baronets to two hundred, so that when any of these titles became extinct others should not be created, and consequently the degree would tend to increase in dignity. This limitation was kept up at first, as is evidenced by the following letter of the 26th June 1623 from the Attorney-General (*State Papers, Domestic Series, James I.*, vol. cxlvii., No. 65) :—

'Sir,

'Having received from you a significacion of his Maties pleasure for drawing up a Bill to create Mr. Corbett a Baronett and conceiving by your letter that the number of Baronettes hath bene once filled and that this man is to come in place of one that is dead without issue I doubted whether his Matie were informed or do remember that by expres covenant with such as have bene formerly advanced to that dignity his Matie hath agreed not only that the number of Baronettes shall never exceed two hundred but that the number being once full if any of them dye without issue male his Matie will create no more but suffer the number to decrease, And therefore though I have prepared the Bill as I am commanded yet I held it my duty to informe you thereof that if his Matie be not already acquainted with it he may not unawares do that which being Rightly informed he would not give way unto.   And so I humbly rest.

'Att your honors commandment
'Thomas Coventrye.'

'Inner Temple, 26 *June* 1623.

'This bearer informes me that it is his Maties intent to discharg the mony usually payed for that degree yor warrant importing not so much I thought not fitt to deliver the patent and discharge to the party but both for that, and for the reason in my letter to addresse it to yow if it be his Maties pleasure that it shall proceed you wilbe pleased to send me warrant for the little bill that is drawne for the discharge as yow have for the patent itself.

(Endorsed) '20 June 1623 Mr. Atturney generall to Mr. Secret. Conwey. Concerninge a Graunt of a Barronnett to Mr. Corbett.

(Addressed) 'To the Right Ho^{ble} Sir Edward Conwey Knight one of his Maties principall secretaries.

In the same collection of papers will be found the following under date 23rd March 1625 :—

'Blank Warrant for the grant of a Baronetcy, in place of Sir Rich. Robartes, Bar^t., now made a Baron.
'Blank Warrant for grant of a Baronetcy, in place of Sir Fra^s. Ashby, dead without issue male.
'Warrant for a grant of a Baronetcy to Hugh Cholmley, in place of Sir Peter Curteen, deceased.'

It would thus appear that the Royal intention of limiting the degree to the descendants of the two hundred Baronets was first altered to limiting the holders of the title to the same number by filling up vacancies which occurred through the extinction of titles. It is however by no means certain that James i. ever really exceeded his own limit, as although his total creations of Baronetcies amounted to 204, yet in defence of this excess of four, it is urged in the essay printed in Wotton's *Baronetage*, the four 'were to fill vacancies that happened, not by death or attainder, but by promotion to a higher dignity, so that he did not go beyond his engagement.' The four Baronets advanced by the King to Peerages were Sir Robert Dormer, Sir Thomas Ridgeway, Sir William Hervey, and Sir Thomas Beaumont. Later on all limitation was withdrawn, and the creation of new Baronetcies is entirely in the discretion of the reigning Sovereign.

V. *No degree, order, name, title, dignity, or state, under the degree, dignity, or state of Barons of England, to be ever created, which would, or could be, superior or equal to the degree and dignity of Baronet.*—This will be found dealt with under VIII.

VI. *If any Baronet of the said two hundred should die without heirs male, no other Baronets of England to be created, but the number of two hundred to diminish accordingly.*—This has been already referred to under IV.

VII. *A newly defined precedency.*—This will be found fully dealt with in Chapter II., where the Royal decree of 28th May 1612 is given at length.

VIII. *A repetition of privilege No. V., etc.*—After the controversy of precedence between the younger sons of Viscounts and Barons and the Baronets had been settled, nothing appears to have arisen to have called for any remonstrance from the members of the Baronetage with the exception of the precedence given to certain Judges who have not attained the degree of the Coif, referred to in the article quoted on pages previous from *The Law Magazine*, until the announcement in August 1897 that the sons and daughters of life peers were to be formed into a special class, having a precedence among themselves, and to take precedence immediately before Baronets. This, however, is referred to later.

IX. *Rights of Knighthood for Baronets and their eldest sons.*—The Letters Patent of 14 James I. finally ratifying, confirming, allowing, and approving of the Hereditary Dignity, State, Title, and Degree of Baronet, with all the rights and privileges of the previous Patents of the 9th and 10th James I., contain the following clause :—'And further of Our special grace, certain knowledge and mere motion, We do hereby declare and express our true intent and meaning to have been, and do hereby promise and grant for Us, our heirs and successors, to and with such Gentlemen as now be, or at any time hereafter shall be Baronets ; That so soon as they or any of them shall attain to the age of one-and-twenty years.   And likewise so soon as the eldest son or apparent heir male of the bodies of them, or any of them, shall during the life of their Father or Grandfather attain to the age of one-and-twenty years ; and that the said Baronets, or the said eldest sons or apparent heirs males, shall be presented to Us by the Lord Chamberlain of our household, or Vice-Chamberlain for the time being, or in their absence by any other Officer attending upon the person of Us, our heirs or successors to be made Knights that they and every of them shall from time to time be made Knights by Us, our heirs and successors accordingly.'   This Hereditary privilege was apparently designed to commemorate the feudal custom incident to a tenure in chivalry, under which the eldest son of the Lord was made a Knight with much ceremony and pomp, while also serving the purpose of giving a title to a Baronet's eldest son, to be enjoyed by law, and not by mere courtesy, as in other Degrees.

As a consequence of these Letters Patent, the Patent of every Baronet created prior to the Revocation by George IV.

of this promise and grant referred to hereafter, contained a clause ratifying the privilege.

The Patents of Baronets of Scotland and Nova Scotia created prior to 1633 contain the following covenant and grant :—

'Moreover We out of our special grace and favor, certain knowledge mere motion and deliberate mind, by these presents, and with the advice aforesaid (viz., of the Privy Council) for Us, our Heirs and Successors, will, concede, declare, and promise, that at whatever time, and so soon as, the Eldest Son and Apparent Heir-male of the said Sir A—— B—— Baronet, or the Eldest Son and Apparent Heir-male of whatsoever Heirs-male succeeding to him, shall attain the age of twenty-one years, that they, and every one of them respectively by Us, our Heirs, and Successors, shall be inaugurated Knights whensoever they, or any of them, shall require that Order without any Fees, or expense whatsoever.'

The Patents of all Baronets of Scotland and Nova Scotia, created after 1633, contain either the above clause or else the following general clause :—

'We give, grant, and confer, on the said A—— B——, and his Heirs-male, for ever, the title, dignity, order and honor of KNIGHT-BARONET, ordaining them, their Wives, and Children to use and enjoy the same title, with all privileges, immunities and honors of every kind belonging to Knights Baronets, in virtue of whatsoever Acts, Statutes, Diplomas, or Customs, existing in these Our Dominions.'

The Parliament of Scotland held at Edinburgh on 28th June 1633, Charles I. being present in person, passed a law, willing, statuting, and ordaining, that the Dignities and Order of Knight Baronet, with all Letters Patent granted therewith to any person or persons whatsoever, together with all Acts of the Privy Council, and Proclamations thereanent, shall stand and continue in force according to the tenor of the same, and in as ample manner as if the bodies of the said Letters Patent, Acts, and Proclamations were therein particularly engrossed and expressed.

On the 10th May 1636, Charles I. issued a Warrant to the Chancellor of Scotland, directing him to knight the eldest sons of Baronets desiring the honour, which was duly recorded as follows :—

'ANENT KNIGHTING OF BARONNETS SONNES.

'Apud Edinburgh 16 Junij 1636.

'Forsamekle as the Kings Majestie having formerlie upon verie good considerations both for freithing his Matie frome truble and saving of the parties whome it concernes frome charges Give warrand and direction to his Ma^teis Chanceller for the time being That the eldest sonnes of all Baronnets being of the age of 21 yeeres sould be knighted whensoever thay sould desire the same according to thair patents under the Great Seale And his Matie being yett willing upon the same consideratiouns that the said course be continued   His Majestie for this effect hes gevin warrand to the Lord High Chanceller of this kingdome to knight the eldest sonnes of all and everie ane of suche Baronnets who being of the perfyte age of 21 years compleit sall desire the same without putting thame to anie charges and expensses As in the said warrant presentit and exhibite this day before the Lords of Secreit Counsell at lenth is conteanit Quhilk being read heard and considderit be the saids Lords and thay with all humble and dewtifull respect acknowledgeing his Majesteis gratious will and pleasure in this mater They ordaine the said warrand to be insert and registrat in the bookes of Privie Counsell and to have the force of ane act of Counsell in time comming To the end the said Lord Chanceller may knight the saids eldest sonnes of all Baronnetts without forder warrand and that all whome it may concerne may take notice of his Majesteis Royall pleasure heerin and ordanis letters to be direct to make publication heirof wherthrow nane pretend ignorance of the same.

'Followes His Majesteis missive for warrand of the Act foresaid.'

'CHARLES R.

'Right Reverend Father in God We greit you weill Whereas We wer pleased by our letter unto our lait Chanceller to give power unto him or anie other for the time being that the eldest sonnes of all Baronnetts might be knighted being of the perfyte age of 21 yeeres whensoever they sould desire the same according to thair patents under our Great Seale both for freing Ws from trouble and saving thame frome charges whiche thair repairing hither for that purpose might procure and now being willing upon the like consideration that the same sould be continued We have thought fitt heirby to renew our pleasure unto yow for that effect and thairfoir We will that yow knight the eldest sonnes of all and euerie one of suche Baronnetts who being of the perfyte age of twenty-one yeeres sould desire the same, without putting thame to anie charges or expensses And Our further pleasure is that yow make ane Act of Counsell heirupon That your successors in your charge of Lord Chanceller doe the same without anie further warrand and that all others whome it may concerne may take notice of our Royall pleasure heerin for doing whairof these presents sall be your warrand We bid you farewell Frome our Courte at Whitehall, the 10 of Maye 1636.'

A Baronet was not a Knight as well as a Baronet until he had actually presented himself before the Sovereign and obtained the honour of Knighthood, as illustrated by the following case :—

Sir Henry Ferrers, Baronet, was indicted by the name of Sir Henry Ferrers, Knight, for the murder of one Stone, whom one Nightingale had feloniously murdered. Sir Henry was accused of being present, and aiding and abetting. Upon this indictment, Sir Henry Ferrers being arraigned, said that he was never knighted, which being confessed, the indictment was held not to be sufficient.   Wherefore he was indicted *de novo* by the name of Sir Henry Ferrers, Baronet.

On the 19th December 1827, an Ordinance was passed by George IV. withdrawing the privilege of claiming Knighthood by those Baronets who were not already Knights, and by the eldest sons of Baronets on their attaining the age of twenty-one, from all creations after that date, in the following words :—

> 'REVOCATION OF THE PROMISE AND GRANT contained in the Letters Patent of 28 May 10 James I. for knighting Baronets and their Heirs Male when they should attain the age of 21.

> 'GEORGE THE FOURTH BY THE GRACE OF GOD. To all to whom these presents shall come Greeting. Whereas Our late Royal Progenitor King James the First by Letters Patent bearing date at Westminster the twenty-second day of May in the ninth year of his Reign for himself his heirs and successors did ordain erect constitute and create a certain State Degree and Dignity name and title of a Baronet within his then Kingdom of England to endure for ever   And Whereas the said King James by certain other Letters Patent bearing date at Westminster the twenty eighth day of May in the tenth year of his reign did make a certain Ordinance Establishment and final decree upon a Controversy of Precedence between the younger Sons of Viscounts and Barons and the Baronets and touching some other points also concerning as well Bannerets as the said Baronets whereby His Majesty was graciously pleased (amongst other things) to Knight the then present Baronets that were no Knights and did also by those Presents of his mere motion and favor promise and grant for himself his heirs and successors that such Baronets and the heirs males of their bodies as thereafter should be no Knights when they should attain or be of the age of One and twenty years upon knowledge thereof given to the Lord Chamberlain of the Household or Vice-Chamberlain for the time being or in their absence to any other Officer attending

upon his Majesty's person should be Knighted by his Majesty his
heirs and successors as by the said several Letters Patent reference
being thereunto had will (amongst other things) more fully and at
large appear Now know ye that we for divers good causes and
considerations us hereunto moving Have thought fit to revoke
determine and make void And by these presents for us our heirs
and successors Do revoke determine and make void the said promise
and grant in the said last mentioned Letters Patent contained with
respect to all Letters Patent for the creation of Baronets to be
made and granted after these presents And that the said Letters
Patent shall be made hereafter without such clause as hereinbefore
mentioned without prejudice nevertheless to any Letters Patents
heretofore granted or to the rights and privileges now by Law
belonging to any Baronet and his heirs male. In Witness &c.
Witness &c. the nineteenth day of December.

'By Writ of Privy Seal.'

Now it will be observed that this Revocation is distinctly
stated to be without prejudice to any Letters Patent granted
prior to its issue ; and although for some reason or other,
difficult to explain, the privilege has been rarely claimed
during the present century, yet until quite recently it was
granted as a matter of course when so claimed.

On the 21st February 1865, the Lord-Lieutenant of
Ireland knighted Mr. George Clendinning O'Donel, eldest
son and heir-apparent of Sir Richard Annesley O'Donel, the
fourth Baronet, in compliance with the clause in the patent
of Baronetcy of 2nd December 1780 ; while on the 12th
February 1874, Mr. Ludlow Cotter, eldest son of Sir James
Cotter, Baronet, was knighted at Windsor on coming of age.

On the 20th July 1836, Mr. Richard Broun, eldest son
and heir to the Baronetcy of Broun of Colstoun, made a
formal application to the Lord Chamberlain requiring that

officer, in terms of the constitution of the Baronetage, to present him to the Sovereign for inauguration as Knight. The application set forth the special clauses in the constitution of the Baronetage which rendered it compulsory on the Crown to discharge this peculiar service ; and it was accompanied by such documents and certificates as were deemed by counsel sufficient to warrant the demand.   A very lengthy correspondence followed, with the result that the claim was not allowed, the decision being communicated to Mr. Broun in the following letter :—

'Whitehall,
'August 4th, 1836.

'Sir,

'I am directed by Lord John Russell to acknowledge the receipt of your letter of the 30th ultimo, and to acquaint you in reply that the application which was made by you to the Lord Chamberlain of His Majesty's Household, claiming the honour of Knighthood, in consideration of your being the eldest son of a Baronet, was referred, by his Lordship's direction, for the consideration of the Kings at Arms, who have reported that inasmuch as the Patent granting the Dignity of a Baronet to your alleged ancestor, Sir James Broun, Bar^t., of Colstoun, did not contain any Clause authorising his eldest son to claim the honour of Knighthood, they are of opinion that you have no claim to that honour upon the ground set forth in your application, and Lord John Russell therefore directs me to express his regret that he cannot recommend to His Majesty to accede to your request.

'I have the honour to be,
'Sir,
'Your obedient Servant,
'(Sgd.) Fox Maule.'

Mr. Broun, however, declined to accept this decision as final, on the ground that the reason for the refusal was unsound, he contending that the grant in favour of the eldest sons of the Baronets of Scotland was made a statute law of Scotland by the King and the Scottish Parliament, on the 28th June 1633, since which time it had been solemnly ratified by the Act of Union. After a series of references and delays, the Lord Chamberlain finally, on the 8th December 1841, declined to grant Mr. Broun's request.

At a meeting of the Committee of the Baronetage for Privileges, referred to later on in this work, held at the Clarendon Hotel, London, on the 10th May 1842, the following resolutions were passed :—

'*First*, That in the opinion of this Committee the course followed by the Crown Officers in the case of Mr. Broun's application for Knighthood, is in direct contravention of the constitution of the Baronetage, a statute law of the realm of Scotland, the Articles of Union, the obligation of the Coronation Oath, and the unbroken precedents of 230 years.

'*Second*, That, after a careful review of the whole proceedings, this Committee do, on behalf of the Baronets of the several creations in the United Kingdom, record their unanimous protest against the irregular opinion of the Attorney, and Solicitor-General of England, upon which the Lord Chamberlain has arrived at the supposition that he cannot consistently with his duty present Mr. Broun to Her Majesty for knighthood.

'*Third*, That Sir Robert Peel, as the head of the Government, be informed that the Lord Chamberlain has refused, on the application of a Baronet's Eldest Son for Knighthood, to discharge the duty imposed upon him by the Constitution of the Baronetage ; and that the Right Honourable Baronet be requested by this Committee, as the immediate adviser of the Sovereign, to interpose his official authority in order that the Lord Chamberlain may be directed to present to Her Majesty the Eldest sons of all applying Baronets for Knighthood according to the tenor of the Letters Patent, Statutes, and other instruments, whereby successive Monarchs have bound themselves and their successors to the Throne.'

These resolutions, together with an abstract of the proceedings of the Committee relating to this case, were transmitted on the following day to the Prime Minister, who replied on the 18th May to the effect that he approved of the course pursued by the Lord Chamberlain, and that he must decline therefore to interpose his official authority for the purpose of inducing the Lord Chamberlain to depart from it.

This reply having been laid before the Committee, they adverted to the subject in the Report made to the Annual Meeting of the Baronetage, held on the 4th of June, in the following terms :—

'Considering that a Petition from the Order praying for a judicial hearing before the Queen in Council has been refused ; that the opinions of Counsel have been taken upon the subject, and that they have reported they think there is no tribunal whereby the Lord Chamberlain can be compelled to discharge the duty imposed upon him by the Letters Patent of the 10th and 14th Jac. 1.; that the compact between the State and the Baronets of Scotland is, that their Eldest Sons shall be inaugurated Knights (Equites Aurati) by the reigning Sovereign, whensoever they, or any of them, shall require that Order ; that the Lord Chamberlain, on the formal requisition of Mr. Broun, has declined to present him to the Sovereign for inauguration as a Knight; and finally, that the Prime Minister by approving of the course taken by the Lord Chamberlain in the face of a recorded Protest of the Committee has sanctioned a transaction of the most illegal, arbitrary, and unprecedented nature, your Committee are of opinion that the time has arrived when it devolves upon the Order either to submit to a course which would countenance the doctrine that the Queen is not bound by

the acts of her predecessors—would warrant the supposition that
there was no faith or honour in the mind of His Majesty King
Charles I., when he promised, on the word of a Prince, for himself
and his successors, that this particular Grant should be onerous on
the Crown—and which would for ever compromise the dearest
rights and immunities of the Baronetage, or else to assert and make
good this vested and indefeasible prerogative, by such acts and
regulation of the Body, as shall comport with the dignity of the
Order—evince its wonted fealty to the Commonwealth—and uphold
those principles of honour, justice and truth, which are the basis of
all Law and Privilege in the Realm.'

At the Anniversary Meeting held on the 4th June the
above proposition was considered ; and subsequently, on the
motion of Sir William Ogilvie, seconded by Sir R. Jodrell,
it was unanimously resolved—

'That the Prime Minister having approved of the course pursued
by the Lord Chamberlain in the case of Mr. Broun's application
for Knighthood, which course the Committee for Privileges, after
mature deliberation, have found and declared to be in direct contravention of the Constitution of the Baronetage, a Statute Law of
the Realm of Scotland, the Articles of Union, the obligations of
the Coronation Oath, and the unbroken precedents of 230 years,
this General Meeting do require of Mr. Broun, in whose person
the national rights of the Eldest Sons of the whole Baronets in the
United Realm have been violated, that he will, in virtue of his
being a Knight *de jure*, as the Eldest Son of a Member of the Order
of ancient creation, vindicate this fundamental and unalienable
privilege of the Eldest Sons of Baronets, by henceforth using, taking,
and enjoying the ancient chivalrous dignity of a Knight (Eques
Auratus) with the immunities and precedencies thereunto belonging : and that the Committee for Privileges do record the same in
the Journals of the Order, that the precedent may rule in future
the cases of all such Eldest Sons of Baronets as may hereafter apply
for Knighthood under the Letters Patent of the 10th and 11th

Jac. I., and experience a similar arbitrary and illegal course of procedure on the part of the responsible Officers of the Crown.'

This Resolution having been passed, Mr. Broun rose and
addressed the Meeting, and formally assumed Knighthood,
throwing the responsibility of his doing so upon the Lord
Chamberlain and the Prime Minister who sanctioned the
Lord Chamberlain's conduct.

On the 17th May 1895, Mr. Claude Champion De
Crespigny, eldest son of Sir Claude Champion de Crespigny,
claimed the honour of knighthood in accordance with the
clause contained in the Patent of the 31st October 1805 ;
and after considerable correspondence on the subject, the
following letter was received from the Home Office :—

'WHITEHALL,

'12th March 1896.

    'SIR,

            'With reference to your letter of 17th May last,
addressed to the Lord Chamberlain, claiming the honour of Knighthood, as eldest son of the present Sir Claude de Crespigny, Bar^t.,
I am directed by the Secretary of State to acquaint you that he has
consulted the Prime Minister on the subject, and is informed that
Lord Salisbury is advised by the Lord Chancellor that the claim in
the Patent of Baronetcy, upon which your application is based, is
not, in his Lordship's opinion, valid, and that accordingly Lord
Salisbury regrets that he is unable to submit your name to the
Queen for the honour aforesaid.

'I am, Sir,

'Your obedient Servant,

'CHARLES S. MURDOCH.

    'C. C. DE CRESPIGNY, Esq.'

It is exceedingly difficult to form any opinion as to why
the clause in the Patents of Baronets granted before the

19th December 1827, relating to knighthood, should not be valid, and the following extract from a letter of Sir William Betham, a former Ulster King of Arms, and a recognised authority on all matters appertaining to Dignities, may be here given :—

'I am surprised to hear such a doubt started by the Law Officers of the Crown, as that the Sovereign has not a right to bind his successors to confer the honor of Knighthood on the Eldest Sons of Baronets; for it was part and parcel of the Constitution at the foundation of the Order, and consequently part of its essence, and therefore inseparable from it.'

It has been suggested that should this privilege of claiming knighthood be definitely abandoned by the Baronets of older creations, a substituted privilege commemorative of their former right might be conceded to them.   The Knights Grand Cross of the Order of the Bath are entitled to bear supporters to their Arms although those holding this distinction rank beneath the Baronetage.

At the present time the Baronets (as such) are not entitled to bear supporters.   In the time of James i. supporters were confined to Peers and Knights of the Garter; and they were not borne by Knights of the Bath until the creation of the Order as a regular Military Order of Knighthood, by George i. in 1725, for which purpose a special statute was issued.

The decree of 1612 assigned the armorial distinction to be borne by the Baronets of England and their descendants, as being 'either in a canton in their coat-of-arms, or in an inescutcheon, at their election, the arms of Ulster, that is, in a field argent, a hand gules, or a bloody hand.'

It does not appear that there is any authority either in their patents or elsewhere for the Baronets of Scotland to bear supporters, although Edmondson in his book on Heraldry (vol. i. p. 193) states : ' The Nova Scotia or Scotch Baronets are by their patents of creation allowed to carry supporters, notwithstanding that privilege was not indulged to the baronets of England at the time of the institution of their dignity. Some of them indeed bear supporters, but it is by virtue of a royal license obtained for that especial purpose.'

In the later Patents of Baronets of Scotland occurs the following clause respecting their armorial bearings : ' Mandamus per præsentes Leoni nostro Regi armorum suisque fratribus fecialibus ut tale additamentum armorum præsentibus insigniis prænominati A—— B—— sicuti talibus casibus usitatum est dent et præscribant.'

This clause is sometimes varied, as, for example, the following :—

' Leoni porro Armorum Regi ejusque fratribus fecialibus additamenta præsentibus insigniis armoriis dicti A—— B—— quæ huic occasioni congrua et idonea videbuntur dare et præscribere imperamus.'

Should supporters be granted to the Baronetage, they might be either at choice or else consist of two Equites Aurati, commemorative of the Order of Knighthood, with which all Baronets created prior to December 1827 and their eldest sons were connected.

Before leaving this subject, the following letter from Sir

Warwick Hele Tonkin, written 1st February 1842, is worth recording :—

'It is clearly established by precedents that there are two ways of conferring the Dignity of Knighthood by the accolade or by Patent.   I take it, therefore, the Baronets are Knights by the latter mode, and I prove it by the following admissions in public ceremonies and Courts of Law.

'When the Installation of the Knights of the Bath took place in Westminster Abbey more than thirty years ago, many Baronets acted as proxies; this they could not have done had they not been Knights by Patent or by being dubbed by the Sovereign: ergo the privilege of the Baronets and Knights are intimately blended together.

'Now, with respect to the open and full recognition in Courts of Law, I will refer you to the last Writ of Rights, tried in England at two different Assizes, consequently before four Judges, where three Baronets and one Knight were summoned to come *girt with Swords and (cum gladio cinctus)* as Knights.

'Of this proceeding you have the date, names, and particulars, and as a trial took place, the event is recorded.   Thus, then, the privileges of Knighthood are recently confirmed, need I add that the girding with a sword of the infant Prince of Wales is the ancient mode of conferring Knighthood.   The Collar of S.S., the Spurs, Signet Ring, and Badge or Star being appended as mere adjuncts of the Sword which was formerly, and is now, in Russia an emblem of nobility.

'The Foreign Office in granting permission, and I am yet to know what legal rights they assume to deny it, to wear a Foreign Decoration, especially assume " the privileges of Knights Bachelor "; now, if you look into Ashmole's *History of the Garter*, you see that the Baronets and Knights are united in the proposed distinction recommended by the then Heralds in 1627.   What is the difference, then, existing between the two Orders, precedence and the transmission of the title to the first, but equal privileges as Knights? The Baronet's eldest son is a Knight *de jure*, since the Knight's eldest son is an Esquire *de facto*; union is strength, let these Knightly Orders coalesce to establish their privileges at Court and elsewhere. The Herald's College are no corporation in Law, the Lord Chamberlain has no legal power, it is to the Throne we all must look for a reception, and not to the minister of the day.   Let a deputation present a petition to the Queen, there are peers who are Baronets as well as Knights, to them delegate your memorial, it will add to the splendour of the dignity of the Throne, and confirm our attachment the stronger to the foundation of all honour.'

In addition to the above letter, Sir Warwick Hele Tonkin wrote the following observations on the Writ of Right :—

'The last which was tried in England, by this it would appear that Baronets were legally allowed to be "Knights," Equites Aurati, since they were summoned as Knights as well as Baronets ; how far such summons was strictly right and legal cannot now be proved, since the Law regarding "Writs of Right" is abolished, and the question cannot now be mooted although it evidently admits of a doubt—the word Knight evidently intending to convey in its meaning simply Knight Bachelor—which dignity every Knight of an Order must have before he can be admitted or wear a Decoration of the Garter, Bath, Thistle, or any other Order of English Knighthood.

'The claim to the title of Knight has been legally established on this Trial, and this admission would entitle any Baronet (not a Knight Batchelor) to all the honors and privileges of the Accolade. The decision is therefore highly important to the Baronets, as it would clearly appear they may wear a Badge or Decoration without the personal honor of being Knighted by the Sovereign.'

The account of what took place on the occasion referred to is recorded in Woolmer's *Exeter Gazette*, as follows :—

'1837.
'Devon and Exeter Lent Assize.
'Writ of Right.
'At half-past 12 o'clock this day four Knights, Sir John Duntze,

Sir John Duckworth, Sir Robert Newman, Baronets, and Sir William Hele Tonkin, Knight, being summoned by virtue of a Warrant from the Sheriff of the County of Devon, appeared in Court each girt with a sword, to be sworn in accordance with the ancient ceremony. It is more than half a century since this curious Law procedure, which is the last resource for the recovery of Real Estate, has taken place in this county, and it may never occur again in England, as the original Statute is repealed, excepting in cases where suits have been previously pending. The names of the parties in this present case are :—

'Henry Richards,   Demandant,
                         'and
'Lewis Gidley,   Tenant.

'The form of proceeding was as follows :—The Counsel moved that the Four Knights be sworn, after which they retired to select Twenty Gentlemen from the Special Jury List, who are termed "Recognitors."

'The Knights then returned into Court and presented Twelve out of the Twenty who had been elected by them at the present Assize to constitute a Jury for the next Summer Assize, which Jury must include the four Knights, and will be denominated The Grand Assize.

'The attendance of the Four Knights girt with Swords is indispensably necessary, as the absence of one would render all the trouble and expense useless.

'Note.—The Knights were sworn in open Court before Mr. Baron Gurney :—All the Knights were in attendance at the following Assize, and all the special Jurymen selected ; the Cause came on, and was tried.

'The presence of all was extraordinary, as some casualty might have intervened.

'It was the last " *Writ of Right* " tried in any county in England.'

X. *Addition of the Arms of Ulster in armorial bearings.*— The Second Letters Patent of the 10th May 1612 enacted:—

'The Baronets and their descendants shall and may bear,

either in a Canton in their coat of arms, or, in an inies-cutcheon, at their election, the Arms of Ulster, that is, in a field argent, a hand gules, or a bloody hand.' This was, of course, to commemorate the fact that the degree had been instituted for the protection of that province.

The Ulster cognisance as usually blazoned is a hand *sinister*, but in Mr. Broun's *Baronetage* for 1843 are engraved two very ancient seals of the Arms of Ulster, in both of which a *dexter* hand appears. One is the copy of an impression of a seal which was found between 1830 and 1840 in the vicinity of Magherafelt, and which is considered to have belonged to Murtogh Roe, or the Red O'Neill, lord of Clanaboy, whose family for seven hundred years were hereditary monarchs of Ireland, and who, according to the annals of the Four Masters, died in 1471. The other is a facsimile of the impression of a very ancient silver seal supposed to have belonged to Hugh O'Neill, King of Ulster, and was in the collection of Sir Robert Walpole, at Strawberry Hill. The inscription bears no date, but is as follows : ' *S. Odonis O'Neill Regis Hybernicorum Ultoniæ.*'

Sylvanus Morgan in his *Sphere of Gentry*, published in 1661, states that the Canton of the Shield or the Escutcheon of Pretence bearing the Ulster Hand is not to be taken up at pleasure, but is to be allowed by a certificate, quoting as his authority one granted by Sir William Segar to Sir Richard Baker, Baronet, as follows :—

'To all and singular persons, as well Nobles, as others, to whom this present Certificate shall come, William Segar Garter, principal King at Arms, sendeth greeting in our Lord God everlasting.

Know ye, that I the said Garter, at the request of the much Honoured Sir Henry Baker, Knight, and Baronet, have added, and annexed to his Antient Coat of Arms, which is Azure, three Swans heads erased proper, an Escoucheon Argent charged with a hand Sinister Gules extended in Pale, being the Arms of the ancient Kings of Ulster in Ireland, and that Honourable augmentation, which now it hath pleased his Majesty to grant and confer unto the Baronets for their more honour, and to their issue for ever, &c.'

XI. *A place near the Royal Standard in battle.*—The Second Letters Patent of the 10th May 1612 enacted :—

'The Baronets for the time being, and the heirs-males of their bodies, shall have place in the Armies of the King's Majesty, his heirs and successors, in the gross, near about the royal standard of the King, his heirs and successors, for the defence of the same.'

This honourable position was valuable only to Baronets created or born within a limited period of the erection of the dignity, and the privilege has become practically obsolete. It appears, however, to have been linked from the first with a recognised right of the Baronetage to be represented on occasions of state ceremony, such as coronations, public funerals, and processions. This indeed was natural ; for in the Royal Founder's Decrees, and in Patents of creation, it is provided that the new Baronet may have and take his appointed place and precedence by virtue of the dignity of Baronet in all 'sermons, conventions, assemblies, and places whatsoever.'

At the funeral of Henry, Prince of Wales, 7th December 1612, the Baronets went above the Prince's Treasurer of his Revenues, the Treasurer of his Household, and the

Master of the Horse to the Prince ; and particular Baronets were in honourable services, as the banner of the earldom of Carrick was borne by a Baronet, when that of Chester was borne by Lord Howard of Effingham; the great standard of the Prince was borne by a Baronet, as was also his coronet ; the canopy of black velvet was borne over his effigies by six Baronets, and ten bannerolls about the body by ten other Baronets. Among the 'blackes' allowed for the several degrees was included seven yards for Baronets and eight for their servants or followers. Early in the procession the servants of Baronets had a place assigned to them after the servants of Knights and before the servants of sons of Barons.

In the procession to Parliament in 1614, Baronets went above the King's Attorney-General, and the Solicitor-General, the King's Sergeants and Knights of the Bath. They also went above those who had been the King's Ambassadors and Lords Presidents in Ireland.

At the funeral of Queen Anne of Denmark, who died 2nd March 1618, and was buried on the 13th May following, Baronets went above the following principal officers of the Prince of Wales's Court, viz.: the Cofferer, the Comptroller and Treasurer of the Household, the Keeper of the Privy Purse, the Master of the Wardrobe, and the Prince's Chief Commissioners, and next above Sir John Bennet the Chancellor to the Queen.

In the solemn procession made by James I. to St. Paul's Cathedral on 26th March 1620, Baronets took place of such Knights as had been Ambassadors, Lords Presidents of the provinces in Ireland, and Lords Deputies of that Kingdom.

In the procession to Parliament in 1620, Baronets went above the King's Attorney-General, and the Solicitor-General, the King's Sergeants and Knights of the Bath, the Master of the Ordnance, Masters of the Requests, Gentlemen of the Bedchamber to the King, the Vice-Admiral and Knight Marshal, the Treasurer of the King's Chamber, and Master of the Jewel Office.

At the funeral of the illustrious Prince Ludowic, Duke of Richmond and Lenox, who was of the royal family, and buried in Westminster Abbey, 19th April 1624, Baronets went immediately after the Chancellor of the Duchy of Lancaster, and their servants accordingly.

At the funeral of George Monk, Duke of Albemarle, who was buried by His Majesty's order in the chancel of Westminster Abbey, 13th May 1670, Baronets in a body went above the Judge of the High Court of Admiralty, the Knights Marshal and King's Cofferer, as also Knights of the Bath ; and themselves immediately next after Sir John Trevat, the principal Secretary of State, and William Pierpoint, Esquire, son of the Earl of Kingston, who walked together.

At the funeral of James I., the Standard of the Crest of Ireland was borne and offered by a Baronet, Sir Thomas Button ; at that of the illustrious Duke before mentioned, in 1624, the Banner of Stewart, quartered, was borne by Sir Robert Napier, Baronet ; and at that of the Duke of Albemarle, Sir Thomas Vincent, Baronet, bore the banner

of Beauchamp, supported by Sir Edward Bray, Knight, on
one side, and Colonel Molesworth on the other.

At the funeral of H.R.H. Henry Frederick, Duke of
Cumberland, in Henry VII. Chapel, Westminster, on the
28th September 1790, the train of the chief mourner
(a Duke) was borne by a Baronet.

In the ceremonial for the public funeral procession of
Lord Nelson from Greenwich Hospital to the Admiralty
on the 8th January 1806, and on the next day to St. Paul's,
Baronets were allotted their place in the procession, as also
at the funeral of William Pitt in Westminster Abbey on
the 22nd of the following month.

XII. *A funeral ceremony ' meane betwixt that of a Baron and
a Knight.'*—The Second Letters Patent of the 10th May
1612 enacted :—

'The Baronets and the heirs-males of their bodies shall
have two assistants of the body to support the pall, a
principal mourner, and four assistants to him at their
funerals, being the mean betwixt a Baron and a Knight.'

XIII. *The right for all Baronets, then and in future, to have
Letters Patent under the Great Seal of England to the effect of
former Letters Patent of creation and of these presents.*—This
right appears to have been strictly adhered to.

XIV. *The Degree of Baronet to be, and be reputed to be, a
Degree of Dignity Hereditary, mean in place betwixt the Degree
of a Baron and the Degree of a Knight.*—It does not appear
that any suggestion has ever been made to create any

hereditary degree since the erection of the Baronetage, and indeed it would be difficult to suggest any useful purpose which would be served by so doing.

Many new orders of Knighthood have been created in order to confer personal distinction ; but for those deemed worthy of receiving an honour to be transmitted to their offspring, the augmentation in numbers of the already established six hereditary degrees has been considered sufficient.

XV. *Eldest sons of Baronets to precede eldest sons of all Knights, whatever their Order; with similar provisions respecting other sons, etc.*—Notwithstanding the fact that Knights of the Garter take precedence of Baronets, yet the eldest sons of the latter take precedence of eldest sons of Knights of the Garter (as such), and consequently of the eldest sons of all other Knights. The younger sons of Baronets take precedence immediately before the younger sons of Knights of the Garter, and consequently before the younger sons of all other Knights.

XVI. *Doubts or questions arising in future concerning precedency, privilege, or other matter touching Baronets to be decided according to the rules, custom, and laws of other Degrees of Dignity Hereditary.*—This privilege was conferred on the Baronetage by its Royal Founder by his Decree of 1616, issued five years after the erection of the Degree. In the interval he had settled the very serious dispute which had arisen at the instance of the younger sons of the Viscounts and of the Barons, recorded in Chapter III., and he evidently intended that any future questions relating to the Baronetage should be regulated according to the rules, customs, and laws of the Peerage.

Unfortunately, however, there is not in existence a single tribunal which even claims for itself the right to deal with doubts and questions relating to the sixth hereditary degree, and as a result there has arisen a very serious abuse in the Baronetage of the assumption of the title in many instances by those who have no right whatever to bear it.

The hostility of the Baronets to the Order of George III., issued in 1783, that every Baronet should register his pedigree in the College of Arms, led, unfortunately, to its revocation. In former times the visitation of the Heralds was to a certain extent a restraint on the unlawful usurpation of any name or title to honour or dignity, as they had the power to reprove, control, and make infamous by Proclamation all such offenders.

Before any Peer can take his seat in the House of Lords, he has to adduce proper legal proof to that body that he is the person entitled to succeed his predecessor in the title ; but on the death of a Baronet there is no tribunal to prevent an unlawful claimant posing as his successor. Where a Baronet has succeeded to the title held by his father, or uncle, it is not, of course, likely that any one will venture to make himself ridiculous by placing himself in competition for the Dignity. A false assumption of a Baronetcy is, as a rule, made by some one bearing the same name, and usually connected with the family of a Baronetcy, which up to the time of the assumption was supposed to have become extinct through failure of issue.

These false assumptions commenced many generations ago, and it is probably no exaggeration to state that many are now wrongfully describing themselves as Baronets who firmly believe they are entitled to do so in consequence of their father, grandfather, or perhaps great-grandfather, having so styled themselves.

The question of how to deal with these false assumptions is at present under the consideration of the Baronetage.

XVII. *Grants of land in Nova Scotia, with plenary baronial rights and jurisdiction, and legislative powers, in that plantation.* —This has been so fully referred to in the preceding Chapter dealing with the early history of the Baronetage of Scotland and Nova Scotia, that it is unnecessary to do more than state that the following Chapter also contains a reference to the efforts made in 1845 by certain Baronets, whose ancestors had not received their lands, to obtain possession of them more than two centuries later.

XVIII. *Precedency above lesser Barons in Scotland.*—The lesser Barons were those persons who had Charters of Barony from the King, *i.e.* had their lands erected into Baronies. They sat in Parliament until 1585, when they were excused from attendance on condition of sending representatives, a measure which had actually been put on record so far back as 1487.

The following is a copy of the Charter granting to James Colvill the Barony of Culross, bearing date the 20th June 1589:—

'CARTA, &c. Jacobi Colvill de Easter Weems, et Hæredibus Masculis de Corpore suo legitime procreatis, seu procreandis, quibus deficientibus, propinquioribus et legitimis Hæredibus suis masculis quibusq. cognomen et Arma de Colvill gerent. omnes et singulas terras, dominia, baronias, quæ ad Monasterium de Culross, et patrimonium ejusd. juste pertinuerunt, quosquidem omnes et singulas terras annexavimus in unum temporalem baroniam omni tempore affuturo cum titulo et nomine BARONIÆ DE CULROSS, nuncupandum dando et concedendo memorato Jacobo Colvill, Hæredibus suis masculis et assignatis prescriptis, Titulum, Honorem, et Statum LIBERI BARONIS ratione dict. terrarum, simiter et adeo libere sicuti aliquis alius BARO infra Regnum nostrum habuit, habet, vel quovis tempore præcedenti habere poterit. Et volumus quod ille honorabitur cum Ditione (*lie* Badge) et Armis LIBERI BARONIS prout congruit imposterum BARO DE CULROSS appellandus, et quod dict. Jacobus Colvill de Easter Weems, Hæredes et successores sui, BARONES DE CULROSS vocabuntur.'

XIX. *Addition of the Arms of Nova Scotia in armorial bearings.*—This privilege can be more conveniently referred to in conjunction with the Badge to which Nova Scotia Baronets are entitled, and is therefore dealt with under No. XXI. It may, however, be here pointed out that the Nova Scotia Arms is the addition which the Baronets were to bear on their shields, while the Badge is a personal decoration not granted until four years later.

XX. *Power to Members thereof to sit and vote by deputy in the Scottish Parliament when absent from the Kingdom.*—It appears to be uncertain whether this privilege was ever exercised by the Baronets entitled thereto.

XXI. *Right to wear about the neck the Badge of Nova Scotia, suspended by an orange-tawny ribbon.*—The distinctive cognisance assigned to the Baronets of Scotland was, on the institution of this branch of the Degree, the arms of Nova Scotia,

'Dicti baronetti gererent vel in paludamentis vulgo lie cantoun in thair coatt of airmis, vel in scutis, thair scutcheonis pro suo arbitrio, arma Nove Scotie.'

It appears from blanks in the early Signatures and Charters that at that date the arms of Nova Scotia had not been decided upon ; but Nisbet, in his work on Heraldry, gives the following description of the arms as granted :—'Argent, a cross of St. Andrew azure (the badge of Scotland counterchanged), charged with an escutcheon of the royal arms, supported on the dexter by the royal unicorn, and on the sinister by a savage or wild man, proper ; and for the crest, a bunch of laurel and a thistle issuing from two hands conjoined, the one being armed, the other naked, with this motto : "Munit hæc altera vincit."'

In 1629, after Nova Scotia had been sold to the French, Charles i. authorised the Baronets of Scotland and their heirs-male to wear and carry about their necks in all time coming an orange-tawny silk ribbon, whereat hung a scutcheon argent, a saltier azure, and thereon an inescutcheon of Scotland, with an imperial crown above the escutcheon, and encircled with the motto : 'Fax mentis honestæ gloria.'

Nisbet, after giving the above description of the badge, adds : 'The wearing of which badge about the neck was never much used, but carried by way of canton or escutcheon in their armorial bearings without the motto '—'by way of canton, dexter, and sinister ; also by way of an inescutcheon. There 's this difference to be observed, when the badge of Nova Scotia is placed in a canton, and when on an inescutcheon ; in the first, the inescutcheon of Scotland is

ensigned with the imperial crown, whereas the canton cannot
be ensigned by reason of its position; in the last, the
escutcheon which it contains is ensigned with the imperial
crown, and not the inescutcheon contained.'

Some Baronets add the badge as an extra-scutal appendage
to their arms, hanging by its ribbon; but it cannot be
charged on the shield.

The terms of the royal letter, dated the 17th November
1629, given in full in Chapter IV., were : 'We authorise
and allow the said Lewetennent [Sir William Alexander] and
Baronettis and everie one of them, and thare heirs male, to
weare and carry about their neckis in all time coming, ane
orange tauney-silk ribbane, whairon shall hing pendant in a
scutchion *argent* a saltoire *azeuer*, thairon ane inscutcheeine of
the armes of Scotland, with ane imperiall croune above the
scutchone, and incircled with this motto, "Fax Mentis
Honestæ Gloria" : Which cognoissance oure said present
Leivetennent shall deliver now to them from ws, that they may
be the better knowen and distinguished from other persones.'

In a very interesting article on 'The Insignia of the
Baronets,' which appeared in the *Scottish Antiquary* for April
1898, written by its learned editor, Mr. J. H. Stevenson,
F.S.A. Scot., he calls attention to the fact that the King's
letter of 1629 does not give the tincture of the oval on
which it is placed, but that the general practice in the Office
of Lyon King of Arms has been to make it blue.   Mr.
Stevenson, however, gives three instances where the oval
is gold—one being on a portrait in the Parliament House,
Edinburgh, and the other two in coats-of-arms in the Lyon

Office.   He also adds that in an Heraldic manuscript in
the Advocates' Library the oval is green.

The practice of wearing the badge by the Baronets of
Scotland and Nova Scotia appears to have fallen into desuetude ; and in 1775 Lyon King of Arms issued a circular
letter to those Baronets of this creation, calling their attention
to this fact.   As a result, a meeting of the Baronets of Scotland took place in Edinburgh on the 14th June 1775, a resolution was passed to resume the badge, and the following letter
was addressed to the Earl of Suffolk, requesting him to lay
the intentions of the Baronets of Scotland before the King :—

'EDINBURGH, June 15, 1775.

'MY LORD,
      'In consequence of a circular letter from the office of
the Lord Lyon King of Arms, directed to the Baronets of Scotland
created before the Union, there was yesterday a meeting of the
Order held here ; where, from respect to the Crown which conferred
these honours, and in justice to their own families, they resolved
unanimously to resume the Badge of their Order.

'They have directed us to inform your Lordship of their proceedings,
and to intreat of you to lay their intentions before the best of Sovereigns.

'We have the honour to enclose a copy of the circular letter sent
us by the Lyon-office; an authenticated extract of the Royal
Warrant for wearing the Badge of the Order; and a copy of the
minutes of the proceedings of yesterday.
'We have the honour to be,

'My Lord,

'Your Lordship's most obedient,

'And most humble servants,

'(Signed)   ROBERT GORDON, Praeses.

WILLIAM FORBES.

HOME JOHN DALRYMPLE.

ALEXANDER MAXDONALD.

A. STIRLING.'

The following letter was also sent to Lyon King of Arms :—

'EDINBURGH, June 28, 1775.

'MY LORD,

'As a Committee of the Baronets of Scotland, who met here on the 14th instant, we have the honour to enclose for your Lordship a copy of the proceedings of the meeting, and of the letter which they wrote to the Earl of Suffolk.

'In conformity to the orders of the meeting, we also, in the name of it, return our thanks to your Lordship, for the obliging attention which upon this occasion you have shown to the honours of your country ; an attention which, while it flatters us greatly, must also add respect to your Lordship, and an office which we consider as one of the guards of the honours of families.

'We have the honour to be with the highest respect,

'My Lord,

'Your Lordship's most obedient

'And most humble servants,

'(Signed)   WILLIAM FORBES.
JOHN INGLIS.
JOHN DALRYMPLE.
ALEXANDER DICK.
JOHN GORDON.'

The *Gentleman's Magazine*, under date 29th November 1775, records the result of this resolution :—'Several Scotch Baronets appeared at Court in the ensigns of an Order which has lain dormant near 150 years. It was originally called "A NOVA SCOTIA ORDER," and has been lately revived.'

CHAPTER VI

LATER HISTORY OF THE BARONETAGE

In the progress of time, as was only natural, abuses crept into the degree, and pretenders to the dignity from time to time appeared, claiming to be the successors of Baronets, the similarity of their family name affording frequently the sole ground for their assumption of the title.

Representations were from time to time made to the Crown by the Baronets, with the result that on the 3rd December 1783 a Royal Warrant was issued with a view to correct the most important abuse, namely, the wrongful assumption of the style and title, and prohibiting the insertion of the title in any commission, warrant, or appointment thereafter to be issued from any of the Public Offices, without a certificate of the right of the respective parties so using the title being first obtained from the College of Arms.

This Warrant was published in the *London Gazette*, 2nd to 6th December 1783, as follows :—

'COLLEGE OF ARMS, Decr 6th 1783.

'His Majesty has been pleased by Warrant under His Royal Signet and Sign Manual, bearing Date at St. James's the 3rd Instant, to declare and ordain, that, for correcting divers Abuses which have of late Years crept into the Order of BARONETS,

(many Persons having assumed that Title without any just Right)
and for preventing the like in future, the Title of Baronet should
not, from the Date thereof be inserted in any Commission, Warrant,
Appointment, or other instrument, thereafter to be issued to any
Person claiming or using the said Title from either of His Majesty's
Offices of Secretary of State, or from any other of His Majesty's
Offices whatever, until such Person so claiming or using the said
Title, or some one on his Behalf, should have proved his Right
thereto in His Majesty's College of Arms, and produced a Cer-
tificate thereof from the said College, under the Common Seal of
that Corporation.

'And that His Majesty's Secretaries of State for the Time being,
should not, from thenceforth, prepare any Warrant to pass under
the Royal Signet and Sign Manual, for the purpose of advancing
any Person to the Degree of a BARONET of Great Britain, until
it should appear, by a proper Certificate, that the Family Arms of
the Person so intended to be advanced, together with so much of
his Pedigree at least as may be necessary to ascertain the Descent
of the Title, should have been duly registered in His Majesty's
College of Arms; and that the Clerk of the Crown for the Time
being should transmit all Patents of Baronets, thereafter to be
created, as soon as might be after they should have passed the
Great Seal, to the Register of the College of Arms, for the Purpose
of an authentic Registry thereof in the said College, which Patent,
so registered, should be returned to the Clerk of the Crown, for
the Use of the Person to whom the same should be granted.

'SURREY, D. E. M.'

On the publication of this Warrant, a number of the
Baronets, although the step taken was intended for their
protection, and made in consequence of the representations of many of their own body, took offence.   At a
meeting of several Baronets held at the Star and Garter,
Pall Mall, on the 12th May 1784, it was resolved that a
General Meeting of Baronets of Great Britain should be

held on the 22nd of the same month ; and accordingly on that day fifty-three Baronets attended, with Sir Henry Hoghton in the chair.

A Resolution was passed electing a Committee of twenty-one Baronets to consider the Warrant of the 3rd December 1783, and what steps would be most proper to take thereupon ; and Mr. Joseph Edmondson, Mowbray Herald Extra, was appointed Secretary.

Accordingly, at a Meeting of the Committee held on the 25th May, the Royal Warrant was taken into consideration ; and Sir Henry Hoghton, Sir Harbord Harbord, and Sir George Allanson Winn were appointed to wait on the Deputy Earl Marshal, and request to be informed of the specific abuses alluded to in the Warrant.

Two days later the Committee met again at their headquarters, the Star and Garter in Pall Mall, when the deputation informed the Committee that they had waited on Lord Surrey and conversed with him on the subject.

His Lordship informed them that the Order arose from a representation to him, that several had assumed the title of Baronet who neither themselves nor Ancestors had been so created, that persons got their names inserted as Baronets in Commissions, which were to pass under the King's Sign Manual, and that from such time they assumed the title.

His Lordship further said he had, from a regard to and a wish to support the Order of Baronets, taken that as the best and most effectual mode in his power to prevent such innovations in future, and that he could not inform the Committee of any mode of removing or getting out of the list those who had thus assumed the title, but was ready to meet the Baronets, to answer any further questions they might have to propose, and also to give up the Order of the 6th December last, if found to be inconvenient, that he should concur with the Baronets and assist them in any other mode of preventing these inconveniences, if they or himself could find out or agree upon a proper and effectual one.

The Committee then passed the following resolutions :—

'That it be recommended to the General Meeting to come to a resolution expressive of the high sense they entertain of the Gracious Intentions of His Majesty respecting their Order.

'That the Order in the *Gazette* of the 6th December last signed Surrey, D. E. M., subjects the Baronets to much inconvenience and expense.

'That it would add much to the Honor and Dignity of the Order if His Majesty should be graciously pleased to grant unto the Baronets of Great Britain the privilege of wearing such mark or marks of Distinction as His Majesty shall be most graciously pleased to direct, and would also be the most effectual means of preventing the abuses mentioned by Lord Surrey, and afford a just and proper opportunity of requiring such Baronets as should be desirous of enjoying that privilege (previous to their being admitted to wear the same) to make such proofs of their title to the Honor as His Majesty in his great wisdom shall be pleased to appoint.

'That a petition be prepared for that purpose and laid before the next General Meeting.'

A General Meeting of Baronets was accordingly held on the 31st May 1784, and after several alterations in the draft submitted to the Meeting, the following Petition was agreed to :—

'To THE KING'S MOST EXCELLENT MAJESTY, the Humble Petition of the Baronets of England and Great Britain.

'SHEWETH,

'That they are fully convinced of your Majesty's most Gracious Intention to support the Honor and Dignity of their Order, and of preventing Persons assuming that title without legal authority, as appears by your Majesty's Royal Warrant in the *Gazette* of the 6th December last.

'We your Petitioners beg leave therefore most humbly to suggest to your Majesty, that since the first Institution of the Order, several applications have been made, and measures adopted to stop all abuses in the said Order, but without the desired effect, that on a General Meeting of the Baronets, to take into consideration the Regulations published in the *Gazette* of the sixth of December last, respecting their Order, and signed Surrey, D. E. M., they were of opinion that it would subject those who are really entitled to that Honor and Dignity to numberless inconveniences and expense, without being an effectual means of preventing such abuses.

'Your Petitioners therefore most humbly pray your Majesty to grant them relief from the inconveniences and expense directed by the said Order and regulation, and humbly apprehend it would tend much to correct the abuses complained of in the said Order of Baronets if your Majesty would be graciously pleased to grant them the privilege of wearing such mark or badge of distinction as is here annexed for your Majesty's Royal Consideration or any Mark or Device your Majesty shall be most graciously pleased to grant them, as your Petitioners apprehend will afford a just and proper opportunity of requiring all persons bearing or wearing such marks of distinction, to produce their title thereto.

'And your Majesty's Petitioners shall ever pray, etc.'

In what way the grant of a further mark of distinction than that given by their Patents, viz. the privilege of bearing in an escutcheon the Badge of Ulster, could have the effect of removing the inconveniences or expense which were apprehended from the provisions of the Royal Warrant complained of, the petitioners did not state.

At a meeting of the Committee held on the 2nd June, it was arranged that Sir Henry Hoghton, Sir Harbord Harbord, and Sir George Allanson Winn should wait upon Lord Surrey, show him a copy of the Petition, and request him to favour them with some plan to be laid before the Committee as should appear to him proper for establishing a Committee of Baronets, who might in conjunction with his Lordship, assisted by the College of Arms, decide upon such disputed claims as might be referred to them, or for any other matters relating to their Order, and to request the attendance of some of his Lordship's Officers, who might inform the Committee in what manner the Baronets' Patents of creation were formerly registered in the College of Arms, and in what manner they were at that time registered.

Two days later the Committee again met, when Mr. Edmondson, their Secretary, submitted a plan 'for the better regulation of the Order and to prevent the abuses therein.' This was read and ordered to be entered in the Minutes.

At a meeting on the 8th June, Mr. Heard and Mr. Brooke, Officers of the College of Arms, attended by order of the Deputy Earl Marshal, and were asked several questions; but not being fully prepared with answers, they were desired to attend the next Committee, and at the meeting on the 11th June they accordingly attended and laid several papers before the Committee for their consideration.

A General Meeting of the Baronets was held on the 29th June 1784, at which it was resolved the Petition to the King should be delivered as soon as convenient, also that fair copies should be made for each Secretary of State, and that a paper setting forth the inconveniences of the Earl Marshal's Order, as also the request of the Baronets for a mode to be established by them for the better regulation of the Order, be given to each Minister.

A considerable number of meetings of the Committee was held; and at a General Meeting of Baronets held on the 19th February 1785, Sir Harbord Harbord read the following letter from Lord Sydney, received by him that morning :—

'Lord Sydney presents his compliments to Sir Harbord Harbord, and in return to the Petition delivered to him by Sir Harbord Harbord, Sir Edward Astley and Sir George Allanson Winn has the honor of acquainting him that there will be no difficulty in recalling the Proclamation of which the Baronets complain, that the King's Servants will be ready to consider of any plan of a Court of Honour or Committee to be established consisting of a number of their own Order to prevent the title of Baronet being assumed by those who have not a right to it. But with regard to the wearing a Badge as an Hereditary Order, many objections have been raised to it, and it seems by no means agreeable to many of the Order of Baronets themselves, so that it will be impossible to comply with that part of the Petition.'

The following resolutions were then passed :—'That the Committee be empowered to take such measures as they shall find necessary to obtain the immediate repeal of the Order of the Deputy Earl Marshal of the 6th December 1783'; also, 'That the Committee be empowered to take such further steps as they shall think prudent relative to the other parts of their petition.'

As a result of this movement, the following Order was issued :—

'COLLEGE OF ARMS,
'February 28, 1785.

'Whereas it hath been represented to His Majesty, that some inconveniences have arisen in carrying into execution part of the regulations contained in His Majesty's Warrant of the 3rd of December 1783 relative to the Order of Baronets His Majesty hath been graciously pleased by another Warrant under His Royal Signet and Sign Manual bearing date the 24th instant to suspend the several Regulations contained in the above-mentioned Warrant of the 3rd December 1783 except the clause which relates to such Persons as shall have been or may be created Baronets after the date of the said Warrant of the 3rd of December 1783 till such other Regulations in this matter shall be adopted as may not be attended with such inconveniences.

'SURREY, D. E. M.'

The prayer for the personal decoration of the Baronets, in addition to the badge enjoyed by the Baronets of Scotland and Nova Scotia, was therefore not complied with, one reason being that it would have tended to reduce in value personal distinctions awarded for public services, naval, military, or civil.

It is recorded in a manuscript book of collections in Heralds' College that Sir Thomas Frankland, Baronet, when upon a mission at the Court of Lisbon, wore as a badge, suspended by a ribbon of three colours, the bloody hand of Ulster enamelled on a white field, and set round with diamonds. This badge is now in the possession of Mrs. Frankland-Russell-Astley of Chequers Court, Buckinghamshire, who has also a similar one set round with coloured stones. It is said Sir Thomas wore the badge appended to his button-hole by a twisted ribbon of three different colours, namely, blue, green, and red.

As long ago as 1627, the Baronets, in conjunction with the Knights Bachelors, endeavoured to obtain a declaration or order from the King that they should wear a distinctive badge upon their bodies to distinguish one Order from another, and give to each respect proper and reverence correspondent.

With this object in view they approached Henry Rich, Earl of Holland, who was Captain of the King's Guard, and the representation set forth in substance that, as the honour of Knighthood in divers degrees, with some additions of title and perpetuity thereof, had been, and was, daily imparted from His Royal Majesty to worthy persons and families within his realm of England and Ireland; 'and as divers were supposed surreptitiously to assume that honour never really conferred by His Majesty, so it seemeth a thing very consonant and much to be desired that His Majesty would be pleased, for a more eminent manifestation of his Royal greatness, and for the discoverie of the aforesaid surreptitious assumers, to institute and appoint some distinctive Badge to be worn and carried by all Baronets and other Knights upon their bodies, in such eminent manner and with such difference of the matter and colour of the said Badge, or of the ribband or other thing wherein it shall be borne, or that every man who shall behold and see any such honoured person, may presently discover his degree and title of honour.'

A cross of gold was suggested as most fitting, and reasons

for the same assigned ; and further, that those taking the said badge should have precedence of all who might refuse to take the same, though they should subsequently take it ; and that no such distinguished Baronet or Knight should have his person arrested without being first called before the Earl Marshal to answer the complaint against him.

As a result of the appeal made to him, the Earl of Holland addressed the following letter to the Officers of Arms :—

'To my very Loving Friends Sir Richard St. George and Sir John Borough, Knights, and the rest of His Majesty's Officers of Arms—or to so many of them as are in town at receipt hereof.
                                                            'HOLLANDE.'

'After my hearty commendations unto you—
'Whereas there hath been a proposition made unto me to move His Majesty to declare His Royal pleasure by proclamation that all Baronets and Knights Bachelors should wear several Orders in Ribands of several colours to distinguish one Order from another, and both from persons of inferior quality, in such sort as the Knights of the Bath by His Majesty's commandment at this time do, I have thought fit to recommend the same to your considera-tion, who are best able to judge of matters of this nature, and to entreat your opinion of the fitness and conveniency thereof on His Majesty's behalf and that of his subjects.
'Whereon desiring your Answer with all convenient speed, I bid you heartily farewell and rest.
                                        'Your very loving friend,
                                                            'HOLLANDE.

'Whitehall, 29th June, 1627.'

To this letter the Officers of Arms sent the following reply :—

'To the Right Hon. our very good Lord Henry Earl of Holland, at the Court.

'Right Honourable and our very good Lord,

'Whereas Your Lordship was pleased by your Letter of the 29th of June last past (inscribed to us Sir George St. George and Sir John Borough, Knights, and the rest of His Majesty's Officers of Arms, or unto so many of them as were then in town), to recommend unto our consideration a Proposition made unto Your Lordship to move His Majesty to declare His Royal pleasure by proclamation that all Baronets and Knights Bachelors should wear several Orders in Ribands of several colours to distinguish one Order from another, and both from persons of inferior quality, in such sort as the Knights of the Bath by His Majesty's Commandment at this time do, and to entreat our opinion of the fitness and conveniency thereof on His Majesty's behalf, and that of his subjects, and hereon declare our answer with all convenient speed, which Letter being delivered unto Mr. Henry St. George, Richmond Herald, upon Saturday, being the 7th of this instant July, we whose names are hereunto subscribed (the rest of our Society being out of town) were forthwith assembled at our usual place of meeting in the Office of Arms, and having with as much deliberation and maturity as the shortness of time would permit, taken into our consideration the premises, we do most humbly Certify unto your Lordship as followeth,—

'As touching differences, and marks upon robes or in apparel, for distinguishing of degrees and orders, we find the same not only frequent among other nations, but by the ancient usages and customs of this Realm, as time and place required, to have been formerly observed in England. For so were, and yet are, the degrees of Princes, Dukes, Marquesses, Earls, Viscounts, and Barons, distinguished by the number of *barrs* on their robes among the greater nobility; And for Distinction of Orders, the Knights of the Garter were formerly distinguished from others, by their *George and Garter*, and not long since by their *Blue Riband* added unto the former. So likewise were Knights (now called Bachelors) anciently known by their Belts, their Collar of S.S. of Gold, their

R

gilded Spurs, and Swords; and Esquires by their Collar and Spurs of Silver. The Knights of the Bath have also lately been distinguished from other Knights by their Carnation Riband and Jewel appendent. Of all which we find not that any one so worn hath at any time been held or considered as unfit or inconvenient either to the King or subject, but taken and esteemed as a peculiar mark of sovereignty in the giver, and an eminent token of Honor in the receiver,—some of them having been by public Acts of Parliament allowed, and none of them (for ought we know) condemned by any. And that formerly all Estates, by their differences in apparel, were thought fit to be distinguished according to their Estates pre-eminences, Dignities, and Degrees, is clearly expressed in the preamble to the Statute on Apparel, 24 Hen. VIII. cap. 4.—

'The consideration whereof showeth us to be of opinion that if there were respective Ornaments worn for the distinction of the Degree of a Baronet, and the Order of Knights-Bachelors, it would no way be unfit or inconvenient either to His Majesty or to His Subjects. But whether His Majesty's pleasure in this behalf should be declared by proclamation, or what the marks of difference in these cases should be, we must, as in duty bound, humbly leave the same to the consideration of His Majesty.

'All which by way of answer to your honourable Letter we do in all humbleness Certify, and remain your Lordship's most humbly to be commanded.

> 'RI. ST. GEORGE, Clarencieux.
> Jo. BOROUGH, Norroy.
> WM. PENSON, Lancaster.
> HEN. ST. GEORGE, Richmond.
> HEN. CHITTINGE, Chester.
> Jo. PHILPOT, Somerset.

'At the Office of Arms,
     16th July, 1627.'

On the 15th December following, Sir Robert Heath, the Attorney-General, wrote to Sir William Segar, King of Arms, as follows:—

'Sir,

'I understand that about July last yourself and the rest of the Heralds, or some of your Society, made a Certificate to his Majesty concerning the Baronets etc.—I have received lately a Commandment from the King concerning that business; and as I shall have use of the said Certificate for his Majesty's service, I pray you make me a copy thereof with all convenient speed.

'So with my love and service to yourself

'I remain your very loving friend

'Ro. Heath.

'15 December 1627.'

It does not appear, however, that the King was advised to comply with the request, as no Order was made, nor any badge, ornament, or vestments assigned to either the Baronets or the Knights.

After the second unsuccessful attempt to obtain a badge made at the same time, the Baronets were successful in their application that the terms of the Royal Warrant of the 3rd December 1783 should be rescinded, no further movement was made by the Baronetage until 1834, when Mr. Richard Broun, heir-apparent to Sir James Broun of Colstoun, Haddingtonshire, a Baronet of Scotland and Nova Scotia, already referred to as having at a meeting of Baronets assumed knighthood on the honour being refused him when claimed, revived all the questions relating to the privileges of the Degree.

After a conference with his friends in the Baronetage, Mr. Broun issued a short statement of the original institution of the Degree, dated the 9th August 1834, to which was annexed a private Circular intimating that it was put

forward by a few members of the Baronetage desirous of a
revival of the rights and privileges which had fallen into
disuse.   The Circular also requested the recipients to communicate whether they would take part in the proceedings
either personally or by proxy.

As a result of this Circular and further correspondence, a
preliminary Meeting of Baronets was held at the Clarendon
Hotel, Bond Street, London, on the 26th May 1835.   The
proceedings commenced by Sir Charles Cockerell, Baronet,
M.P. for Evesham, expressing the hope that the circumstance of his having been one of the Baronets who had taken
an interest in originating the measures before the Meeting,
would be considered as an apology for taking a lead in the
proceedings.   He then proposed that Sir Francis Shuckburgh,
the senior Baronet present, should preside upon the occasion,
which was unanimously approved.

Sir Francis Shuckburgh having taken the chair, observed
that the object of the meeting over which unexpectedly he
had the honour to preside was, as stated in the second para-
graph of the Circular convening it, for the purpose of
taking into consideration a case that had been prepared to
establish, by charter and other documentary evidence, the
right of the Order to enjoy the style of ' The Honourable,'
the conjunct dignities of ' Knight & Baronet,' to wear the
Collar of S.S., etc., to bear Supporters, etc., and to determine what further steps should be adopted for the revival of
their privileges ; also to take into consideration a proposal
which would be submitted for petitioning His Majesty to
grant that the Ulster Badge might be worn upon the person.

Sir Francis then requested Mr. Broun to read the Case referred to in the Circular.

After a few preliminary remarks, in which he referred to the number of Baronets who were in sympathy with the movement, Mr. Broun read the Case which he had prepared, the object of which, as stated in the preamble, was by adducing in detail from official records, ancient manuscripts, and the writings of genealogical and heraldic authorities, extracts and notices corroborative of their truth, to establish *seriatim* the accuracy of the conclusions arrived at.

The Case stated that the Inquiry divided itself into four branches :—

1. To establish the right of the Baronets, individually and conjunctly, to enjoy the honorary epithet of 'The Honourable.'

2. To prove that the Baronetage is, like the Peerage, a union of Dignities ; and that the members of it are entitled to enjoy the style of 'Knight & Baronet,' together with the immunities and insignia pertaining to both.

3. To prove that the Baronetage, in right of its being a conjunct Dignity, is privileged to wear the Collar of S.S., etc.

4. To show that the Baronetage are entitled to bear Supporters, Coronets, etc.

It is not necessary to give any extracts from the Case, as the various points raised in it have either already been referred to in preceding chapters, or will be mentioned later on. At the conclusion of Mr. Broun's reading, the Chairman expressed the strong sense which he entertained of the satisfactory and conclusive nature of the evidence adduced in support of the rights and privileges of the Baronetage; and eventually a resolution was passed for convening a General Meeting of Baronets on the 22nd June following to pass resolutions declaratory of the intention of the Degree to reserve the rights and privileges pertaining to the Baronetage, which had fallen into disuse, and also to petition the Crown that the Ulster Badge should be worn upon the person.

A Provisional Committee was appointed, Mr. Richard Broun being requested to act as its Honorary Secretary; and a subscription list was opened.

As a result, two petitions were presented to the King, setting forth the grounds on which the Baronets claimed to have prefixed to their names the style of 'Honourable,' praying for grants of Supporters to their arms, vestments, and other decorations of estate, and a distinctive badge; also to hold a Chapter.

These petitions were eventually referred to the College of Arms through the Earl Marshal, who, after consideration, issued the following Report :—

'Report of the COLLEGE OF ARMS upon the Petition of certain Baronets of England, Scotland, and Ireland and of the United Kingdom, addressed to His Majesty King William IV., and through the Earl Marshal referred to the consideration of the College of Arms, 29 August, 1835.

'COLLEGE OF ARMS, 31st October, 1835.
'My Lord Duke,
'The Members of this College, assembled in Chapter,

having, in obedience to your Grace's commands, signified in your letter of the 29th of August last, transmitting two Petitions addressed to the King by certain Baronets of England, Scotland, Ireland, and of the United Kingdom, taken the same and the accompanying Papers and Drawings into their consideration, have the honour to report to your Grace their opinion thereon.

'The Prayer of one of these Petitions is, that his Majesty would be pleased to direct and command the proper Officers,

'1stly. To receive, consider, and report to his Majesty upon the evidence to be produced in support of the claim of the Petitioners to the style of " *The Honourable*" :

'2ndly. To issue His Royal Warrant to Garter King of Arms, and his fraternity, to assign *Supporters* to all Baronets :

'3rdly. To issue a similar Warrant to the Master of the Robes, or other proper Officer, to assign to the Petitioners appropriate *Vestments and other Decorations of Estate*, in virtue of their conjunct dignities of Baronet and Knight, according to the relation of the Order to the Orders of Nobility, and the principle laid down in the final decree in 1616, of King James the First :

'4thly. To approve the formation of a *Chapter of Baronets* for the regulation of the Order by statutes to be prepared by the Petitioners, and afterwards submitted for His Majesty's royal approval and sanction.

'The Prayer of the other Petition is—

'That His Majesty would be pleased, by His Royal Warrant, to grant permission to the Petitioners to wear, with an appropriate ribbon suspended on their persons, when they approach the Royal Presence (as usual with all other degrees in the State similarly privileged) *the Badge* which was conferred upon their ancestors by the illustrious Founder of their Honours.

'1. In regard to the claim of the Petitioners to be styled " *The Honourable*"—

'We beg leave to observe that the evidence, adduced in the

subjoined case of the Petitioners, in support of the allegation, "That the Order of Baronets did, before as well as subsequently to the Revolution, enjoy such style, though it has now fallen into disuse," and consisting of instances of the attribution of such style in printed Books, Deeds, Letters, Monumental Inscriptions, and elsewhere, cannot be received as authority for the same. If Baronets have been so addressed on the occasions mentioned, such address has been no more warranted by authority than when the same style has been applied to Field Officers in the army and others, and been, in such cases, an evident infringement on the style which is given by courtesy to the sons of Earls, Viscounts, and Barons, whilst the style, place, and precedence of Baronets were definitely fixed by the Decree of King James the First, to be *after* the younger sons of Viscounts and Barons.

'The style of "*The Honourable*' is given to *the Judges* and to *the Barons of the Exchequer*, with others; because, by the Decree of the 10th of King James the First, for settling the place and precedency of the Baronets, the Judges, and Barons of the Exchequer, as well as others therein mentioned, were declared to have place and precedence *before* the younger sons of Viscounts and Barons.

'But the Patents of Baronets, having expressly designated and fixed what their style shall be, viz. that the appellation of "*Sir*" shall be prefixed to their Christian names, and that of "Baronet" added to their surnames, we humbly conceive that no other appellation was intended by the Founder of the Order to be given to them; and that the style of "*The Honourable*," if conceded, would create such confusion, and interfere with and intrench upon the privilege which courtesy has assigned to the sons of Peers of the Realm, and others adverted to.

'2. On the arguments for conceding to the Baronets the privilege of bearing *Supporters* to their arms—

'We have the honour to observe, with reference to the *four* grounds upon which the claim to such Privilege is stated by the Petitioners to rest—

'1. That the Letters Patent of King James the First, and Charles the First, do not contain, as inferred in the case of the Petitioners, any direction whatever, positive or implied, upon the point in question :

' 2. That the Provision, cited from the Decree of the 10th James the First, for ordering and adjudging any question that might thereafter arise touching the privileges or other matters concerning Baronets, according to the usual rules, customs, and laws by which matters concerning other degrees of dignity hereditary are ordered and adjudged, could not have contemplated any question concerning the bearing of Supporters, the right to which was then limited to the Peers of the Realm and the Knights of the Garter :

' 3. That the exceptions to the general rule, by which the bearing of Supporters is now limited to the Peers of the Realm, the Knights of His Majesty's Orders, and the Proxies of Princes of the Blood Royal at Installations, have been, by the especial grace and favour of the Crown, either in reward of eminent services and merits, or upon consideration of the weight of which the Sovereign alone, as the Fountain of Honour, has the right of judging.

' We do not feel it necessary to offer any observations upon the practice referred to under this head, in the case of the granting Supporters to Baronets by the Lord Lyon King of Arms in Scotland, which, not being founded, so far as we are apprized, upon any authority emanating from the Crown, can surely not be adduced as examples for imitation in this part of the United Kingdom.

' The assertion, in the case of the Petitioners, " that the Charters of the Royal Founders of their Order expressly and specially warrant and empower the King of Arms to assign *Supporters and a peculiar Coronet or Cap of Estate* to the Baronets," requires no comment ; as, upon reference to the Letters Patent cited, they are found to contain no words which could bear that construction.

' 4. That the grants of Supporters to the Knights Grand Crosses of the Order of the Bath, which are founded upon

a statute of that Order, upon its Institution in 1725, being
for special, military, naval, and diplomatic services, and a
personal distinction, and coupled with a personal decoration by the hands of the Sovereign, cannot be considered
as a precedent for *perpetuating* that Distinction in the
Families of Baronets, although they have a higher place
in the Tables of Precedency.

‘If the right to such honourable distinction were to be determined by Precedency, the younger sons of Peers, and the
Judges and others, who by the Decree above referred to
have higher place than those younger sons, and consequently take precedence of Baronets and Knights Grand
Crosses of the Bath, would, upon the same principle, have
a claim thereto : and the Privilege, if conceded upon such
ground, would come to be so diffused and common as to
render it of little value to those who, by ancient usage, or
by especial Grace and Favour of the Crown, are now or
may become entitled thereto.

‘Finally, we beg leave to remark, upon this part of the case
of the Petitioners, that the armorial Distinctions of the
Baronets are clearly defined by the Decree of the 10th of
James the First, before cited, which declares that they
shall bear, either in a canton in their coat of arms, or in
an inescocheon, at their election, the *Arms of Ulster*, a
privilege which was afterwards set forth in the Letters
Patent of Creation of Baronets down to the present time.

‘3. The claim of the Petitioners to *Vestments and other Decorations of Estate* is stated, in their case, to rest partly upon the Charters
of the Royal Founders of their Order, viz. “that Baronets shall be
ordered and adjudged, in all matters, as the other degrees of *dignity
hereditary* are ordered and adjudged,” and partly “upon the usual
rules, customs, and laws for place, precedence, and privilege,” and
the circumstance “that all the various degrees of *dignity personal*
have had assigned to them Vestments of Estate.”

‘Upon this claim we humbly submit that neither do the Charters
or Letters Patent referred to bear out this assertion, nor is there

any analogy established, in the case of the Petitioners, between a supposed right to particular Vestments of Estate, in virtue of their dignity, and the rights of the Peers of Parliament to Robes of Estate and parliamentary, or the rights of the Knights of the Royal Orders to particular Robes under the Statutes of the Orders to which they respectively belong.

'The "*other Decorations of Estate*" alluded to, are enumerated in the case of the Petitioners, and delineated in the accompanying drawings, as follows :—

> ' " 1. The Baronets claim the right of wearing *a dark-green dress*, as the *appropriate* costume pertaining to them as *Equites Aurati*.
>
> 2. The Collar of SS.
> 3. The Belt.
> 4. The Scarf.
> 5. *A Star*.
> 6. A Pennon.
> 7. A White Hat and Plume of White Feathers.
> 8. The Thumb Ring and Signet.
> 9. The Sword, Gilt Spurs, &c."

This claim purports to be founded upon the clause heretofore contained in Patents granting the dignity of Baronet, whereby the King, in pursuance of an ordinance to that effect contained in the final decree before referred to of the 10th of James the 1st, covenanted and granted to and with the person advanced to the dignity that His Majesty, his heirs and successors, would immediately after the passing of the same create and make the Grantee, being of full age, a Knight, and also confer the same honour upon his first-born Son or Heir male apparent, being of full age, *upon Notice given to the Chamberlain or Vice-Chamberlain of the Royal Household for the time being.*

'This promise and grant were revoked, determined and made void, by Letters Patent dated the 19th December in the 8th year of His late Majesty King George IV., with respect to all Letters Patent for the creation of Baronets to be granted after that date ;

saving, of course, the rights and privileges then by law belonging to any Baronet.

'Upon a reference to the Record of Knights it appears that, in pursuance of the Ordinance in question, thirteen Baronets were (in order, probably, to place them on the same footing with others who had been knighted previously to their advancement to the Baronetage, and to enable them to use the same style of "Knight and Baronet") knighted by King James the First within the two years following the date of the Ordinance; and we find no instance of such knighthood during the remainder of that and the whole of the succeeding reign.

'Without entering, therefore, into a discussion how far "the Decorations of Estate" claimed by the Petitioners are to be classed amongst the appendages of Knights Bachelors, or considering the numerous objections applying to the Drawings of Decorations accompanying the Petition, we shall only beg leave to observe that the allegation, reiterated throughout the case of the Petitioners, that Baronets are seized of "the conjunct dignities of Baronet and Knight," is not supported by historical fact; Knighthood being a strictly *personal* honour, conferred only by the Sovereign or his Lieutenant or Commissioner, or by Letters Patent under the Great Seal.

' 4. Upon the prayer of the Petitioners that there may be formed "*a Chapter of Baronets* for the regulation of the Order by Statutes to be prepared by them and submitted for His Majesty's approval."

'It is our humble opinion that the Baronetage being an herditary dignity, whose privileges are already clearly defined and established by the several Letters Patent and other Acts of the Crown by which they are governed, as well as set forth and recited in every Patent conferring the honour, there does not appear to us to be any necessity for assimilating them to the Royal Orders of Knighthood by constituting them a capitular body.

'With reference to the Petition praying that the Baronets may wear suspended by a ribbon on their persons "*the Badge conferred upon their ancestors*," we submit the following remarks:—

'There is not any record of a Badge having been, as here assumed,

conferred upon the Baronets of England, Ireland, Great Britain, or
the United Kingdom, who by their Patents are to " bear either in
a canton in their coat of arms, or in an escutcheon, at their pleasure,
the arms of Ulster (to wit) a Hand Gules or a Bloody Hand in a
Field Argent."

'This distinction is purely *armorial*; and the option of bearing
the Arms of Ulster, on a canton or upon an escutcheon *in their
coat of arms*, was given only in reference to the possible description
of heraldic charges which might render the one mode of displaying
the added bearing more convenient than the other. That this is
the true construction of the Ordinance is evident from the practice
which has always obtained, of placing the Ulster Arms either in
canton, or in an escutcheon on a chief, or in the body of the coat
of arms.

'King Charles the First having thought fit, for the advancement
of the Plantation of Nova Scotia, to extend, in 1625, the Order of
Baronets, by creating Baronets of Scotland, the Patents of creation
granted thereupon were precisely in the same phraseology, in regard
to the style, place, precedency, and other privileges, as those of the
Patents of Baronet granted by his royal predecessor; but with
different armorial distinctions, the Baronets of Scotland being
directed to bear, as an addition to their arms, either on canton or
inescutcheon at their option the Ensign of Nova Scotia being
Argent the ancient Arms of Scotland upon a Saltire Azure supported on the dexter by the Royal Unicorn and on the sinister
by a Savage proper, and for the crest a Branch of Laurel and a
Thistle issuing from two hands conjoined, the one being armed
the other naked, with this motto, " Munit hæc et altera vincit."
And we have no evidence of any Ordinance having been issued,
between 1625 and the date of the Union, for altering the mode so
prescribed of distinguishing the Arms of Baronets of Scotland.

'It appears that King Charles, by his Royal Warrant of 17
November 1629, without reference, however, to his prior Ordinance
in regard to this armorial distinction, was pleased to grant a part
of it in the form of a Badge to Sir William Alexander, His Majesty's
Lieutenant in Nova Scotia, and the Baronets so created " for the

better advancement of the Plantation of New Scotland," and their heirs male, permitting them to wear about the neck "an orange-tawny silk Ribbon whereon shall hang pendent in an Inescutcheon Argent a Saltire Azure thereon an Inescutcheon of the Arms of Scotland with an Imperial Crown above the Scutcheon and incircled with this motto: 'Fax mentis Honestæ Gloria'; which cognisance His Majesty ordains his said then Lieutenant shall deliver to them, 'that they may be the better known and distinguished from other persons.'"

'The Warrant also ordains that "from time to time, as occasion of granting or renewing their patents, or their heirs succeeding to the dignity, shall offer, the said power to them to carry the said Ribbon and cognisance, shall be therein particularly granted and inserted'; but we do not find, upon examining such Patents of Baronets of Scotland, after the date of the said Royal Warrant, as we have had the opportunity of inspecting, that the direction to grant and insert in subsequent Patents the permission to wear such Ribbon and Badge was complied with. It may therefore be questionable whether the distinction of a Badge so granted by that Royal Warrant was not intended to be limited to those upon whom the honour had been conferred in reward for their exertions in the settlement of the Colony of New Scotland.

'It is undoubtedly in the power of His Majesty, in his wisdom and in the exercise of his Royal Prerogative, to assign to Baronets, Knights, and any other class of his subjects a Badge, in imitation of the grant made by his Royal Predecessor King Charles the First to the Baronets of Scotland: but we humbly submit how far an *hereditary* personal decoration in the nature of a Ribbon and Badge (which, if conferred upon the Baronets, would at once decorate upwards of 900 persons, and entail such decoration upon the heirs male of their bodies for ever), would not be an anomaly in this country where personal decorations have been hitherto received only from the hands of the Sovereign by the Knights and Members of his Royal Orders, or by Individuals who have been honoured with medals in commemoration of eminent services rendered to the State.

'To this observation we may be permitted to add that, in the year 1784, a Petition, having a similar object, was presented to His late Majesty King George the Third; but it does not appear that His Majesty was pleased to accede to the prayer thereof.

'By order of Chapter,

'CHAS. GEO. YOUNG,

'To His Grace   York Herald and Register.

'The Earl Marshal,

'&c., &c., &c.'

As a consequence of this Report, the prayer of the petitioners was not conceded by the Crown, notwithstanding which Mr. Broun and the Baronets associated with him persevered in their endeavours.

The Committee of Baronets took into special consideration so much of the Report of the Officers of Arms as related to the Badge, and submitted for the consideration of the Secretary of State for the Home Department some special observations, with the hope of removing his impression that he could not advise the King to comply with the prayer of the Baronets.

Correspondence took place between the Committee and the Home Office, and also between both and the College of Arms.

On the 30th May 1836, a general meeting of Baronets was held, at which the following Address and Petition to His Majesty King William IV. was adopted, and copies were sent on the 13th June to Lord John Russell, M.P., the Home Secretary, who on the same day replied he would be happy to receive a deputation from the Baronets three days later at the Home Office.

'To His Most Excellent Majesty
'King William the Fourth
'&c. &c.

'The Most Humble and Dutiful Address of the
'Baronets of Ulster.

'Sire,

'We whose names are hereunto annexed Baronets of Ulster of the various creations of England, Ireland, and the United Kingdom, approach your Majesty with sentiments of the most profound attachment to your Royal Person, and of loyalty to that Throne of which those enjoying the Hereditary Dignity we represent have ever been the strenuous supporters.

'Sire, on the 8th of July last, on the occasion of our laying before your Majesty certain proceedings instituted by us with a view to restoring our Order to the original excellence on which it was placed by its Royal Founder King James I., we embraced the opportunity of praying Your Majesty to grant us, as a boon proceeding from your Royal grace and favour, the privilege of wearing as a Badge, on our persons at Court and on other suitable occasions, the cognizance or device assigned to our Order to commemorate the objects for which it was erected.

'Sire, Your Majesty having been pleased to receive that Petition in the most gracious manner, and to assure the deputation who presented it that your Majesty would take a personal interest in our wishes, it is with deep regret that we learn by a communication from Your Majesty's Secretary of State for the Home Department, dated the 23rd November last, that obstacles have interposed to delay the fulfilment of Your Majesty's most gracious intention.

'Sire, after the lapse of two centuries during which every class of Your Majesty's subjects have received large accessions of rights and privileges, we approach Your Majesty, the FOUNTAIN OF HONOUR, and sole Arbiter in all matters of Dignity, most humbly representing the anomalous condition in which we are placed when compared with our Brethren of Nova Scotia.

'Sire, we cannot but more strongly hope for the sympathy of your Majesty the supporter, as well as the distributor of all State Honours, when we inform Your Majesty that our Order and Rank are neither understood, nor appreciated at the various Courts of Your Majesty's allies, and that we are often when present at those Courts set aside and postponed to our acknowledged inferiors in rank, solely because our personal distinction has no outward decoration or Badge.

'Sire, most humbly hoping that your Majesty, in furtherance of already expressed gracious intentions towards our body, will be pleased to put us on the same footing with the Baronets of Nova Scotia (who are of subsequent creation) as regards a Badge, and praying that your Majesty may long continue in peace, prosperity and happiness to sway the Sceptre of this great Nation.

'We remain, Sire,

'With the most profound respect, loyalty, and veneration

'Your Majesty's most obedient, most dutiful,

'and most faithful Subjects and Servants.

'Signed in the name, by the authority, and on the behalf 'of the following Baronets concurring therein.

ROGER GREISLEY, Bar^{t}.

Chairman.

(Names follow.)

The result of this Petition is shown in the following letter:—

'Whitehall,

'July 8, 1836.

'SIR,

'I have had the honour to lay before His Majesty a copy of the Address of the Baronets intended for presentation to His Majesty.

'His Majesty was pleased to say that he would receive the Address of the Baronets at the Levee whenever they wished to present it, and that he should then refer it to me, as his Secretary of State for the Home Department.

'Having considered the object of the Address, and the Report of the Herald's College, my impression undoubtedly is, that I cannot advise his Majesty to comply with its prayer.

'I have the honour to be

'Your most Obedient Servant,

'Sir R. Greisley Bar^{t}.   'J. RUSSELL.

'&c. &c. &c.'

S

At a special meeting of the Baronets' Committee, open to all Baronets and their eldest sons, held at the house of Sir Robert Fitzwygram, Baronet, Connaught Place, London, Sir Francis Shuckburgh, Baronet, in the chair, Mr. William Crawford, Barrister-at-Law, Standing Counsel to the Committee, read a most able address of great length on the subject of the Chartered Rights and Privileges of the Degree.

This Address, which was subsequently printed in 1837, and privately reprinted in 1898, after setting out the First Patent of James 1., his Decrees of 1612 and 1616, proceeded to refer to the privileges of the Degree, and gave very numerous examples to show that the style of ' Honourable' was commonly applied to Baronets for at least 150 years after the erection of the dignity. He then cited many examples to prove that Baronets claimed and enjoyed the personal dignity of Knighthood, and subsequently proceeded to expose many fallacies upon which the Officers of Arms had founded the opinions expressed in their Report of the 31st October 1835 to the Earl Marshal.

In all the Royal and state processions (five in number) which occurred in the reign of James 1., subsequent to the erection of the Degree, the Baronets enjoyed their place and precedency, they also attended their Royal Founder's funeral.

In consequence of the plague raging in London at the time of the coronation of Charles 1., no public ceremonial took place. In the list, however, of the nobility privately present on that occasion, the names of many Baronets appear. The rights of the Degree were practically in abeyance during the civil wars, and the Baronets allowed them to remain dormant since.

It appeared, therefore, to the Committee of Baronets that a suitable occasion on which these could be revived would be on the coronation of Queen Victoria, and accordingly they resolved to present the following Petition to Her Majesty, which was adopted at a General Meeting of the Baronetage, held on the 22nd March 1838 :—

'TO HER MOST GRACIOUS MAJESTY THE QUEEN

'The Petition of the Baronets of the Realm of the various Creations—English, Scottish and Irish,—

'Most Humbly Sheweth,

'That from the foundation of the Monarchy down to the period of the erection of the Baronetage in the year 1611, by the ancient rules, laws, and customs of the Realm, all classes of Dignity Hereditary have enjoyed and exercised the privilege of attending their Sovereigns on all great State occasions in the proper place appertaining to their several dignities.

'That in the year 1611, King James 1. erected the Order of Baronets, being the sixth degree of Dignity Hereditary in the Realm.

'That in the year 1616, King James 1. by a final decree and establishment ratified and confirmed the privileges of the Baronets, conferred by former charters, and granted in addition (among other things), "that the said title, stile, dignitie and degree of Baronet, shall be and shall be reputed and taken to be a title, stile, dignitie, and degree of dignitie hereditary, meane in place betwixt the degree of a Baron and the degree of a Knight."

'That by the same charter it was also granted, "that if any doubts or questions not heereby nor by any our recited letters pattents cleared and determined doe or shall arise concerning any place, precedency, priviledge, or other matter touching or concerning the same Baronets, and the heires males of their bodies, such doubts or questions shall be decided and determined by and according to such usuall rules, custome, and lawes for place, precedency, priviledge, and other matters concerning them, as other degrees of dignity hereditary are ordered and adjudged."

'That the confusion of hereditary and other honors, which obtained during the Commonwealth, caused the chartered rights and privileges of the Order to which your Majesty's Petitioners belong, to become dormant; but they most dutifully submit to your Majesty, that, as those rights and privileges arising out of charters and decrees of your Majesty's Royal Predecessors, are still in full force and operation, it is fully competent for your Majesty graciously to carry into effect the distinguished favor of which their ancestors were the immediate objects, at the period of the erection of the hereditary degree of Baronet.

'That your Petitioners hailing with the most devoted loyalty and attachment to your Majesty, your Majesty's happy accession to the Throne of these realms, are most desirous of testifying their veneration and loyalty to their august Sovereign, by attending in their proper place to do suit and service with the other hereditary degrees of dignity at the Coronation of your Majesty.

'That, although your Majesty's Petitioners never undervalued or lost sight of the distinguished privileges attaching to the Order, by virtue of its Royal Charters, yet they never so highly appreciated their value as at the present auspicious moment, when the destinies of this great and happy Country are committed to the hands of a Princess who so abundantly merits, and so fully enjoys, the confidence, the love, and loyal attachment of all classes of her subjects.

'Wherefore may it please your Most Gracious Majesty to take the premises into your favorable consideration, and to issue your Royal Commands to the proper Officers of the Crown, to provide a suitable place, and befitting vestments of estate for your Petitioners, at the approaching ceremonial of a Coronation; and in the event of your Majesty requiring the advice of the Law Officers of the Crown, that your Majesty's Petitioners may be at liberty to appear by Counsel in support of the same; And your Majesty's Petitioners, as in duty bound, will ever pray.'

This Petition was forwarded to the Queen through the Home Office on the 9th April 1838, and was referred to the Earl Marshal, who reported it to be his opinion, that there could be no ground for such a claim, and that a compliance with its prayer would lead to very great embarrassment.

In order, therefore, to have a judicial determination upon the claim of the Baronets for place at the coronation of the Sovereign, the Committee on the 28th April presented a petition to the Lords and others of the Privy Council, sitting as a Court of Claims.

The Privy Council heard the application of Counsel in support of the claim on the 26th June, but came to the conclusion that they were not competent to entertain the Petition. They stated, however, that it was open to the Baronets to petition the Queen to refer the claim to the Attorney-General and Solicitor-General, or to bring it by petition before the Queen in Council.

Had the Committee in the first instance adopted the latter suggestion, there would not have been time to obtain a decision before the Coronation took place; they, therefore, on the 8th June, presented a petition to the Queen, praying a reference of the claim to the Law Officers of the Crown. On the 22nd of June, the Secretary of State informed the Committee that 'Her Majesty had not given any commands on the subject of the Petition.'

A General Meeting of Baronets took place at the Clarendon Hotel on the 10th July 1838, at which the events just recorded were reported and a number of resolutions passed, including one to prosecute the rights and privileges of the Degree and other matters to an issue, by seeking by petition a hearing of, and judicial determination upon, its claims before the Queen in Council, that tribunal being the one before which, in 1612, the question of precedency between the Baronets and the younger sons of Viscounts and of Barons was argued and decided.

At a Special Meeting of the Committee held on the 14th May 1840, it was resolved to issue a Report to the Baronetage, together with a notice inviting them to attend a special meeting to be called for Thursday the 28th May.

The Report referred to previous Reports made explaining the proceedings of the Committee from the period of its formation on the 22nd June 1835 to the 10th July 1838, and then referred to the unsuccessful attempt to obtain from the Crown recognition of the right to obtain Knighthood by the eldest sons of Baronets on attaining the age of twenty-one. After some general remarks on the Baronetage, the Committee recommended that a permanent Committee should be named by a General Meeting with full power and authority to attend to the common interests of the body, to collect and preserve Records, etc., and that it should be composed of 100 Members, viz. 20 Baronets of England, 16 of Scotland, 14 of Ireland, 22 of Great Britain, and 28 of the United Kingdom.

The Report concluded with a recommendation that the attention of the Order should in the first instance be concentrated on the maintenance of the chartered rights of Baronets and their eldest sons to receive Knighthood, the Riband and Badge, upon Supporters, etc.

A Meeting was accordingly held on the 28th May 1840 ; and at an adjourned General Meeting of the Baronetage held at the Clarendon Hotel, London, on the 15th June 1840, over which Sir Henry Martin, Baronet, presided, a series of resolutions was passed, forming a permanent Committee of Privileges for the Baronetage, 'with full power and authority to attend to, and act for, the common good and benefit of the Order in all matters appertaining to its state and dignity, to collect and preserve records, and otherwise to carry into effect such special instructions as, from time to time, General Meetings of the Order, by resolutions duly proposed, deliberately discussed, and afterwards registered, shall give and ordain.'

The Meeting then adjourned until the 15th July following, on which date 'The Committee of the Baronetage for Privileges' was founded, and consisted of Baronets and their heirs, while such Peers and Privy Councillors being Baronets as concurred in the proceedings were *virtute officii* Honorary Members. Sir Francis Shuckburgh, Baronet, was appointed Treasurer ; Mr. Richard Broun, Honorary Secretary and Registrar ; and Committee Rooms were taken at the Clarendon Hotel.

On the 2nd February 1841 a special Report on Supporters, etc., was adopted by the Committee, and the following Recommendations were agreed to :—

'That Supporters, and the other Exterior Heraldic Ornaments, of right incidental to the Baronetage, be adopted by a formal and solemn resolution of the Order, grounded upon this Report ; which Resolution shall be binding henceforth and for ever upon all such

Baronets of the several creations as shall concur in its justice and propriety.

'That, as Exterior Ornaments only indicate political rank, and do not particularize families, it is advisable that Supporters be brought within the influence of the laws which regulate heraldic accompaniments in general; and accordingly, that power shall be given by the Order to this Committee to assign such Supporters, and other external ensigns, to members, on their individual application, as shall appear to the Committee best calculated to avoid confusion, and to accomplish all the objects which such additamenta are designed to effect.

'That every Baronet taking Supporters, or other Exterior Ornaments, in virtue of the recommendation above given, shall register them in the Heralds' Colleges of his native kingdom, or in the office of "The Committee of the Baronetage for Privileges," in order that such a record may be made of the same as shall perpetuate their descent with his family honours for ever.'

At a General Meeting of the Baronetage held on the 14th May 1841, the Special Report from the Committee on Supporters, etc., dated 2nd February 1841, which had been communicated to the Members of the Baronetage, was taken into consideration; and it was stated that no replies had been obtained from any Member dissenting from the clauses therein drawn, or objecting to the course of the recommendations set forth in it; and after reciting various documents, including Mr. Crawford's Address upon the Chartered Privileges of the Baronetage, dated 15th July 1837, it was unanimously resolved and declared—

'That the RECOMMENDATIONS set forth in the Special Report from the Committee for Privileges, on Supporters, and other exterior Heraldic Ornaments shall, as finally revised and settled this day, have the strength and effect of RESOLUTIONS to be acted upon by all such

Members of the Order of the several creations (Ulster, Nova Scotia, British and United Kingdom) as now, or at any time hereafter, may concur in their propriety, and, accordingly, that the Committee for Privileges shall be empowered to register the Arms of all such Baronets as shall make application to that effect, with Supporters, and other exterior Heraldic Ornaments, in accordance with the principles laid down in the said Recommendations and the rules and customs which regulate the Armories of the other Degrees of Dignity Hereditary ; such rules and customs having been expressly laid down and appointed by King James the First, the Royal Founder of the Baronetage (for himself, his heirs and successors), as standing and certain Laws whereby the Arms of Baronets at all times, and in every reign, are to be charged and augmented.

'That the ancient honorary style of "The Honourable" which was attributed to the Order by its Royal Founder, and universally ascribed to Baronets and Baronetesses in former reigns, shall be resumed.'

At a General Meeting held on the 4th June 1841, the following Resolution, together with a number of others, was passed :—

'That all Baronets in future be requested to put Baronet, or its abbreviation, after their names on their cards of address, and also after their signature in all writings and namings, etc., as a proper and suitable distinction of their rank.'

On the 18th September 1841, after applications had been reported from a number of Baronets intimating their intention to act on the Resolution passed on the 14th May, and requesting that their Arms might be registered in the books of the Committee, the Hon. Secretary, Mr. Broun, laid before the Committee an heraldic drawing, showing the manner in which it was suggested the Resolution of the General Meeting might be carried into practical effect, and then read a very long Exposition, showing that Baronets are privileged to augment their Arms with such exterior Heraldic Ornaments as indicate Baronial and Equestrian Dignity.

The Applications to the Committee were made in the following form :—

'TO THE COMMITTEE OF THE BARONETAGE FOR PRIVILEGES.

'NOBLE SIRS,

'It being my intention to act on the Resolutions of the General Meeting of the Order, passed on the 14th of May last, relative to Supporters and other exterior Heraldic Ornaments, I request that my Family Arms, as described on the margin, may be registered in the Books of the Committee, with Supporters and other exterior Heraldic Ornaments, in conformity with the principles laid down in the said Resolutions.

'I have the honor to be,

'Noble Sirs,

'Your most obedient Servant,

....

'Bar^t.'

In Accordance with these applications the Committee issued Certificates on vellum in the following form :—

'COMMITTEE OF THE BARONETAGE FOR PRIVILEGES.

'London,   184

'The Royal Founder of the Baronetage having for himself his Heirs and Successors granted and appointed that the usual Rules and Custom which regulate the Armories of the Other Degrees of Dignity Hereditary shall be standing laws whereby the Arms of all Baronets shall be charged and augmented, And the Honourable Sir —— —— Baronet of —— having intimated to the Committee for Privileges his intention to act upon the Resolutions of the General Meeting of the Order held on the 14th day of May

1841 relative to Supporters and other Exterior Heraldic Ornaments,

'This is to certify that in terms of a minute passed in Committee on the 5th of June last the Arms of the said noble Baronet have been duly registered in the Books of the Committee with the Insignia of right incidental to Baronetage and Knightly Dignity and as exemplified upon the margin are as follows :—

'Coat.............................

'Supporters. Two Equites Aurati proper.

'Crest...........................

'Motto............................

'Coronet, Mantle, Helmet, Collar of S.S., Badge and Wreath as blazoned in the Atchievement.

'Given under the Seal of the Order this —— day of —— 184 .

'(Signed)   R. BROUN, Eq. Aur.,

'Hon. Secretary and Registrar.'

SEAL

At a Meeting of the Committee held on the 10th May 1842, Sir Henry Mervyn Vavasour, Baronet, in the chair, the Committee took into consideration a Memorial from Mr. Broun relative to his application to the Lord Chamberlain to present him to the Queen for inauguration as a Knight. The result of this application, and the consequent proceedings at the Annual Meeting on the 4th June following, when Mr. Broun formally took upon himself knighthood, have already been narrated in the previous chapter.

At a Meeting of the Committee held on the 20th June 1842, letters were read from Members who had been absent

from the Meeting of the 4th, offering to the Honorary
Secretary their congratulations on the manner in which he
had been called upon to assert his natitial dignity ; and in
consequence of suggestions to that effect from various
quarters, a resolution was passed to the following effect :—

'That a Testimonial, comprising the insignia appertaining to the
degree of Eques Auratus, should be presented to Sir Richard Broun
on the occasion of his taking up his Knighthood under the requisition of a General Meeting, as a pledge of their approbation of his
conduct, and their determination to revive all the rights and ornaments belonging to that ancient equestrian honor.'

A number of Baronets were appointed Trustees, and
empowered to take whatever steps were necessary to carry
this resolution into effect.

As a result, the so-styled Sir Richard Broun, at a Meeting
on the 27th May 1843, was presented with a Testimonial
which comprised a golden Collar of S.S., a Sword, Ring,
Spurs, etc.

It is exceedingly doubtful whether the Collar of S.S.
ought to have been included in the insignia of Knighthood,
as it is by no means clear whether this Collar has ever, at
any time, had any connection with Knighthood.

Its origin is at the present time unknown, and the number
of attempts to solve the enigma has caused it to be described
by Mr. Albert Hartshorne, who wrote a very able article
on it in *The Archæological Journal*, vol. xxxix., the *crux
antiquariorum*.

Its meaning has been variously explained as derived from
—(1) St. Simplicius, (2) Salisbury (Countess of), (3) Soissons

(Martyrs of), (4) Silentium, (5) Societas, (6) Souvenez, (7) Souverayne, (8) Seneschallus, (9) Sanctus.

Mr. Hartshorne considers that the testimony for the first six is very dubious, while there is more or less indirect evidence in support of the other three. There is a good deal to be said in favour of 'Seneschallus,' for John of Gaunt was Seneschal, or High Steward of England, and the employment of the Collar of S.S. as the 'Livery' of the great Lancastrian party during the reigns of Henry IV., Henry V., and Henry VI. is a matter of history.

The earliest pictorial example noticed is a drawing in the British Museum by Nicholas Charles, Lancaster Herald, from a window of old St. Paul's, of the arms of 'Time-honoured Lancaster,' within a Collar of S.S. of the early form, namely, a buckling-strap with S's upon it at intervals.

The earliest sculptured example appears to be that repre-sented on the effigy of Sir John Swinford, who died in 1371. Now, even if it could be shown that this effigy was sculptured many years after his death, Mr. Hartshorne points out that the fact still remains that this Knight was entitled to wear a Collar of S.S., and it consequently follows that this decora-tion was an established collar of livery when Henry of Lancaster, Earl of Derby, was yet a boy, since he was not born until 1360. This would seem at once to dispose of the favourite conjecture that the collar was first devised by Henry IV., when he was Earl of Derby, in allusion to his motto, 'Souverayne.'

In support of 'Sanctus,' it may be urged that Church vestments were frequently powdered with S's for Sanctus.

Mr. J. G. Nichol, in an article in *Notes and Queries*, is in favour of the theory that the S is derived from Seneschallus. It still forms part of the official dress of the Lord Chief-Justice of England, and the Lord Mayor of London, which is also in favour of the assumption that it was originally a livery collar of a high functionary.

At the same time, an Act passed in 1532-33, being 24 Henry VIII. c. 13, enacts 'That no manne, onelesse he be a knight . . . weare any coler of golde named a coler of S.' And in a *Chaucer*, printed in 1598, occurs 'lyeth buried . . . with his image lying over him . . . a collar of esses gold about his necke . . . being the ornament of a knight.'

These two references, however, must not be taken as proving anything—the writers in both may have been mistaken : many writers have ignorantly assumed that the collar of the Order of the Garter is a Collar of S.S., which it certainly is not, any more than are the Collars of the other Orders of Knighthood. Should it be decided later to accord a Collar to the Baronets, a special one should be designed.

In the chapter dealing with the early history of the Baronetage of Scotland and Nova Scotia, the narrative was carried down to 1709, two years after the Union. A succession of historical events occurred to cause their rights to fall into a state of desuetude. These events were the rebellions of 1715 and 1745, the revolt of the United States of America in 1776, and the French Revolution, with the long Continental wars following.

In 1691 the territories and colonies known by the name of the Colony of Massachusetts Bay, the Colony of New

Plymouth, the Province of Maine, and Nova Scotia, were, in terms of a charter known as the Massachusetts Charter, united and incorporated, and a tract of land within was assigned to some Protestants from Ireland and the Palatinate.

This led the inhabitants of Massachusetts Bay to claim not only a right to the government, but also to the territory, although up to this time they had neglected this particular tract of land. In consequence of this claim, a case was submitted, in August 1731, to the Attorney-General and Solicitor-General, asking for their opinion on the following points :—

1. Whether the pursuers, if they ever had any right to the tract claimed, had not by their neglect, and even refusal to defend, take care of, and improve the same, forfeited their said right to the government, and what right they had under the charter, and now have, to the lands?

2. Whether by the said tract being conquered by the French, and afterwards re-conquered by General Nicholson in the late Queen's time, and yielded up by France to Great Britain by the Treaty of Utrecht, that part of the charter relating thereto became vacated? And whether the government of that tract, and the lands thereof, are not absolutely re-vested in the Crown; and whether the Crown has not thereby a sufficient power to appoint governments, and assign lands to such families as shall desire to settle there?

To these questions the law officers of the Crown replied that they were of opinion the pursuers had not been guilty of any laches of a kind to create a forfeiture of the rights conveyed by their charter; that the country not having

been yielded by the Crown of England to France by any
treaty, the conquest thereof by the French created—according to the law of nations—only a suspension of the property
of the former owners and not an extinguishment; and that
upon the re-conquest of it by General Nicholson, all the
ancient rights, both of the province and of private persons,
subjects of the Crown of Great Britain, did revive, and
were restored *jure postliminii*; that the Crown had not power
to appoint a particular governor of this part of the province,
or to assign lands to persons desirous to settle there; and
that upon the whole matter, they considered the pursuers
ought not to be disturbed in their possession, or interrupted
in carrying on their settlement of the lands granted to them
within the district in question.

In 1734, between two and three years after this opinion
had been given, in a case which appeared to be identical with
the claims of the Baronets of Scotland to the grant of lands
in Nova Scotia comprehended in their Patents, meetings of
these Baronets took place in London; but there do not
appear to be any records in existence showing what tran-
spired, or the result of their deliberations.

In 1763, Nova Scotia was restored to the British Crown
by the Treaty of Paris; and fourteen years later, on the 19th
February 1777, the Baronets of Scotland held a meeting in
Edinburgh relative to their lands in that province, with the
Earl of Home as 'Preses,' and appointed a standing committee. Lord Elibank, a member of this Committee, drew
up an address to Lord George Germaine on the Claims of
the Baronets.

This address, after being referred to Sir Harry Mon-
creiffe and Sir James Foulis, was finally approved by the
Committee in Edinburgh, on the 25th March 1777, and
was forwarded to London to be presented to the Minister.

The actual date of the Address was 27th March 1777,
and it was signed on behalf of the Baronets of Scotland and
Nova Scotia by five of their number. The Preamble adverts
to the institution of the dignity, to the Acts of Parliament
confirming its rights, to the endeavours made by the first
created Baronets to improve their new acquisitions in Nova
Scotia, to the calamities of the latter portion of the reign of
Charles I., which soon diverted their attention from that
country, to its seizure by the French, and its restoration to
the English Crown. It then proceeded: 'The Baronets of
Nova Scotia presume that no prescription of land can operate
against them while their property was forcibly withheld from
them by a hostile nation. They can, therefore, have no
doubt that their lands have now legally reverted to them,
and have directed us to solicit your Lordship's countenance
and assistance in making application to His Majesty to
restore them to those rights of their ancestors.

'The difficulty of assembling so many different claimants
may have hitherto prevented a general application. And
the impropriety of separating particular pretensions from
the general interest of the Order may have hindered individuals from advancing their particular claims. But we
flatter ourselves your Lordship will not think a general
application now too late. We ask not for new rights; we
ask only the possession of rights already established. We

T

have the honour to rank ourselves with those friends of
Government whose attachment to the laws and liberties of
their country hath taught them zeal for the dignity of the
Crown, and affection for the person of the Sovereign. If
His Majesty should be pleased to reinstate us in our ancient
properties, we know that the influence which might arise
to us upon the continent of America would be faithfully
employed in His Majesty's service ; and, we flatter ourselves, might be of some importance in disseminating the
principles of genuine patriotism and loyalty.'

This Address appears to have been presented in May
1777, but what answer, if any, was made to it does not
appear. Since then the revolt of the United States, the
French Revolution, Continental wars, and the insurrection
in Canada prevented the Baronets of Scotland and Nova
Scotia from taking any steps for the revival of their rights
and privileges in Nova Scotia, until Mr. Richard Broun
(who, as has already been narrated, took up the cause of the
Baronetage as a whole in 1834) espoused the cause of the
Baronets of Scotland and Nova Scotia two years later.

A General Meeting of Baronets of Scotland and Nova
Scotia, attending personally or by proxy, took place in
Edinburgh on 21st October 1836, Sir John Campbell,
Baronet of Ardnamurchan, being in the chair. A case was
read by Mr. Broun, showing the right of each Baronet to
have a grant of land in Nova Scotia of 16,000 acres in
extent ; that there were then existing about 150 Baronets ;
that during the reign of Charles i., one hundred and eleven
had their grants assigned to them by Charter ; that these

grants had been twice ratified by Acts of the Scottish Parliament, and were declared to be valid and effectual notwithstanding non-user, presumption, and any other casualty whatsoever. The case was ordered to be printed and circulated, preparatory to a special General Meeting being held to consider what further measures should be adopted.

On the 11th of May 1837, a Meeting of Nova Scotia Baronets was held in London, and another on the 15th of the same month. On the latter occasion a document was drawn up and signed by the Marquess of Downshire, Lord Kilmaine, Major-General Sir James Cockburn, B^t., Sir Archibald Murray, B^t., Lieutenant-General Sir F. G. Maclean, B^t., and Sir F. G. Cooper, B^t., stating 'that having considered the instruments, and the statement laid before them in reference to the claims of the Nova Scotia Baronets, they were of opinion that these claims were such as to render any proposal for their revival entitled to the best consideration and support of the Members of the Order ; and farther, that they should be ready to attend to any proposals that a competent assemblage of the Baronets in Edinburgh might think it right to suggest.'

A third Meeting of the Nova Scotia Baronets took place on the 29th May in Edinburgh, when it was resolved that a Case should be drawn up for the opinion of Counsel, and that a fund to defray expenses should be raised.

Throughout the greater portion of 1837 and 1838, the most alarming distress prevailed in the Western Highlands and Islands of Scotland, and a public Meeting on the subject took place at the Mansion House, London, on the 11th March 1837, which resulted in the formation of a Relief Committee, of which Alderman Sir John Pirie, B^t., was nominated the Treasurer. Owing to the distress, and also to an outbreak in Canada, no Meetings of the Nova Scotia Baronets took place in 1838.

On the 26th June 1839, the 'London Highland Destitution Relief Committee' presented a representation to the Government recommending the immediate adoption of a systematic plan of emigration by whole families as the only means of preventing a recurrence year after year of the same distress to which the Highland peasantry were subjected ; and on the 1st August, Dr. Rolph and Bishop Macdonell arrived at Liverpool from Canada on a mission to promote emigration to these colonies. On the 4th October, the former was present at the General Meeting of the Highland Society at Inverness, and on the 18th of the same month he attended a large public meeting in Glasgow.

A day or two before the General Meeting of 'The Central Agricultural Society,' held in London on the 12th December 1839, Dr. Rolph called upon Mr. Broun, and expressed a wish to attend the meeting and dinner. The Central Society, of which Mr. Broun had been one of the founders, and of which he was one of the Honorary Secretaries, enrolled about eighty of the local associations. Finding from Dr. Rolph that his mission to this country was to promote emigration to Canada, it led to him and Mr. Broun eventually co-operating to found a public company for emigration and colonisation.

Accordingly, on the 10th January 1840, Dr. Rolph attended a great public Meeting of Highland proprietors and others, held in Edinburgh, and presided over by the Duke of Argyll, and as a result of this and other Meetings 'The North American Colonial Committee' was on the 6th May formed, with Dr. Rolph as Honorary Secretary.

In the meantime the House of Assembly of Upper Canada addressed Her Majesty on the 8th February, praying her to promote emigration; and during the latter half of the year Dr. Rolph was engaged in Canada, and was appointed by Lord Sydenham Emigration Agent for the Canadian Government. He returned to England in January of the following year, and was engaged continually with Mr. Broun on the proposed Company.

On the 20th February it was settled that the seignories of D'Aillebout and de Ramsay should be purchased as a basis for the Company's first operations. Dr. Rolph was the Agent for their sale, and it was arranged they should be taken in Mr. Broun's name, the price ultimately being arranged at £20,000, payable in five yearly instalments.

A Meeting of Nova Scotia Baronets was immediately summoned, which met on the 11th March 1841, the Marquess of Downshire being in the chair. The copy of a proposed memorial to the Colonial Minister on behalf of the Baronets was laid on the table, also the prospectus of a proposed public Company for colonising such lands as might be given in lieu of the original grants.

Another Meeting was held on the 6th April at the Thatched House, St. James's, the Marquess of Huntly being in the chair, and a further Meeting on the 28th of the same month, at which it was resolved an Association should be formed for the combined purposes of promoting emigration, establishing the rights, and managing the properties, in Nova Scotia, of the Baronets who should join it.

A Circular was accordingly issued from 21 Wigmore Street, Cavendish Square, dated the 7th July 1841, and signed by Mr. Broun, announcing the passing of this resolution, and that since the meeting arrangements had been made to carry the objects contemplated into effect, the Scottish and British-American Association having been formed on the principles adverted to in the abstract from its constitution which accompanied the Circular.

The Circular then went on to state that, to enable the Association to carry out effectively its joint views, it had already acquired by purchase two valuable seignories in North America, comprising eighty thousand acres of valuable soil, to which would progressively be added the grants of the concurring Baronets, or such new lands as the Government might give in exchange for them.

It also suggested that by the plan proposed, the Baronets joining the Association would be relieved from the trouble and expense connected with prosecuting their respective claims in Nova Scotia, and, in the event of the claims being established, from the additional trouble and expense of planting their particular grants. It pointed out that rights having a legal existence, but not reduced into actual possession, and therefore comparatively valueless, each concurring Baronet would on their being realised receive £10,000 worth of paid-up shares in the Capital Stock of the Association, and £6000 in money, deducting only from the amount of the latter sum the expenses connected with prosecuting and establishing the joint claims.

Accompanying this Circular was the abstract from the Constitution referred to, which was headed by the name of the Association; a statement that its capital was one million pounds in fifty-pound shares, on which was to be paid a deposit of five pounds a share; and a steel-engraved map of the ancient province of Nova Scotia, showing the position of the lands originally granted to the Baronets of Scotland and Nova Scotia.

The object of the Association was stated to be the promotion of the settlement of Nova Scotia, and the establishment of the rights and the administration of the properties of such of the Baronets of Scotland as should consent to join it. The constitution was stated to contain provisions to the following effect :—

'1st. That the Association shall purchase the grants of each of the one hundred and eleven Baronets of Scotland created prior to 1638 who actually had lands assigned to them on the following terms, viz. at a rate not exceeding £1 per acre; two-thirds of the purchase money to be liquidated in paid-up shares of the capital stock of the Association, the remainder in cash, subject only to the deduction of any expenses that may be incurred by the Association in recovering the same.

'2nd. That the Association will purchase the claims which each Baronet of Scotland, created from 1638 to the Union, has against the Crown for a territorial qualification in Nova Scotia of 16,000 acres, in virtue of the Constitution of the Baronetage, upon the same terms and conditions as above set forth.

'3rd. That the Association, immediately on a contract having been made with each concurring Baronet to the effect above specified, shall pursue, promote, and realise the claims and interests of the said Baronets, either with the Crown, the Treasury, the Colonial Office, or in such other way as the Board of Commissioners and their legal advisers shall deem most expedient.

'4th. That each Baronet of Scotland, being a peer, who shall join the Association on the terms laid down, shall be a Vice-President of the Association, and as such have a voice and control in the management of its affairs.

'5th. That each Baronet of Scotland not being a peer, who shall join the Association, shall be a member of the Consulting Council of the Association, and as such have a voice and control in the management of its affairs.

'6th. That the executive management of the Association shall be in a Board of Commissioners, composed of Baronets and Share-holders. The Commissioners to be the owners of properties containing at least 10,000 acres of land in North America, conveyed to the Trustees of the Association in furtherance of its objects, or the holders of at least £1000 stock each in the capital of the Association. Which Board of Commissioners, aided by the Consulting Council (which will be composed of the President, Vice-President, Trustees, and concurring Baronets), shall have the power to realise the residuary rights and privileges of the Baronets, either by a process of law, or by a compromise with the Government, as shall be deemed most advisable.

'7th. That no Baronet shall have any interest or benefit in the Association who shall not signify his concurrence in the above plan, in writing to the Commissioners, prior to the 1st day of September next.'

Meetings were held on the 4th, 6th, and 7th of May, and on the 10th May a Draft Prospectus of the proposed Company was read, corrected, and ordered to be printed, Dr. Rolph reporting that the Duke of Argyll had stated his willingness to receive a deputation from the Company. The

Prospectus was revised at a Meeting on the 13th, and on the 17th a series of resolutions for the formation and management of 'The Scottish and British-American Association for Emigration and Colonisation' was adopted.

Inter aliâ, these set forth that the seignories of D'Aillebout and de Ramsay should, with the baronies of New Carnoustie and Banff Ogilvie (Sir William Ogilvie's grants which he agreed to convey to the Company), be the basis of the Company's operations. The most ample powers were taken under the Articles of Agreement for the executive management of the Company, and Mr. Richard Broun and Dr. Rolph were empowered as a deputation to wait on the Nova Scotia Baronets in London and procure their adhesion.

In accordance with his promise, the Duke of Argyll received on the 25th May a deputation from the Company, consisting of Mr. Richard Broun and Dr. Rolph; and after ascertaining the principles on which it was to be constructed, consented to become its President, and a few days later a Prospectus, with His Grace's name printed thereon as President, was forwarded to the Marquis of Downshire.

Mr. Richard Broun, on the 7th July, sent a Circular Letter to the Baronets of Scotland, informing them of the resolution come to at the Meeting of the 28th April in favour of the formation of a public Association, for the combined purpose of promoting emigration, establishing the rights, and managing the properties in Nova Scotia, of the Baronets who should join it. The fact of the Duke of Argyll having consented to become President of the Association was set out in the Circular.

This was followed by Mr. Richard Broun arranging with
Dr. Rolph to hold meetings in Scotland to further the objects
of the Company, but the latter was suddenly recalled to
Canada.   He sailed on the 8th of August, three days after
the constitution of the Company was signed.

Nothing of moment occurred until the 2nd February the
following year, when a Meeting of Nova Scotia Baronets
was held at the house of Sir Frederick Hamilton, and a
resolution was passed that in the opinion of the Meeting the
Scottish and British American Association was well adapted
to relieve Scotland of her surplus population, to strengthen
British interests in North America, and to effect the combined objects of establishing the rights and making available
the properties in British America of such Baronets as should
join it.   It was further resolved that the concurring Baronets
who were Peers should be added to the list of Vice-Presidents, and the Baronets not Peers to the list of the Consulting
Council, and that the proceedings of the Meeting should be
communicated to them.

Dr. Rolph returned from Canada on the 23rd March
accompanied by Sir Allan Macnab, who was shortly afterwards elected a Commissioner.   On the 18th April they
had an interview with the Duke of Argyll, who appointed
the following Friday, the 22nd inst., for a Meeting of the
Consulting Council of the Scottish and British-American
Association.

The first Meeting of this Consulting Council took place
accordingly on the day appointed, the Duke of Argyll, as
President, being in the chair.   Various Reports were made,

including one from the Board of Commissioners, setting
forth that the Constitution had been carefully revised since
the meeting on the 2nd February, and that during the same
time arrangements had been entered into for the purchase of
several extensive seignories. The Report having adverted
to Lord Stanley's reply to the Memorial of the Nova Scotia
Baronets, a long discussion ensued upon the propriety of
making the revival of the rights of the Baronets too pro-
minent a feature in the operations of the Company, instead
of the first resolution on the paper of business, which was
to the effect ' that the Association should substantiate by all
legal means the rights and privileges of the Nova Scotia
Baronets, and that a deputation should wait on Lord Stanley
on the subject.' It was then proposed and carried ' that
the general objects of the Association—namely, emigration
and colonisation—should be immediately proceeded with ' ;
and the consideration of the other matters was adjourned
until the Friday following, the 29th inst.

At this adjourned Meeting of the Consulting Council, the
Marquis of Downshire filled the chair, a letter from the
Duke of Argyll regretting his absence being read. The
attention of the Council was drawn to a variety of documents relative to the state of distress in Scotland, and the
necessity for emigration, and a Report from the Board of
Commissioners was read by Dr. Rolph. The Prospectus
was revised, and the title of the Association was amended by
striking out the words ' Scottish and.' After other business
had been transacted, including the authorisation of a Deputation from the Board of Commissioners to visit Scotland, it

was ordered that copies of the Prospectus, together with the proceedings of the Meeting, should be communicated to the absent members of the Scottish Baronetage. This was followed by public Meetings in Edinburgh and Glasgow.

The third Meeting of the Consulting Council took place on Wednesday, the 8th June 1842, the Duke of Argyll in the chair. A Report from the Board of Commissioners was read as to business transacted since the last Meeting, including the entering into contracts for the acquisition of land in Prince Edward's Island, and in Canada East four seignories. The Report also set forth that the Commissioners expected to send a body of emigrants to Prince Edward's Island before the close of the season; and having immediate reference to the completion of the purchases already made, and the advances which might be required to promote emigration to the properties of the Association, it recommended that the sum of £50,000 should be raised by the issue of Debentures.

A considerable discussion took place on this proposition, and the clause relative to Debentures was altered to the effect that the Commissioners proposed to raise the sum required by an issue of 10,000 shares in the capital stock of the Association in this country, and by an equal amount of land shares in Canada. It was then resolved that a subscription should be immediately opened for shares. The Report of the Council was printed and circulated immediately afterwards.

A few days afterwards a Share-list was issued with the following heading :—

'BRITISH AMERICAN ASSOCIATION.

'We, whose names are hereunto annexed, do agree to subscribe for the number of shares and amount of stock of the above Association set opposite to our respective signatures, and to pay a deposit of £5 per share thereon to the Bankers of the Association when shares to the amount of £50,000 have been taken, upon having twenty-one days' notice thereof.'

The subscription was started by the Duke of Argyll, who subscribed for fifteen shares for himself and ten for his son, the Marquis of Lorne.

Immediately after this, the Association was advertised in the newspapers. The Prospectus was headed with the name of the Company, the 'British American Association for Emigration and Colonisation,' round the Arms, Supporters, Crest, and Motto of Nova Scotia. The capital was £1,000,000 in £20 shares, with a deposit of £5 per share. The President was the Duke of Argyll; fifteen Vice-Presidents, all Peer-Baronets, followed; and then a long list of the Consulting Council, consisting almost entirely of Baronets, the exceptions being the Lords Provost of Edinburgh and Glasgow, The Chisholm, and three other gentlemen. There were seven Commissioners, of whom six were Baronets, together with the usual Officers; and the Headquarters of the Association were at 29 New Bridge Street.

The Prospectus stated that the object of the Association was 'to promote the Colonisation of our North American Provinces by a transfer of the surplus population of the

United Kingdom upon a national scale, and by such an infusion of capital into them as shall lead to an immediate and wide development of their inexhaustible resources.'

The Prospectus also contained the following clause :—
'There is one feature in the constitution of this Association as connected with Scotland, and with the interests of the Scottish Emigrant, too important to be passed over. The undertaking will be supported by an union with the Baronets of Scotland and Nova Scotia, an Order originally created to further the settlement of British North America, by which its objects are closely interwoven with the interests of a large portion of the Scottish Nobility ; and by the members of that Order, assisting in its Councils, and conducting its management, a careful supervision is provided over all the interests, not only of the shareholders, but more especially of the emigrants confided to its care—a supervision not ceasing with their landing in a new country, but continuing till they shall be located on their settlement, and providing for their future happiness and advantage.'

At a Meeting of the Board held on the 8th July, an arrangement was entered into with Mr. Maitland, the proprietor and editor of the *Emigrant's Gazette*, to take 250 copies weekly for circulation, and from this time until the breaking up of the Institution these papers were sent weekly to the Duke of Argyll, the Baronets of Scotland, and others. In these papers the advertisement of the Company continually appeared, and it contained weekly a notice of the proceedings of the Company.

The Duke of Richmond presided at a dinner given by

the Commissioners on the 15th July to Sir Allan Macnab, previous to his departure for Canada, to commence his duties there as Chief Commissioner for the Company. The party was a very influential one, including five ex-Governors of Canada.

Sir Robert Barclay withdrew from the Board on the 26th July.

Sir Allan Macnab left for Canada on the 2nd August, followed by Dr. Rolph on the 19th of the same month, Mr. Broun being engaged shortly afterwards in connection with the sailing of a ship, the *Barbadoes*, chartered by the Association to take out Mr. Haldon and a few workmen engaged by him to the estates contracted for in Prince Edward's Island. Mr. Broun opened the banking account of the Association on the 23rd September by paying in £250, being the deposit of £5 per share on fifty shares taken by him. This and the same amount paid in by Sir William Ogilvie and Dr. Rolph, in all £750, appears to have been the only money paid in to the account of this unfortunate enterprise, which was shortly afterwards broken up.

The *Barbadoes* left for Gravesend on the 19th September, and sailed finally on the 1st November with 20 men, 12 women, 16 children, and 14 crew, 62 in all; but she was recalled in consequence of the following circumstances. Her sailing had previously been delayed by the institution of certain inquiries by Lord Stanley, the Secretary of State for the Colonies, instigated by some one whose name he refused to divulge.

On the 22nd September a complaint was laid at the Mansion House before Sir John Pirie, Baronet, the Lord Mayor, at the instance of some men who had entered into an agreement with Mr. Haldon. At the instigation of the Lord Mayor, the matter appears to have been amicably settled, the men on the 25th October executing a receipt for moneys paid them by Mr. Haldon, and expressing their entire approval of all his acts in connection with their engagements with him.

For some reason, however, Sir John Pirie made some injurious remarks against the British-American Association, and wrote to the Duke of Argyll, asking His Grace whether he was a shareholder in the Company, and considered himself liable for the pecuniary transactions of the parties in London who had the management of its concerns.

In reply, the Duke wrote the following letter, which appeared in the *Times* newspaper of the 2nd November 1842 :—

'TO THE LORD MAYOR.

'MY LORD,

'I am very much obliged to your Lordship for your communication of the 25th instant. I certainly took a deep interest in the British American Emigration Society, having upon my estates in the Western Highlands and Islands too large a population for the space inhabited by them, and wishing, of course, that many of them should have the opportunity, if they wished it, of emigrating to North America, in such a manner as would be most advantageous for themselves, I consented to be named President of the Society ; but from several of their proceedings lately, I am now desirous of withdrawing my name from the roll of subscribers or shareholders, as they are called ; and I have desired my agent, Mr. Nettleship of

4 Trafalgar Square, to inquire into the late proceedings before your Lordship, and to acquaint you with the result.

'I certainly do not consider myself responsible for any of the pecuniary transactions of the parties in London, who assume the management of the Company's affairs at present.

'I subscribed in June last £500, upon the implied and understood condition, that no step involving any expenditure of money was to be undertaken on the part of the company till the sum of £50,000 was duly certified to have been subscribed or placed to the company's credit by some means or other; and I was quite surprised to observe the question brought before your Lordship lately as to wages, etc., to be paid to some operatives and emigrants upon the company's account. Referring your Lordship to my agent, Mr. Thomas Nettleship, 4 Trafalgar Square, for any further information relative to my connection with the company.

'I remain, your Lordship's obedient servant,

'ARGYLL.

'Inverary Castle, Oct. 27.'

The same post which took the Lord Mayor's letter to the Duke conveyed one also to him from Mr. Broun, explaining that the complaints made against Mr. Haldon in no respect affected the Association, but of this letter the Duke took no notice; and on the 9th November there appeared in the *Times* newspaper a letter from his solicitors to the effect that he was not a shareholder in the Association, that he had never contemplated deriving personally any profit from its operations, and that he had also withdrawn from the office of President.

A Committee of Inquiry into the affairs of the Association was appointed which sat from the 9th to the 23rd December 1842, during which time the Committee had before them the books, documents, papers, and accounts connected with the formation and objects of the Association, and subjected the whole of the executive officers to a strict *viva voce* examination, after which they issued a report to the effect that the objects of the Association were worthy of support; that the properties acquired, consisting of 443,594 acres, had been selected with care; that the affairs of the Association had been administered with economy, none of the principal officers having received any remuneration for their services, and regretting the attack which had led to the breaking up of the Association.

A Meeting of a public character was held in the City of London on the 23rd December, Sir William Ogilvie, Baronet, being in the chair, at which this report was read.

Lord Stanley, the Secretary of State for the Colonies, having in his place in Parliament, on the 24th April 1843, made some observations with reference to the British-American Association which were, in the opinion of Mr. Broun, not in accordance with the facts, that gentleman addressed a public letter to his lordship explanatory of the charges made against the Association, showing that to the Colonial Land and Emigration Commissioners, or to Sir John Pirie, were justly to be ascribed the whole losses sustained, sufferings endured, and distresses occasioned, by the destruction of the Company, and asking at his lordship's hands justice and reparation for the wrongs which had been inflicted.

To this letter Lord Stanley made no reply; and as he also refused to give up the name of the individual who addressed to him the letter which had occasioned the delay in the sailing of the *Barbadoes*, and had thereby originated the series of casualties which terminated in the destruction of the Association, a petition was presented to the House of Commons from Mr. Broun on the 24th April 1844 asking the House to move an address to Her Majesty for the production of the letter, and to appoint a Select Committee to investigate all the circumstances of the case.

About this time the Duke of Argyll was, in an action tried before Lord Chief-Justice Denman, found liable as one of the shareholders of the British-American Association. The day following the *Globe* newspaper introduced into its leading article certain statements with regard to its executive officers which caused Mr. Broun to bring an action for damages against its proprietors.

In the meantime the following Petition was presented to the Queen through the Home Office :—

'TO HER MOST GRACIOUS MAJESTY QUEEN VICTORIA

' *The Petition of the undersigned Knights Baronets of Scotland and Nova Scotia,*

' HUMBLY SHEWETH,

' That Your Majesty's illustrious Ancestor King Charles the 1st of happy memory established the Noble Order of Knights Baronets of Scotland and Nova Scotia, to which your petitioners have the honor to belong by descent, and amongst other valuable privileges which he bestowed on it, was that of His Majesty's Hereditary Lieutenant of Nova Scotia being entitled to convene the Baronets in an Assembly or Chapter. That the dormancy of the said hereditary office of Lieutenant has prevented any such Chapter from having been held for many years, and that thus abuses are said to have arisen and rumours throwing doubts on the validity of

some of the titles on the Roll of the Baronets of Scotland and Nova
Scotia have been frequently and widely circulated especially of late
years to the great prejudice of your petitioners and the Order to
which they belong for if it were true that any of these titles had
been taken up without any just right, it would be not only a
disgrace to the Order itself, but it would imply a serious breach of
Your Majesty's Royal Prerogative ; Your Petitioners therefore do
most humbly implore Your Majesty that you would be graciously
pleased to allow their Order an opportunity of wiping off all such
foul aspersions, by issuing Your Royal mandate that a Chapter of the
Order shall be forthwith held at Edinburgh, to meet afterwards as
occasion may require in time coming and that all individuals for the
first time requiring admission to the said Chapter, shall be called
upon to produce such reasonable proofs as may satisfy Your Majesty's
Lord Advocate or Solicitor General for Scotland, or any other Law
Officer that Your Majesty may be graciously pleased to appoint for
this purpose, that their titles to seats thereat are admissable ; And
may it please Your Majesty farther to ordain, that the Baronet of
Eldest Creation present shall always preside at all meetings of any
such Chapter.   We also crave Your Majesty that powers may be
granted to the said Chapter to regulate and determine all matters
concerning the Baronetage of Scotland and Nova Scotia that may
be brought before it and afterwards sanctioned by Your Majesty ;
and Your Petitioners would especially beseech Your Majesty that in
order to secure the future purity and integrity of the Order, and as
a safeguard for Your Majesty's Royal Prerogative, You would be
graciously pleased to ordain that no Baronetage of Scotland and
Nova Scotia dormant or otherwise shall in future be taken up by
any individual whatsoever until he shall have produced satisfactory
proof of his right thereto before the said Chapter, always excepting
from this the eldest legitimate Son or Nephew of a Baronet of
Scotland and Nova Scotia, directly succeeding to the title of his
Father or Uncle deceased or a younger brother succeeding to that
of an older.

    'Humbly beseeching Your Majesty most graciously to Grant
       this their Petition, or to afford such other remedy for the

evil complained of, as to Your Majesty may appear to be most fitting your Majesty's Petitioners as in loyalty and duty bound, will ever most anxiously Pray for Your Royal Person.

'Edinburgh, 8th June 1842.

'(Signed)   CAITHNESS.
'&c., &c.'

At a meeting of Baronets of Scotland and Nova Scotia held in London on the 31st October 1843, the Marquis of Downshire presiding, a resolution was passed to the effect that negotiations should be continued through Mr. Woodman of Amherst with the Colonial authorities in New Brunswick relative to the territorial rights of the Baronets. By a letter dated from Fredericton, June 14, 1843, that gentleman reported that, in accordance with the instructions he had received, he had made a journey to Fredericton and opened a communication with Sir William Colebrooke, the Lieutenant-Governor of New Brunswick, on the subject of a grant of land in that province for the Baronets ; that he found Sir William a zealous and active personage in the cause of colonisation and emigration ; that by the settlement of the Boundary Question nearly the whole line of road between Nova Scotia and Canada would have to be altered and made anew ; that Sir William had suggested that the grant should be taken on the line of road and in separate selected tracts, by which the best lands might be secured, the onus of settling them, and making the road through them, to be undertaken by the Baronets, at periods to be stipulated with the Government ; and that a Petition on the subject should be presented to the Colonial Minister.

This letter was accompanied by the copy of one dated 3rd June 1843, which Mr. Woodman had previously received from Sir William Colebrooke, and in which his Excellency says—'That he had considered the conversation which he had had with him on the subject of the views of the Nova Scotia Baronets ; and taking, as he did, great interest in them, it has occurred to him to suggest that these views might be much advanced by employing Dr. Gesner to examine the lands, which are vacant in various districts, and to report on their capabilities' . . . 'that the application of the Baronets should specify the condition upon which they desire to acquire lands wherever they may be found suitable ; and that in the course of the summer Dr. Gesner would obtain such information as would enable them to make a selection with full confidence.'

A General Meeting of Baronets of Scotland and Nova Scotia was held in Glasgow on the 8th August 1844, at which Sir John Campbell, Baronet of Ardnamurchan, was in the chair; and after a number of documents had been laid before the meeting, Sir R. Broun read a Report of the steps which had been taken since 1835 for the revival of the territorial rights of the Baronets of Scotland and Nova Scotia in British America, and of the circumstances which had occurred to suspend the proceedings since October 1842.

At the conclusion of the reading of this Report a resolution was passed directing it to be printed and circulated amongst the Members of the Nova Scotia Baronets preparatory to a meeting to be held later in Edinburgh.

A resolution was also passed directing that copies of the Prospectus of 'The Scottish Company for advancing the Plantation of Nova Scotia and Canada' should also be sent to each Member with a request that they would communicate with Sir R. Broun whether they would consent to join it or not.

A General Meeting of Baronets of Scotland took place on 7th November 1844, at which a Committee was appointed.

At a Meeting of the Committee of Baronets for Nova Scotia Rights, appointed by the General Meeting on the 7th November 1844, held in Edinburgh the 9th September 1847, after the business had been transacted, a Report was read by Sir Richard Broun relative to the proceedings then in progress in London for the revival of the rights of the Degree, by means of a 'Petition of Right'; a copy of the joint legal Opinion of Messrs. M. D. Hill and J. Chisholme Anstey, M.P., was also submitted.

According to the latter, the two Counsel concurred in thinking that the Baronets of Scotland, created from 1625 to 1638, held their respective Baronies of 16,000 acres in Nova Scotia, given with their titles, in feu blanch farm, and as liege regal Fiefs, immediately of the kings of Scotland; that the Baronets created between 1638 and the Union in 1707 had the same equitable rights to Baronies of 16,000 acres in Nova Scotia as they would have had if their Charters had been made out; that the rights and privileges of the whole Body were valid and subsisting, not having been extinguished or impaired by statutes of limitation, adverse possession, foreign conquest, non-usage, or any other cause or circumstance whatsoever; and that it was open and competent to the Baronets to recover the same by an application to the Sovereign in person as the Fountain of Justice, through the legal medium of a Petition of Right.

The attention of the Committee was specially called, first, to the fact that, on the erection of the Scottish Baronetage, it was made a covenant between the Crown and the nation that no Baronet ever should be created within the Kingdom of Scotland except for the express purpose of advancing the plantation of Nova Scotia (which comprehends New Brunswick, Gaspe, Cape Breton, Prince Edward's Island, etc.), and that each Baronet, in consideration of the contribution of 3000 merks towards the plantation, should receive, as a territorial qualification for his title, 16,000 acres in one or other of the districts of the Province, the same to be held of the Scottish Crown as a free Barony and Regality, with seat and voice in the Provincial Parliaments, and other great and important privileges; second, to the circumstance that the Crown Precepts to the Baronets created subsequent to 1638 authorised their patents to be so prepared as to convey to them and their heirs all rights, privileges, and immunities whatsoever, that are vested in the senior Members of the Order *quasi Baronets*; and third, to the comprehensive binding and effectual words used in the Patents of the junior Members, which declare and provide that they shall be Baronets with 'no less liberty and extent of right in all respects than is enjoyed by those of prior creation, under whatsoever laws, statutes, customs, commissions, or constitutions.'

The Committee, having taken the Report and statements into consideration, passed, in addition to others, the following resolutions :—

'1. That the Committee, as representing the general interests of the Order, receive with satisfaction the Report as to the progress of business now made, approve of the presentation to her Majesty of a Petition of Right, in accordance with the Opinion of Counsel, and direct that all due diligence be used to urge forward the proceedings to an immediate conclusion.

'2. That the Members present are unanimously of opinion, under the present distress existing in the British Islands, that the due location and settlement of the common properties of the Baronets in Nova Scotia as originally bounded, could not fail to prove highly beneficial both to the mother country and the colony, and that every possible effort on the part of those interested should now be directed to that important end.'

On the 2nd June 1848 a deputation of Baronets of Scotland waited upon Lord Grey, the Colonial Secretary, pursuant to a series of resolutions which were passed by the Committee at a meeting held in London on the 23rd of May, and placed in his hands a Memorandum and Protest, which commenced by stating that the objects for which the deputation had been appointed were threefold :—

'(1) To present a copy of a compilation entitled "The Nova Scotia Question, with observations geographical and statistical—Historical summary of events relative to the Baronetage of Scotland and Nova Scotia—Roll of existing Members—List of charters, and opinions of Counsel."

'(2) To submit on behalf of the Order, that, in lieu of all territorial claims, a consolidated grant shall be made to the Baronets of 2,500,000 acres of the vacant land in New Brunswick, upon the line of the proposed Railway between Halifax and Quebec.

'(3) To place in the hands of her Majesty's Government a formal protest against the sale, grant, or concession of any of the vacant territory within the province of New Scotland, as originally bounded, pending the settlement of the Claim of Right now urged by the Baronets.'

This preamble was followed by arguments in support, the document being signed by order of the Committee by Sir W. A. Maxwell, B^t., as Preses, and Sir Richard Broun, B^t.

Meetings were held in 1849, at which a 'Petition of Right' and an Address to the Queen were discussed and agreed upon, but no practical result was obtained by the Baronets of Scotland and Nova Scotia in connection with their claim in respect of lands under Charters granted to their predecessors more than two centuries earlier.

The Committee of the Baronetage for Privileges were equally unsuccessful in obtaining for the Degree generally the various claims they had from time to time put forward, and it was consequently dissolved. The failure of these two movements should not, however, be any discouragement to the Baronetage in the prosecution of their undoubted rights to the removal of abuses connected with their Degree and the maintenance of their covenanted privileges.

The enormous support accorded to Sir Richard Broun is a proof of the necessity felt half a century ago by the Baronetage of an organisation to protect these privileges. It is, however, to be regretted that a pugnacious attitude was adopted, and that proposals for a fancy dress and the formation and promotion of commercial enterprises in connection with the Baronetage of Scotland were included in the programme.

On the 27th August 1897, a notice appeared in the newspapers of that date to the effect that the Queen had issued an Order that the sons and daughters of Life Peers should in future bear the title of ' Honourable,' and have a precedence amongst themselves according to the date of their fathers' patents ; whereupon a long correspondence appeared in the newspapers, commencing with a letter signed ' Justitiæ Tenax,' protesting on behalf of the Baronets that this Order was an infringement of their privileges. This letter, together with the most important ones connected with the correspondence which followed, will be found in the Appendix.

A few days afterwards the authorship of the first letter was owned by Sir Charles H. Stuart Rich, Baronet, of Shirley, who put himself in communication with other Baronets, as a result of which a Meeting was held at the Bristol Hotel, London, on the 10th November following.

At this Meeting Rear-Admiral Sir Lambton Loraine, Baronet, was voted to the Chair, and a Committee was appointed to make arrangements for holding in London a General Meeting of the Baronetage in order to form a permanent Society. Sir Charles Rich, Baronet, F.S.A., and Mr. Francis W. Pixley, F.S.A., were appointed Honorary Secretaries of this Committee.

Unfortunately, at the same time, an attempt was made by a well-known genealogical writer to form what he called a Committee of the Order of Baronets with Vice-Presidents, Companions, etc., and there is no doubt that the circulars issued by him to this end led away many who were as yet ignorant that a Society was in process of formation by the Baronets themselves. The attempt, however, to exploit the Baronetage as a private venture collapsed almost immediately, and many who had supported the movement deserted it in favour of the real and properly appointed Provisional Committee.

The General Meeting of the Baronetage convened by this Committee was held on the 26th January 1898, at the Hotel Victoria, London, Sir Lambton Loraine, B^t, being voted to the Chair. At this Meeting the Honourable Society of the Baronetage was formed, with Sir Charles Rich, B^t, as its Treasurer, and Mr. Pixley as Registrar. An Executive Committee was appointed, and instructions for their guidance were passed.

A very large number of Baronets (about one hundred and eighty) were enrolled at this Meeting as the first Members of the Honourable Society, and their names published on the following day.

The Royal Warrant giving precedence to the children of Life Peers and erecting them into a special class between the younger sons of Barons and the Baronets was published in the *London Gazette* of the 16th August 1898, and was as follows :—

'*Whitehall, August 15th*, 1898.
' THE QUEEN has been pleased to issue a Warrant under Her Majesty's Royal Sign Manual to the following effect :—

'*VICTORIA*, R.

' VICTORIA, by the Grace of God, of the United Kingdom of Great Britain and Ireland, Queen, Defender of the Faith, To Our

Right Trusty and Right Entirely Beloved Cousin and Councillor Henry, Duke of Norfolk, Knight of Our Most Noble Order of the Garter, Earl-Marshal and our Hereditary Marshal of England, Greeting !

'Whereas We did by a Warrant, under Our Royal Sign Manual and Signet, bearing date the twenty-second day of December, one thousand eight hundred and seventy-six, declare that the wife of a Lord of Appeal in Ordinary then appointed or that thereafter might be appointed, whose husband was not otherwise entitled to sit in the House of Lords, should be entitled, so long as she continued his wife or remained his widow, to the style, rank, and precedence, of a Baroness of these Our Realms, together with the rights and privileges thereto appertaining, according to and from the date of his appointment, and did therein and thereby declare that nothing contained in the said Warrant should be deemed or construed to authorise or permit any of their children to assume or use the prefix of Honourable, or to be entitled to the style, rank, or precedence, of the children of a Baron :

'Now Know Ye that We deem it expedient to assign and grant to all the children lawfully begotten of the said Lords of Appeal in Ordinary heretofore appointed, or that may be hereafter appointed, certain style, title, rank, and precedence, as is hereinafter declared.

'We hereby revoke and altogether make void so much of Our aforesaid Warrant of the twenty-second day of December, one thousand eight hundred and seventy-six, as is inconsistent with, or contrary to the provision of, this Our present Warrant, and We do hereby declare with respect to all of the surviving children of the undernamed persons, all of whom either were formally or are now Lords of Appeal in Ordinary, namely :—Colin Blackburn, Lord Blackburn, deceased ; Edward Strathearn Gordon, Lord Gordon of Drumearn, deceased ; John David Fitzgerald, Lord Fitzgerald, deceased ; William Watson, Lord Watson ; Edward Macnaghten, Lord Macnaghten ; Michael Morris, Lord Morris ; James Hannen, Lord Hannen, deceased ; Charles Synge Christopher Bowen, Lord Bowen, deceased ; Charles Russell, Lord Russell of Killowen (now Lord Chief-Justice of England) ; and Horace Davey, Lord Davey ;

as also with respect to the children of any Lord of Appeal in Ordinary hereafter to be appointed and created a Lord of Parliament for life; that such children shall have and enjoy on all occasions the style and title enjoyed by the children of hereditary Barons of these Our Realms, together with the rank and precedence next to and immediately after the younger children of all hereditary Barons now created or hereafter to be created, and immediately before all Baronets.

'Our Will and Pleasure, therefore, is that you, Henry, Duke of Norfolk, to whom the cognizance of matters of this nature doth properly belong, do see this Our Order kept and observed, and that you do cause the same to be recorded in our College of Arms, to the end that Our Officers of Arms and all others upon occasion may take full notice and have knowledge thereof.

'Given at Our Court at *Saint James's*, the thirtieth day of *March*, One thousand eight hundred and ninety-eight, in the sixty-first year of Our reign.

'By Her Majesty's command.

'*M. W. Ridley.*'

This document, not issued until more than four months after signature by Her Majesty, had taken about a year altogether to prepare, for its purpose was publicly acknowledged in August 1897, as already shown.

The Honourable Society of the Baronetage lost no time in making a protest as public as the Warrant itself, by means of a letter, signed by its Registrar, addressed to the leading London newspapers, a copy of which will be found in the Appendix.

APPENDIX

LETTERS TO NEWSPAPERS REFERRING TO THE PRE-
CEDENCE GIVEN TO CHILDREN OF LIFE PEERS AND THE
ROYAL WARRANT OF THE 30TH MARCH 1898.

The Times, 31st August 1897.

'TO THE EDITOR.

'SIR,

'I see in the daily papers of the 27th inst. that in future
the children of legal life peers are to be styled "Honourable" and
to take precedence immediately after the children of barons and
before all baronets. Surely this is a direct infraction of the undertaking given by James I. when he instituted the Baronetage, that
neither he nor his successors would at any time create any dignity
whatsoever mean between the barons and the baronets.

'I wonder what the barons would say if the children of bishops
were given precedence of their children, or the rest of the Peers if
the Lord Chancellor's or Lord Chamberlain's children were suddenly
given a new and unprecedented place in the social scale.

'For many years the Baronetage has been slowly but surely dis-
credited. The baronet's position *quasi* baronet has long been ignored
in State functions. Their ancient privileges have disappeared, and
the style of Honourable, justly accorded them until the latter part
of the last century, has long been denied them ; and now an edict
has gone forth lowering the order in the social scale.

'Only last year we had an instance of this when a baronet's eldest
son claimed his knighthood on attaining his majority, yet, in defiance
of the statutes of the Baronetage, the Lord Chamberlain refused to
recognise the validity of the claim.

'Surely it is time that the baronets as a body took some steps to protect their rights and the ancient dignity of their order. They are a powerful body, and it rests largely with themselves whether they will calmly sit still and allow their honour to be surely but steadily discounted. If the legal life peers' children had been placed on a par with the barons' children, perhaps the baronets could not have objected ; though it is, I think, unprecedented for official rank to convey precedence to children. But I cannot think that the baronets will submit to a further infraction of the covenants of the order without striking a blow in their defence.

' I am, Sir,

' Your obedient Servant,

' JUSTICIÆ TENAX.'

The Times, 18th August 1898.

'THE BARONETAGE AND THE CHILDREN OF LORDS OF APPEAL.

'TO THE EDITOR.

' SIR,

' Observing that the Royal warrant giving titles to the children of Lords of Appeal in Ordinary with precedence before all baronets is now gazetted, I am instructed to inform you that the Honourable Society of the Baronetage has from the first called in question, as it does still, the legality of the advice given to the Sovereign which has led to the issue of this warrant.

' The warrant, in itself a curiosity for the genealogist, is in direct, I might say flagrant, contravention of James I.'s decree, dated May 28, 1612. In this instrument the King binds not only himself, but his heirs and successors also, not at any time to erect, create, or constitute any degree, order, name, title, style, dignity, or state, nor to give place, precedency, or pre-eminence to any person or persons, whatsoever beneath the degree of Lords of Parliament which should be or accounted to be higher, before, or equal to the degree, dignity, or place of baronets.

' The warrant, moreover, rides roughshod in quite an easy way over Royal covenants, expressed in the language of the decree, made with individual baronets in their patents of creation.

'The baronetage is not aware of any definite repudiation of James's decree, or of the individual covenants having been made by the Crown.

'Had her gracious Majesty elevated the persons concerned into any existing degree or order, baronets could have nothing to say, but as the Royal warrant involves a clear breach of one of the privileges which, held by them in trust for their posterity, it concerns their honour to defend, they will have no option as to the course now incumbent upon them.

'The Honourable Society, intending to petition the Crown, has hitherto scrupulously avoided publicity, and my committee regret the necessity now forced upon it to depart for a moment from this principle.

'I have the honour to remain, Sir,

'Your most obedient servant,

'FRANCIS W. PIXLEY,

'Registrar of the Honourable Society
of the Baronetage.

'58 Coleman Street, London, E.C., August 17.'

The Times, 22nd August 1898.

'TO THE EDITOR.

'SIR,

'In *The Times* of the 18th inst., a gentleman in the City writes on behalf of the "Society of the Baronetage" to complain of the Royal Warrant of March 30, regarding the style and rank of the sons and daughters of life peers.

'It is a new proposal to regulate the fount of honour from Coleman Street; but if the baronets will employ some clearer-minded agent than their new "Registrar," they will discover that titles divide themselves into two classes—first, actual; and secondly, courtesy; that the titles now held by life peers' children come under the second heading; and, further, that the March warrant hardly creates any fresh dignity, but rather cancels the peculiar disability under which certain peers' sons and daughters suffered

x

since 1876. They were the sons and daughters of a baron and a baroness, the former ennobled for higher reasons than generally influence the creation of a peerage, and yet they were practically illegitimatised. This probably lowered the value of their high position in the estimation of those peers who were called on to represent the House of Lords in its double capacity. Such peers are now, by an alteration of the 1876 Act, lords of Parliament for their natural life—like all other barons—and the usual courtesy precedence is accorded to their wives and children. No new degree "beneath a lord of Parliament" has been created now or since 1876.

'I am, etc.,

'A. B. C.

'August 20.'

The Daily News, 22nd August 1898.

'To the Editor.

'Sir,

'The gentleman who in "*The Daily News*" of Thursday signs himself as the Registrar of that somewhat mysterious body "The Honourable Society of the Baronetage" should moderate the ardour of his claims. The demand for precedence over the sons of Life Peers, which he bases on the original charter of James I., only recalls the degraded origin of the title. Till that time knighthood was the most honourable of English dignities, and Queen Elizabeth added lustre to the status of a peer when she dubbed him knight for valiant deeds. But when that most despicable of English Kings, James VI. of Scotland, arrived from the North, he was sadly in want of funds, and proceeded to sell for ready cash hereditary knighthood to those who could afford to pay his price. This course was worthy of the man who put that true knight Raleigh to death. But what should we think to-day if the Victoria Cross were made an hereditary decoration? Since the time of James I. baronetcies have been granted for services rendered, and any payments in return have been decently veiled in contributions to party needs. But those baronets who are particularly proud of their ancestry as holding an original title of James I. creation should let sleeping dogs lie. At present the newly-formed Honourable Society of the Baronetage is becoming ridiculous.

' Historian.'

The Daily News, 23rd August 1898.

' To the Editor.

' Sir,

' I shall be obliged if you will allow me to say one word in respect to your article on the protest of the baronets. The contention that the Sovereign has power to revoke engagements entered into by her predecessors on the Throne appears to me a somewhat dangerous doctrine for a Liberal paper to enunciate. I had imagined that this question had been settled even as recently as the Wensleydale case in the House of Lords, when the Peers, not a very revolutionary body, clearly laid down the doctrine that the power of the Sovereign in the creation of honours was limited by Parliament, and the contract entered into between the Throne and Parliament at the time of the Act of Succession. Were it otherwise, no man, or order of men, would be safe.

' It may be argued that precedency is a small matter—in this case a very small one, for the number of the children of life Peers is limited, nor is it likely that a baronet of ancient and territorial rank is likely to suffer in influence or power through the interpolation of a few not very influential persons between himself and the peerage ; but what is of importance in the State is that contracts entered into shall be carried out, and that the Sovereign, being the chief of all orders in the land, shall be as jealous of their privileges as they are themselves. And, on the whole, is it more curious to observe the baronets as a body crying " Privilege," " Privilege," than to observe the same phenomenon in, say, the House of Commons, and is the right of the baronets of Nova Scotia to wear a ribbon and jewel very much more absurd than that which allows a bishop to wear a mitre, a judge a wig, an officer a sword, a member of Parliament a

hat within the precincts, or a County Council labourer to have the
privilege of preventing his colleague from working more than eight
hours a day ?   All orders of mankind have and should have their
privileges and should be jealous of them, and it is no more ridiculous
for the upper classes to fight for theirs than for the middle or lower
classes to maintain theirs, and each class deserves the sympathy of
just men when they combine to defend them.   The fact that I do
not understand the importance of wearing or refraining from wearing a hat in the presence of the Speaker gives me no warrant for
saying that this is absurd, nor does the maintenance of the rank
granted by the Sovereign to the ancestors of the baronets justify
you, Sir, in ridiculing it as worthless on the ground that you do not
understand its importance.

' I remain, Sir,

' Your obedient Servant,

' Heir Presumptive.'

The Times, 24th August 1898.

' To the Editor.

' Sir,

' " A. B. C.," in your columns of to-day, claims that the
" titles now held by life peers' children " come under the heading
of " courtesy titles."   Courtesy titles indeed !   Since when have
" courtesy " titles been created by Royal Warrants ?

' I hold that no style and title at all are given in the Warrant of
March 30, because no such belongs in law to the children of
hereditary barons, although they are held in the Warrant to " enjoy " them.   Precedence is all that is given, and such grant is, as
Mr. Pixley has conclusively shown (and " A. B. C." cannot abridge
his quotation at his pleasure), in flagrant opposition to the binding
promises made by the fount of honour to whom the erection of the
baronetage is due.

' Do any of us deny the Queen's power to bind her successors to
a certain line of conduct when vested interests are affected ?

'Can any instance be adduced where the covenant of a Sovereign has been overridden without a repudiation of the same in terms?

'May I add that the constitution of the baronetage as a sixth hereditary degree rests on three letters patent of James I., which must be carefully read by those who wish to understand its historical position. The unrest which has from time to time characterised it is most plainly due to the strange views acted upon by King James, as follows—

'He had created baronets to occupy, in his own Royal language, the mean position "betwixt a baron and a knight"; that is to say a baronet would be between these in the scale of precedence, just as a baron would be between a viscount and a baronet. But when this well-understood and natural English scheme of precedence regulating the position of all members of their families had been assumed by the first ninety-two baronets created, the King, after long controversy with five of their number, refused to allow them precedence over barons' sons and younger sons of viscounts, on this most strange assumption—namely, that as these honourable persons (esquires by law) were "sprigs of their fathers' nobility," therefore they were more fit to be placed on a level with the very honourable head of an ennobled family (enjoying his baronet's title by law) than with the sprigs of this father's nobility.

'So it came about that any landless cadet born in the degree next immediately above baronet was appointed a higher place than the great landed proprietors and manorial lords who received baronetcies. For two and a half years afterwards no one accepted a baronetcy.

'At this present period of Queen Victoria's glorious reign it is not agreeable to find her Majesty's advisers counselling her Majesty to imitate, with aggravation, the crowning mistake of James I. Far better would it have been for a dignity, which it is the true interest of the Crown to support, if, as a Jubilee or Diamond Jubilee commemoration of so splendid a reign, our gracious Sovereign had released the Baronetage from its anomalous position by promising to restore it gradually to the position rightly taken by the ninety-two baronets aforesaid, under the saving clause contained in James's final decree dated 1616.

'In itself the giving of rank to the offspring of office-holders is quite a new departure, rights of precedence having been limited heretofore to the holders of high office themselves. Your correspondent hardly improves matters by laying down the very funny doctrine that without certain rights of rank or precedence the children of life peers are "practically illegitimate."

'Personally, like others, I care little for the trumperies of precedence; but, possessing, as I do, a king's solemn promise made to my ancestors, myself, and my posterity in letters patent under the Great Seal, I would rather be a man defending that promise than a person clamouring for distinction, with pretensions which I do not think any baronet is legally obliged to recognise.

'I have the honour to be, Sir,
'Your obedient servant,
'A BARONET (English creation).

'August 22.'

The Daily News, 27th August 1898.

'TO THE EDITOR.

'SIR,
'I have just seen a letter in your issue of the 22nd inst., carrying the signature "Historian" beneath the usual misrepresentations and parrot-cries concerning the baronetage. In these days of shallowness it is customary for ignorance to be paraded as knowledge, but better things are expected from "Historians."

'Your correspondent begins with a blunder in speaking of "the demand for precedence" (over others) as though it originated with the baronetage. Any ordinary observer knows that it is the sons of Lords of Appeal who have been demanding precedence, and titles too, and thereby seeking to disturb the whole fabric of English rules of precedence, since never before has rank been given to the issue of office-holders, as such, either in the House of Lords or out of it.

'"Historian" then runs amuck at the origin of the baronetage and shows either his absolute ignorance of the service to the King and State rendered by the early baronets, or else purposely suppresses it. Where is the fool who does not know that service to the State is either personal or pecuniary, or both, and in all ages has been a fit subject for reward? Who but "Historian" and his kind think any the worse of, (say,) the Duke of Westminster's ancestors because a baronetcy was the first hereditary title conferred on the family of Grosvenor, and was the only one belonging to them for seven generations? Who but they are unaware that the family of their leader, Lord Rosebery, was first ennobled by a baronetcy, and that nearly one-sixth of the baronetage of "degraded origin" (*sic*) is represented in the peerage, while one of the "degraded origin" persons is actually a life peer?

'Of course our "Historian" knows nothing about the sale of peerages and knighthoods in Stuart times; and to judge from the tenour of his letter he thinks that modern people acquiring great riches in trade, or turning their political coat, and in both cases giving contributions to the party chest, "decently veiled," are more worthy to be honoured as baronets than men of the olden time who furnished regiments for the King's service, guarded his standard in battle, and bequeathed to the nation men, plenty of whom have been among our foremost statesmen, administrators, diplomatists, soldiers, and sailors. He is heartily welcome however to his opinion.

'Then we have "Historian" talking about "hereditary knighthood," a thing which has never existed, for knighthood has always been personally bestowed. He means by this name, I suppose, to designate the baronetage, and here again, Sir, is exhibited culpable ignorance on the part of a person claiming to write fact. A baronet's patent of creation is like that of a baron, and constitutes him a baronet simply, with remainder. Originally this was all he had; but at a later date James, by a well-known edict, ordered to be added (among others) a clause enabling any baronet and his eldest son, who should desire it, to claim knighthood in person from the Sovereign as an additional dignity. Thus was provided by charter a second title to be borne at will by a baronet's eldest son, while second titles of peers so borne by their sons remained a matter of courtesy; but some ninety-two baronets already created at the time of the edict did not, of course, have any option of a secondary honour contained in their patents.

'As "Historian" considers knighthood to have been the most honourable of English dignities, it may help him to find out a little more about "degraded origins of titles" if I inform him that it can be seen in the list of the said ninety-two baronets that fifty-six of them were created from the ranks of the knights themselves, while all were heads of great families.

'I trust, Sir, I am not making inordinate demands on your space, but sometimes it is as well not to let ignorance and presumption have it all their own way.

'I have the honour to be, Sir,
'Your obedient servant,
'BARONETTUS.

'August 25.'

INDEX

329

DESORMAIS

www.armorial-register.com

www.ingramcontent.com/pod-product-compliance
Lightning Source LLC
Chambersburg PA
CBHW060326100426
42812CB00003B/893